TEACHING THE BIBLE

AS LITERATURE

TEACHING THE BIBLE
AS LITERATURE

Roger G. Baker

Christopher Gordon Publishers, Inc.
Norwood, Massachusetts

CREDITS

Every effort has been made to contact copyright holders for permission to reproduce borrowed material where necessary. We apologize for any oversights and would be happy to rectify them in future printings.

The Sacrifice of Isaac by Rembrandt Harmensz van Rijn. Reprinted by permission of The State Hermitage Museum, St. Petersburg.

Bible Citations were made using Logos Library System 2.1b licensed to Roger Baker, Logos Research Systems, Inc. http://www.logos.com Copyright © 1885, 1996, 1997.

Bible Works for Windows licensed to Roger Baker, Windows95/NT Release version 4.0.026e, http://www.bibleworks.com/, Copyright © 1998 Bible Works, LLC.

The Holy Bible: King James Version.-Electronic edition of the 1769 edition of the 1611 Authorized Version. – Oak Harbor, WA: Logos Research Systems, Inc., 1995.

The New Revised Standard Version, Citations longer than 500 verses or a complete book are quoted by permission of the National Council of the Churches of Christ in the United States of America. Used by permission. All rights reserved. The Holy Bible: New Revised Standard Version/Division of Christian Education of the National Council of Churches of Christ in the United States of America.-Nashville: Thomas Nelson Publishers, © 1989.

The Hebrew Bible, Biblia Hebraica Stuttgartensia [computer file]: with Westminster Hebrew Morphology. – Electronic ed. – Stuttgart; Glenside, PA, German Bible Society: Westminster Seminary; 1996, c1925; morphology c1999 by Westminster Seminary, Glenside, PA.

BHS [or WTT]_ Biblia Hebraica Stuttgartensia BHS (Hebrew Bible Masoretic Text or Hebrew Old Testament), edited by K. Elliger and W. Rudoph of the Deutsche Bibelgesellschaft, Stuttgart, Fourth Corrected Edition, Copyright © 1966, 1977, 1983, 1990 by the Deutsche Bibelgesellschaft (German Bible Society), Stuttgart. Used by permission.

The Gates of the Forest, by Eli Wiesel, © 1996 by Holt, Rinehart, and Winston. Reprinted by permission of Henry Holt and Company, LLC.

Rainbow Connection by Paul Williams and Kenny Asher © 1979 Jim Henson Productions. All rights administered by Sony/ATV Music Publishing, 8 Music Square West, Nashville, TN 37203. All rights reserved. Used by permission.

The Priestly Benediction on a Silver Amulet, Jerusalem, Ketef Hinnom, Israelite period, late 7th century BCE reproduced with permission of the Department of Image Resources and Copyright Management of The Israel Museum, Jerusalem.

Excerpt from *Canaanite Myth and Hebrew Epic: Essays in the History of the Religion of Israel* by Frank Moore Cross, p. 194, Cambridge, MA: Harvard University Press, Copyright © 1973 by the President and Fellows of Harvard College. Reprinted by permission of the publisher.

Excerpt from Faith, Hope, and Clarity, by Robert Nash, page 50, New York: Teachers College Press. ©1999 by Teachers College, Columbia University. All rights reserved. Used with permission.

64 verses of Susanna from the New Revised Standard Version of the Bible © 1989 by the Division of Christian Education of the National Council of Churches of Christ in the USA. Used by permission.

[I]t might well be said that one's education is not complete without a study of comparative religion or the history of religion and its relationship to the advancement of civilization. It certainly may be said that the Bible is worthy of study for its literary and historic qualities. Nothing we have said here indicates that such study of the Bible or of religion, when presented objectively as part of a secular program of education, may not be effected consistently with the First Amendment.

—U.S. Supreme Court

Abington School District vs. Schenepp, 1963

CONTENTS

ix	Foreword
xiii	Annotated Contents
1	Chapter 1. The Bible in Our World: Why We Should Teach It
13	Chapter 2. Legal Issues Teaching Bible in the Public School Classroom: Teaching without a Lawsuit
33	Chapter 3. What We Should all Know about the Bible: Finding a Common Understanding at the Start
45	Chapter 4. Introducing the Bible: First Lessons and Resources for the Teacher
69	Chapter 5. The Creation Narrative: In the Beginning
77	Chapter 6. Cultural Perspectives: Three Ways of Reading about Abraham and Isaac
95	Chapter 7. Teaching Literary Symbols: Finding Literary Meaning
113	Chapter 8. Teaching Biblical Poetry in Both Testaments: Writing Psalms and Proverbs
133	Chapter 9. Teaching Critical Thinking: It Improves in the Translation
149	Chapter 10. Teaching about Bible Sources: Looking for the Author
159	Chapter 11. Teaching Parables as Short Stories: Stories That Still Speak
167	Chapter 12. Teaching a Grand Theme: The Universal Problem of Suffering
179	Chapter 13. Teaching Dual Narratives: Deborah the Prophetess
189	Chapter 14. Teaching Famous Last Words: Writing Epitaphs
207	Chapter 15. Recognizing Satire: Is Jonah a Fish Story or What?
221	Chapter 16. Artists Imagine Bible Characters: Joseph as a Developing Character
229	Chapter 17. Teaching the Bible as Myth: Myth Is Why We Believe
255	Chapter 18. The Gospel of Mark: Reading a New Genre
265	Appendixes
303	Works Cited
313	Index of Bible Citations
319	General Index
321	About the Author

FOREWORD

The title of this book is *Teaching the Bible **as** Literature*. There are other possibilities: Teaching the Bible *in* Literature, the Bible *and* Literature, the Bible *with* Literature, Literature *about* the Bible, or the Bible *as Religious* Literature. There is also devotional Bible reading, reading for guidance, or reading to prove belief—all important ways of reading the Bible. The way of reading that I propose in this text for teachers does not diminish the other options for students or teachers. It is a way of reading that is familiar in our schools and a way of reading the Bible encouraged by the Supreme Court. It is the way we read in most literature classes as we consider the symbols, metaphors, themes, and literary qualities of a text.

There is a Bible narrative that explains how I personally read. It demonstrates how reading as literature can enhance other readings. It explains how the Bible speaks to me, so perhaps this is something that the reader should know at the beginning. Elijah challenges the priests of Baal to see whose god be God,[1] and the god that "answereth by fire, let him be God." The priests of Baal build an altar and call on their god to burn the sacrifice. All the while Elijah taunts them: Perhaps your god is sleeping or pursuing or talking or on a journey—call louder. (Elijah's sarcastic words here are one of the best examples of satire in the Hebrew Bible.) The priests cut themselves and dance on the altar to show that they are serious, but it does no good. No fire comes from the heavens to take their sacrifice. Then Elijah does the following:

1. He builds an altar on Mt. Carmel (symbolic home of the pagan gods).[2]

2. The altar is made of twelve stones (symbolic of the twelve tribes of Israel).

3. He places the bullock (symbol of Baal, a fertility god) on the altar.

4. He pours on water (symbol of another god, Yam, whose dominion is the sea).

5. At the symbolic evening offering hour, he calls on God using parallel poetic language.

6. "Then the fire of the Lord[3] fell, and consumed the burnt sacrifice, and the wood, and the stones, and the dust, and licked up the water that was in the trench." (In parallel verse the whole pantheon of gods is destroyed one at a time).

7. After a scrimmage with the priests, killing the priests of the groves, and a 40-day journey (a symbolic length of time), he escapes to a cave on the mountain where God spoke to Moses (a symbolically sacred place) and experiences wind, earthquake, and more fire.

8. He then learns that the Lord is not in the wind or in the earthquake or in the fire (the four classical elements are water, air, earth, and fire), but in a "still small voice."

9. His experience shows that he is a developing character, crafted by a literary writer.

Notice how "still small voice" is punctuated. There is no comma between *still* and *small*. Instead of the voice being still and small, it is, after all, a small voice. It is "still" a small voice, in the English translation.

As a literary text, this highly symbolic narrative includes biting sarcasm, satire, parallel poetry, allusion to mythic gods, and a developing character. Yet I read this only to learn that, metaphorically, God speaks with a small silent voice. In more modern Bible translations like the New Revised Standard Versions (NRSV), this voice is "a sound of sheer silence,"[4] a wonderful oxymoron—a silent voice.

This narrative is a cautionary metaphor. The voice of the Lord was not in the fire. Reading the Bible is not calling fire from heaven to consume sacrifices and convert pagans. Bible *as* literature speaks with a quiet, symbolically intense voice, a sound of silence that speaks to individuals and enhances other readings. It is a sparse understated literature in which one must listen carefully to hear the literary qualities, the allusion, the poetry, and the metaphor in a way that complements other kinds of Bible reading or even stands alone as a literary reading. As a fringe benefit, readings outside the Bible are enhanced when one understands biblical allusions.

This book is intended to help teachers find the quiet voices of a literary Bible. Some chapters will offer specific lesson ideas that teach literary principles. Other chapters serve to strengthen the teacher with literary context. In all cases I've tried to carefully document the ideas of others so that teachers can find primary scholarly support for teaching the Bible as literature. The first five chapters are written to establish a rationale and foundation for teaching the Bible as literature; they follow a pedagogical sequence. It is assumed that teachers will read them in order. From chapter 6 on, the teacher is invited to pick and choose from lessons and ideas that don't have to be taken in order. The goal is to make better student readers who will understand the literature that most of us have in common, the biblical literature of our cultural DNA. The Bible as literature helps us to recognize biblical metaphor and allusion in other literature and speaks in a quiet voice to our literary imagination. Teaching from the Bible is teaching literature from a good book, or the Good Book.

Most Bible quotations are from the King James Version (KJV) unless noted. The KJV translators used italics to indicate translation challenges. I hope retaining these italics is not too disturbing for the reader. The language of the KJV is both poetic and sometimes archaic. Teachers are encouraged to use multiple translations but should know that the KJV is one of the few English translations in the public domain.

Footnotes

1   This narrative is in 1 Kings 18–19. The citations are from the King James Version (KJV).

2   *El* means "might, strength." In Hebrew it designates "the divine being."

3   "Lord" is the KJV translation of the Hebrew YHWH. Modern Bible translations often retain the Hebrew term instead of offering any translation. The term is often translated with vowels, such as Yahweh.

4   Could the lyrics of Simon and Garfunkel's "Sounds of Silence" include a biblical allusion?

Annotated Contents

Chapter 1   The Bible in Our World: Why We Should Teach It 1

The Bible is an important part of the cultural DNA of Western civilization that can't be ignored in our schools. It is significant that 81% of high school English teachers reported that it was important to teach some Bible literature, yet only 10% taught a Bible unit or course.

Chapter 2   Legal Issues Teaching Bible in the Public School
Classroom: Teaching without a Lawsuit 13

The reasons given for not teaching the Bible as literature include an argument about lawsuits. There are more than a dozen federal cases in which justices have ruled that the study of the Bible as literature in the public schools is constitutionally protected and even desired. In addition, the American Civil Liberties Union has collaborated with important religious groups who have agreed to some specific guidelines. Since the guidelines were written, many interested religious and academic groups have signed on to what is now called a Statement of Current Law. This chapter highlights the court cases and the Statement of Current Law. In addition to this statement, the First Amendment Center at Vanderbilt University has drafted guidelines that are helpful for parents and teachers. This information should provide safe guidelines for teachers, administrators, and parents.

Chapter 3   What We Should All Know about the Bible:
Finding a Common Understanding at the Start 33

It is easy for a teacher with some background in world literature and the Bible to make assumptions about what students bring to class. Because the Bible is the most-read book in our cultural world, it is easy to assume that we are all on the same page, so to speak, when we talk about the Bible in class. The truth is that we aren't all together and it isn't just a matter of how people read this text. This chapter sorts out common denominators and describes the Bible we have today. This chapter is the beginning of cultural literacy about the Bible.

Chapter 4   Introducing the Bible: First Lessons and Resources
for the Teacher 45

It isn't easy to offer comfort to the student who has his or her own way of reading a sacred text. It isn't easy to assure a skeptical student that the school class won't become a Sunday School class. The first lessons must address both groups of students and their parents, and teachers must have the resources to offer a scholarly study of biblical literature. This chapter offers a place to start.

Chapter 5   The Creation Narrative: In the Beginning 69

The creation narrative is not an eyewitness account. No one was there to see it. The approach here is to ask what the narrative says. Students read the narrative closely, using a long established academic approach. They are also invited to discuss a basic question proposed in the *Great Books* series.

Chapter 6   Cultural Perspectives: Three Ways of Reading about Abraham and Isaac 77

Each person reads through a cultural template. The story of Abraham and Isaac is a wonderful example of what this template does for Islamic, Christian, and Jewish readers. This chapter includes the story from the Bible and the Qur'an. It is supported by commentary and art that shows how narratives become part of our cultures. Students will better understand their own cultural template.

Chapter 7   Teaching Literary Symbols: Finding Literary Meaning 95

The Bible is the source of many literary symbols. In the literary world there are forbidden fruits, serpents, rainbows, and amazing coats that mean more because they are symbolic. Much of this symbolic meaning is in the biblical text. This chapter makes connections between the literary symbols of the Bible and the literary symbols of other literature. The chapter cites allusions from William Wordsworth, Mick Jagger, and Kermit the Frog and suggests teaching resources.

Chapter 8   Teaching Biblical Poetry in Both Testaments: Writing Psalms and Proverbs 113

Biblical literature shares a quality with other sacred poetry of the world's great religions that puts it in a poetic class by itself. The quality ensures that the poetry of the Bible is translatable from language to language while preserving the essential quality that makes it poetry. Students understand that a translator can't translate both the rhyme and meter of a poem, but the poetry of the Bible does not have this problem. What is translatable is the parallel structure of biblical poetry. The parallelism of biblical poetry is much like the binocular vision we have that allows us to see objects from two slightly different perspectives. The result of this binocular vision is depth perception. Depth perception is the translatable consequence of parallelism in biblical poetry. The chapter also points out other poetic forms in the Bible, such as the proverb, and describes psalm and proverb writing assignments.

Chapter 9   Teaching Critical Thinking: It Improves in the Translation 133

There are 26 full or partial English translations of the Bible in the parallel Bible entitled *The Word*. The obvious question from teachers is "Which one for class?" The best pedagogy is to leave this decision to individual students and use the multiple translations to teach critical thinking. There are literary advantages to having multiple translations in the same classroom. There are also advantages in explaining to parents that students can use the Bible that, for whatever reason, may be the choice of their particular religious tradition. Students will find literary ways to defend their translation and will better understand the translations used by others.

Chapter 10   Teaching about Bible Sources: Looking for
the Author 149
It may not be the most important question students ask, but it is the most frequent and suggests a way to teach source criticism. They want to know who wrote the Bible. There is something about reading the work of anonymous writers that is disquieting to students. Some believe that God, in a very literal way, dictated the words to Moses and others. The teacher is not an iconoclast intent on breaking this image. The teacher should, however, have enough understanding to answer questions about authorship and present options. The goal of this chapter is to arm teachers with a brief outline of the current scholarly thinking on this important question. Students will learn ways of looking for the author that will transfer to other literary texts.

Chapter 11   Teaching Parables as Short Stories: Stories
That Still Speak 159
The heart of New Testament literature is the parable, which may be the most read part of the Bible. Students find parables readable and interesting and try to transpose them from the culture that produced them to our modern world. This chapter reviews the parabolic form, provides exercises for some of the parables, and cites some rabbinic parables so that students can have the experience of hearing a simple, difficult story for the first time. Some fables are compared to the parables as teaching lessons.

Chapter 12   Teaching a Grand Theme: The Universal Problem
of Suffering 167
When students experience Job, they have a question: "Was Job a real person?" Some teachers answer with the question: "Was the Good Samaritan a real person?" The students are quick to answer: "But that's different." They are right. In the instance of the Good Samaritan, we are reading a parable. Job reads more like a history or a drama. The idea is to teach students to identify what they are reading. This chapter provides teachers with background, text analysis, and exercises to qualify them to teach this universal story of suffering.

Chapter 13   Teaching Dual Narratives: Deborah the Prophetess 179
The story of Deborah is in the Bible twice. First it is told as a story, then it is told again in a poem. It is the oldest extended Hebrew poem and could be studied as a historical artifact. The two versions, poetic and narrative, can be compared and contrasted. There are good questions for students. Is one or the other version more historically cor-

rect? Is the poem more accurate than the narrative, or is less poetic license taken by the narrative writer? Were both poem and narrative written at the same time, with the victory song (poem) sung by Deborah recounting what happened?

Chapter 14   Teaching Famous Last Words: Writing Epitaphs 189
David is an interesting case. This is an opportunity to teach about last words and epitaphs. It is a chance for students to evaluate the life of the developing character named David based on his last words. It is also an opportunity to look at the last words of others. Some students like to write some possible last words to put in the mouths of famous people, not to mention their own last words. It is fun stuff.

Chapter 15   Recognizing Satire: Is Jonah a Fish Story
or What? 207
"It Ain't Necessarily So," according to Ira Gershwin. He specifically referred to the story of Jonah and the "Great Fish" in these lyrics from *Porgy and Bess*. Maybe it *is* necessarily so. Students will start with some historical criticism and consider the possibility. They will then consider whether this story might be a parable or a prophecy. Last and most difficult, they will consider the possibility that a crafty author has written a satire. It is hard for young readers to recognize irony and satire, but after experiencing this narrative they will have some tools that will help.

Chapter 16   Artists Imagine Bible Characters: Joseph as a
Developing Character 221
The musical is one way that artists have imagined Joseph. He is also portrayed in film and art. The numerous imaginings allow students to see how others view this developing character. It is one way of teaching character development. It also helps that Joseph has a foil to strengthen him.

Chapter 17   Teaching the Bible as Myth: Myth Is Why
We Believe 229
The teacher says "myth," and the students think "untruth." It takes some instruction for students to understand that myth is why we believe. In fact, the evidence required for "true" myth is much lower than the standard for historical "truth." This chapter uses the story of Elijah, who calls fire from heaven, to illustrate the power of myth. It also points out many biblical creation myths and compares one creation myth to the myths of other civilizations.

Chapter 18   The Gospel of Mark: Reading a New Genre 255
Gospel is a genre unique to the Bible. It is a proclamation of "good news." It is also an opportunity for students to consider the description of tragedy formulated by Aristotle and to read a story that can be literal, symbolic, or political commentary (Mark 5:1–20).

Appendixes 265
    A: Finding the Bible in Our World: Borrowing from Bartlett
       and others.. 265
    B: Gold, Frankincense, and Myrrh: Gifts of Wise Men 277
    C: Samson as Archetype 283
    D: Samson as Foil 285
    E: Literary History of Psalm 23: Comparative Translations and
       Metaphor 289

Works Cited 303

Index of Biblical Citations 313

General Index 319

About the Author.. 321

Chapter 1

THE BIBLE IN OUR WORLD: WHY WE SHOULD TEACH IT

O ne of the best arguments for teaching the Bible in the public
schools is that it is part of our cultural DNA, a book most of
us read. We have read it for generations and it is the most-
read book in the United States. It is probably the most loved book in
the world. The widely reported Gallup survey, conducted in 1990 on
the fiftieth anniversary of National Bible Week, suggests that we are
a nation of Bible readers. "The Bible undoubtedly is the most widely
read book in America," the survey concludes. Of the adults surveyed,
17% read it daily and an additional 23% read it weekly. This means
that 40% of us are reading the same book every week. Only 20% of
the respondents said that they read the Bible rarely or never. The survey did note that despite the high number of Bible readers, Bible reading has declined in the United States over the past decade.

The Gallup organization tracks Bible reading as part of its Religion Indicators, and its report of October 2000 shows that nearly six
in ten Americans (59%) say that they read the Bible at least on occasion.[5] This is a decline from the 1980s, when 73% were at least occa-
sional Bible readers.

Not only do people say they are reading the Bible, many tell the
pollsters that they take it seriously. "Sixty-five percent of Americans
agree that the Bible 'answers all or most of the basic questions of life.'
Almost half of [the] people who believe this about the Bible read it at
least weekly," the Gallup poll of 2000 reports. There is some irony,

however, in this professed belief in the Bible, because 28% of the people who say that the answers are in the Bible also say they rarely or never read it. This is where schools can help. Students can be introduced to what most in our country say is our most important literature.

One would think that in spite of the people who miraculously find answers without reading, most of us share some common knowledge with all this Bible reading, but we don't even agree on what to call the Bible. The *Hebrew Bible* is the correct name for the Christian Old Testament. It was the Hebrew Bible long before it was part of the Christian Bible. When Christians use the term *Bible*, they refer to both testaments, but for Jews there is no "New" Testament and therefore no need to refer to the other testament as "Old." Even referring to the Bible as "sacred text" is loaded. For some, "sacred text" is an editorial comment or a statement of belief. For others it simply describes the text, putting it in a category often called *scripture*. This category includes the Vedas, the Brahmanas and Aranyakas, the Upanishads, Sastra Literature, Sutra Literature, and the Qur'an, all texts sacred to some people and all texts that can be read for their educational value.

Besides the lack of agreement on what to call the Bible and "despite the impressive statistics concerning Bible reading and study, it is apparent that ignorance of its contents is widespread" (Gallup and Newport 3). After reviewing the survey results, a cynic could suggest that people may even lie about Bible reading in order to give a favorable impression to the person taking the survey. It is terribly embarrassing to admit to the value of the Good Book and in the same breath admit the "sin" of not reading it. Contradicting the high reading statistics of the 1990 Bible Week survey and subsequent tracking is the fact that "only half of the adults interviewed nationwide could name any one of the four Gospels of the New Testament. Just 37 percent could name all four, compared to 42 percent who were able to cite the four titles correctly in 1982." Many surveyed could not say who delivered the Sermon on the Mount. The most frequent wrong answer was Moses (Gallup and Newport 3).

The Barna Research Group's annual report, "The Faith Practice of America," released in March 1999, is more comprehensive than the Gallup data and is part of a longitudinal study that reports data starting ten years ago. In addition to the longitudinal data, different questions are asked each year. The 1993 survey reported that the typical U.S. home has three Bibles in it, but fewer than four in ten people read one there. In the same year the survey discovered that "almost every household in America (92%) owns at least one copy of the Christian Bible. This includes most homes in which the adults are not practicing Christians as well as the homes of hundreds of thousands of atheists."

This Barna survey of one thousand adults discovered interesting facts. (The year of each survey finding follows in parenthesis.) Some of these facts are evidence that the Bible is very much part of our culture, despite the ignorance of what it says.

- Nearly six out of ten adults (58%) maintain that "the Bible is totally accurate in all of its teachings." (2000)
- Of born-again Christians, 13% percent disagree that "the Bible is totally accurate in all of its teachings." (2000)
- Almost half of the population (45%) believes that the Bible is absolutely accurate and everything in it can be taken literally. (1994)
- Most people take the Bible at face value when it comes to the descriptions of the miracles that took place, and 73% believe that all of the miracles described in the Bible actually took place. (1994)
- Of those surveyed, 80% name the Bible as the most influential book in human history. (no date given)
- Of those surveyed, 38% read the Bible during a typical week, not including when they are at a house of worship. They spend an average of fifty-two minutes a week doing it. (no date given)
- Of those surveyed, 22% say they have read the entire Bible. (no date given)

Still, Bible ignorance is rampant, according to this survey. Of those surveyed,

- 80% of the born-again Christians say that the Bible specifically says that "God helps those who help themselves." (1997)
- 56% say that a good person can earn his or her way into heaven. (no date given)
- 42% know that it was Jesus who preached the Sermon on the Mount. (no date given)
- 12% say that the name of Noah's wife was Joan of Arc. (1997)

The longitudinal data from the annual Barna survey is available at http://www.barna.org. Table 1 shows a rather steady rate of Bible reading in the United States. Bible study in small groups has also remained somewhat constant.

TABLE 1

BARNA SURVEY OF BIBLE READING

	2000	1999	1998	1997	1996	1995	1994	1993	1992	1991
Bible Reading*	40%	36%	38%	36%	34%	31%	37%	34%	47%	45%
Small Group*	18%	18%	18%	18%	17%	18%	12%	17%	No data	No data

* measured as involvement "in the past seven days"

As interesting as the data are, a video clip may make the Bible literacy point better than the survey data. There is a good Jay Leno "Walkabout" video clip in which he asks Bible questions and gets uninformed and funny answers. I like to show this in class along with an old Art Linkletter "Kids Say the Darndest Things" clip in which Summer Bible School students tell Linkletter what the Bible really says. The two-decade gap between the clips provides fodder for good class discussion. Has the way we read the Bible really changed in twenty years? Both of these resources are listed in the Works Cited.

Perhaps the same cynics who suggest that people lie about Bible reading could also argue that the lack of knowledge of the Bible is fortunate if they agree with at least one naysayer who doesn't think the Bible is such a good book. When Gene Kasmar complained to the Brooklyn Center Independent School District in July 1992 about the use of the Bible in the schools, perhaps the issue was more religious than biblical. "The lewd, indecent and violent contents of that book are hardly suitable for young students . . . The Bible quickly reveals its unsuitability in a school and learning environment" because the Bible's passages "have no historical, scientific, literary, artistic or political value. They would be offensive to even the average adult, and only have appeal to prurient interests." If people agree with this, they will probably object to Bible reading in the schools and even a course in Bible as literature.

Kasmar's complaint, which is reported in the September 24, 1992, *Salt Lake Tribune*, is that "there are frequent biblical references to concubines, explicit sex, child abuse, incest, scatology, wine, nakedness and mistreatment of women. He cites 20 pages of examples." It may be that if students really understood this, the Bible would be more widely read, Bible as literature courses would be oversubscribed, and the words that William Shakespeare gives Antonio in *The Merchant of Venice* would be prophetic:

> Mark you this, Bassanio,
> The devil can cite Scripture for his purpose.
> An evil soul producing holy witness
> Is like a villain with a smiling cheek,
> A goodly apple rotten at the heart:
> O, what a goodly outside falsehood hath! (1–3)

In spite of the seldom-heard criticism of Kasmar, most teachers seem to think that the Bible should be part of the public school curriculum. In a survey published in 1998, Marie Goughnour Wachlin noted that "81 percent of high school English teachers reported it was important to teach some Bible literature." The irony, she discovered, is that "only 10 percent taught a Bible unit or course; in fact, English teachers were more than twice as apt to be teaching religious literature other than the Bible." Wachlin's review of textbooks showed that "high school textbooks averaged 261 literary readings; however, only one fourth of one percent (.26 percent) was from the Bible" (31).

Wachlin also discovered that although 55% of college English instructors personally recommended that secondary English majors take a biblical literature course, only 38% of secondary English majors had done so. No state post-secondary school and only 38% of private post-secondary schools surveyed required Bible literature. The purpose of this text is to give savvy high school English teachers who have not taken a Bible as literature course some help in including biblical literature in their courses. The effort here is to help the 81% who think it is important to teach biblical literature for educational purposes.

However, even though most teachers think that teaching Bible as literature in the schools is a good idea and even though surveys suggest that there is a lot of Bible reading in our world, there are some pitfalls and some self-doubt connected with this enterprise.

Regina M. Schwartz teaches English and Religious Studies at North-western University:

> There are days when teaching the Bible feels like being a prophet:
> you are slow of speech like Moses, want to escape to the ends of
> the earth rather than convey certain messages like Jonah, you
> feel alone like Amos (who was not in one of the professional
> bands of prophets) as you forge ahead, interpreting the Bible
> without the authorization of a church community, and you feel
> persecuted by everyone—by those who think you ought to be
> teaching the canon of Western literature and by those who won-
> der why you are not doing something hip and noncanonical
> rather than the Bible, so in general you often wish you had never
> been born, like Jeremiah. But there are also days when you do
> feel inspired like the prophets, not because the word of God has
> been conveyed to you, but because you have to rise to the chal-
> lenge of making the most familiar myths of Western culture, sto-
> ries like the Creation, the Fall, and the Flood, unfamiliar to students,
> and because you must face the challenge of making unfamiliar
> stories, like the rape of the concubine in Judges 19, alien purity
> laws in Leviticus, and horrific curses in Deuteronomy, sound less
> strange. There are freedoms gained by teaching narratives that
> enjoy such cultural currency. (186)

In case the self-doubt of Schwartz isn't enough, a look at a pit-fall may help those who want to teach biblical literature to go in with open eyes. The pitfall is in something that could be heartening to teachers. In some segments of society, Bible reading is thriving, but the reason it is thriving is a signal for caution and a sign of a teacher trap. The caution is that Bible reading is often promoted for commercial reasons. According to an Associated Press release pub-lished in the *Desert News* in 1998, there are a "growing number of devotional and study Bibles aimed at specific groups—women, men, blacks, mothers and teenagers among them." One can even find *The Bible in Cockney* compiled by Mike Coles, head of religious edu-cation at Sir John Cass Church of England high school in Stepney, east London. The article also noted that "some have voiced concern that marketing and packaging could overshadow these Bibles' ba-sic message" (E8). Some suggest that the real goal of special-seg-ment Bibles is to prove or reinforce the ideas of the special segment. From the perspective of someone teaching biblical literature in public schools, the dramatic increase of these special-segment Bibles is evidence that many seem interested in promoting devotional Bible reading at the same time that educators may be more interested in educational Bible reading.

An example of a special edition of the Bible with important goals is The *Black Bible Chronicles*. This book does not claim an editor or a translator. P. K. McCary is the "interpreter." The preface by Andrew Young—former UN ambassador, congressman, and Atlanta mayor—sets forth the purpose of this interpretation of the Bible.

> The *Black Bible Chronicles* is an attempt to put the most important message of life into the language of the streets. This is in keeping with the very origins of the Bible. The New Testament was originally written in Koine Greek, the street language of the people. Subsequently, Martin Luther and others translated the Bible into the language of the people of their day. The *Black Bible Chronicles* stands in this tradition, bringing the Word to our younger generation in contemporary language." (vi)

The purpose of this special-segment Bible is evidence of a land mine for Bible as literature teachers. The purpose of the literature teacher is not "to put the most important [biblical] message of life" into the schools. The purpose of teaching the Bible as literature is to put some of the world's most important literature into the schools, literature that has the qualities of very good literature and that speaks to the imagination.

In "The Commandments," cited in *The Black Bible Chronicles*, which, by the way, doesn't indicate that there were ten such commandments—is this "message of life." "You shouldn't diss the Almighty's name, using it in cuss words or rapping with one another. It ain't cool and payback's a monster." The biblical injunctions against murder and adultery are interesting when cast into a modern vernacular. "Don't waste nobody. Don't mess around with someone else's ol' man or ol' lady" (117). These interesting and imaginative translations make for spirited student discussions and undoubtedly speak to the audience for whom they were written. They are also evidence that the Bible is important to our students and their parents for reasons other than its literary value.

People who want the Bible in the classroom for reasons other than its literary value include members on the United States House of Representatives. On June 17, 1999, the House voted to permit the posting of the Ten Commandments in schools and state public facilities. Supporters of this provision said it would help to promote morality across the country.

However, what version of the commandments should we post? Do we include the version in *The Black Bible Chronicles,* or one of many other versions used by Christians and Jews, who disagree on the wording and numbering of the commandments? There is more on this in chapter 3, "What We Should All Know about the Bible."

This confusion of commandments points in ten directions at the pitfall of trying to teach the Bible as something other than literature in the public school classroom. Fortunately, literature teachers recognize that very little of the Bible seems to be editorial or prescriptive like the Ten Commandments. The Hebrew Bible (Christian Old Testament) may be editorial for the Orthodox Jew, who finds 613 laws (some suspended now because there is no Temple in Jerusalem), but the narrative seems to resonate louder than editorial in the version posted on the school wall at the request of the U.S. House of Representatives. In it are some of the best stories ever told and poetry remembered in literary allusions and song by Bible readers and non–Bible readers alike. Whatever else the Bible is to each of us, it is its value as literature that qualifies it for the school curriculum. It is the educational value of the Bible that makes teaching it in the schools legal. This will be discussed in the next chapter, but you can also read about the current state of the law at http://www.aclu.org/. The American Civil Liberties Union (ACLU) and major religions and associations in the United States have agreed on some guidelines regarding religion in the schools, and the ACLU website has posted the agreement. The statement includes Bible reading guidelines.

The idea of reading the Bible as literature is not without detractors, as we saw in the petition to the Brooklyn Center Independent School District by Gene Kasmar. Some take a different approach from Kasmar and insist that reading the Bible as literature demotes the Good Book from scripture to story. C. S. Lewis said, "Those who talk of reading the Bible 'as literature' sometimes mean, I think, reading it without attending to the main thing it is about." Lewis claimed that the Bible is "a book so remorselessly and continuously sacred that it does not invite, it excludes or repels, the merely aesthetic approach" (33).

> T. S. Eliot also had a special disdain for those who come to the
> Bible first as literature: The persons who enjoy these writings

solely because of their literary merit are essentially parasites; and we know that parasites, when they become too numerous, are pests. I could easily fulminate for a whole hour against the men of letters who have gone into ecstasies over "the Bible as literature" (qtd. in Longman 8).

It is interesting to note that Mark Twain put commentary on the Bible in the mouth of Satan in his *Letters From the Earth*:

> One of his principal religions is called the Christian. A sketch of it will interest you. It is set forth in detail in a book containing two million words, called the Old and New Testaments. Also it has another name—The Word of God. For the Christian thinks every word of it was dictated by God—the one I have been speaking of.
>
> It is full of interest. It has noble poetry in it; and some clever fables; and some blood-drenched history; and some good morals; and upwards of a thousand lies.
>
> This Bible is built mainly out of the fragments of older Bibles that had their day and crumbled to ruin. So it noticeably lacks in originality, necessarily. Its three or four most imposing and impressive events all happened in earlier Bibles; all its best precepts and rules of conduct came also from those Bibles; there are only two new things in it: hell, for one, and that singular heaven I have told you about. (qtd. in DeVoto 20)

If one is to make an argument that the Bible is great literature that should be included in the schools, perhaps it is only fair to first recognize that at one time parts of the Bible were already firmly entrenched in the curriculum—some parts as literature and some as doctrine, theology, or devotion. Even today, most college-level world literature anthologies include readings from Genesis and the Book of Job. Many school texts also include Genesis and Job along with some psalms.

The creator of the American dictionary, Noah Webster, thought that the best reader for schoolchildren was the Bible. He thought that he could teach them to read and write by providing an American translation of the Bible (Rollins 117–118).

It may be that we are less likely to see Bible stories in the curriculum now than in the past, but past school practice has made the Bible part of our U.S. culture. Evidence of religion in general and the Bible in particular is in some of the first readers used in U.S. schools. The revised edition of *McGuffey's Eclectic Primer*, first published by Van Antwerp, Bragg in 1881, ended with a little story about how God made the earth (59–60).

In the *Third Eclectic Reader*, students read a rhymed version of The Lord's Prayer (90), and the *Fourth Reader* includes a fairly sophisticated commentary on the Golden Rule:

> A man may be perfectly honest and yet very selfish: but the command implies something more than mere honesty; it requires charity as well as integrity. The meaning of the command is fully explained in the parable of the Good Samaritan. The Levite, who passed by the wounded man without offering him assistance, may have been a man of great honesty; but he did not do unto the poor stranger as he would have wished others to do unto him." (140)

McGuffey's Fifth Eclectic Reader includes difficult passages from the King James Version (KJV) on "The Goodness of God" (167–168) and an argument from Thomas S. Grimké titled "The Bible: The Best of Classics" (350–351). The first paragraph of Grimké is quoted here not only to remind us that the Bible is very much part of our culture and schools, but also as an example of the sophistication of fifth-grade readers in the late 1800s:

> There is a classic, the best the world has ever seen, the noblest that has ever honored and dignified the language of mortals. If we look into its antiquity, we discover a title to our veneration unrivaled in the history of literature. If we have respect to its evidences, they are found in the testimony of miracle and prophecy; in the ministry of man, of nature, and of angels, yea, even of "God, manifest in the flesh," of "God blessed forever." (350)

McGuffey's Sixth Eclectic Reader includes a "Speech of Paul on Mars' Hill" (160). This speech is from Acts 17:22–34. This same reader for sixth grade students includes "God's Goodness to Such as Fear Him" (189–191); this is Psalm 37. "The Death of Absalom" (420–423) is 2 Samuel 18. In literary terms, sixth-grade students were reading an example of a carefully crafted speech, complex poetry, and a scene culminating a great tragedy, all from the KJV. This is clearly the Bible as literature, which would stand any court test today.

These biblical texts are in perhaps the most important school reader of the early 1800s. Sales figures are estimated to have reached forty-seven million copies between 1836 and 1870 (Gutjahr 119 Cremin).

Another artifact from the past that used the Bible to teach is the

1906 style handbook written by Charles Sears Baldwin, *How to Write: A Handbook Based on the English Bible*. This presumes to teach students how to write using texts from the Bible.

Further evidence of the practice of teaching Bible in the schools is in the comprehensive work of Thayer S. Warshaw, published in 1978. In Warshaw's *Handbook for Teaching the Bible*, he not only establishes a rich history of teaching "Bible as Literature, Bible in Literature, and Bible and Literature," he offers two important lessons for students and teachers that are prerequisites to effectively teaching biblical literature in the public schools: "(1) Nearly every question about the Bible has alternative answers, and (2) no religious (or nonreligious) position is to be ridiculed" (Warshaw 76)

The readings chosen by McGuffey, Baldwin, and Warshaw qualify as great literature and sacred text, but to read them as literature in the classroom demands something that mundane literature does not demand: that the value as sacred text be suspended to make way for literary criticism by informed literary readers. I call this an educational reading. A reader is allowed to say whether a work by William Shakespeare or James Joyce is significant and is also allowed the presumption of making the same judgments of biblical texts, but the nature of religious text does not easily allow this judgment for many readers. The text is more than "just literature," and people claim to know it when they read it and often don't judge it by literary standards. It should be some consolation, to those reluctant to temporarily suspend the text's sacredness in favor of literary reading, that a critical approach has not seemed to hurt the value or the popularity of the text for a thousand years or more.

The challenge is that there are those who have tremendous reverence for *the Word*. Others, particularly those of us in love with language and literature, have reverence for the words. Some, of course, elevate both words and *the Word*. The call for papers for the 2001 Conference on College Composition and Communication (CCCC) convention even rhetorically asked how we can help students become "doers of the word."

In biblical literature the world was created with words. "In the beginning was the word" (John 1:1). God says, "Let there be light," and there is light (Genesis 1:3). The psalms venerate the power of words and recognize that in the words recorded in Genesis, God created the world. "And God said, Let there be light: and there was light" (Genesis 1:3). It is clear that the power is in the words. "By the word of the Lord were the heavens made; and all the host of them by the breath of his mouth" (Psalm 33:6). "Let them praise the name of the Lord: for He commanded, and they were created" (Psalm 148:5).

As Jesus was tempted in the wilderness, he recognized the power of words and quoted the words of the law. "Man doth not live by bread only, but by every word that proceedeth out of the mouth of the Lord doth man live" (Deuteronomy 8:3). The power of words to become "words of delight" (Ecclesiastes 12:9–10) is in the definition of ideas that could be abstract but are illustrated with words in imaginative biblical literature.

I hope that those who wish to teach the Bible as literature will forgive the decontextualization of this play on *word* and *Word*. It is a way of reading the Bible as prooftext, not as literature, but the allusions make the point that we create with words just as the God of the Bible creates Adam with words and, having created the animals, shows them to Adam, who names them and by doing so shares in the creation (Genesis 2: 19–20). The animals are nothing until Adam names them. The words of Adam create the animals. This is imaginative literature at its best.

The Bible is therefore pervasive in our world. It has been part of our schools since we first had schools. It is on our billboards and in our hotel rooms. It is on our lips and we scarcely realize it. It is in our literature and our newspapers. This portable library we call the Bible is part of who we are. It is part of our language, our music, our art, and our movies. Its language is somehow imprinted on our cultural DNA. Beyond this, it is imaginative literature that can be used to teach the characteristics of good literature in our schools and to provide literary examples that will help students to understand secular literature. If teachers can look beyond the self-doubt expressed by Schwartz and the pitfalls of strident belief while at the same time allowing this belief, they will have words of delight in the classroom.

Note

5   The Gallup tracking of Bible reading and Religion Indicators can be found at http://www.gallup.com. It is helpful because all of the Gallup information is there in one place rather than in disparate annual reports and news releases.

Chapter 2

LEGAL ISSUES TEACHING BIBLE IN THE PUBLIC SCHOOL CLASSROOM: TEACHING WITHOUT A LAWSUIT

There are at least two reasons that teachers don't teach the Bible as literature—or any Bible for that matter—in the public schools. The first, according to a survey conducted in 1998 by Wachlin, is that the teachers lack the academic background. The Bible as literature is seldom a required course for English majors or English education majors. The main purpose of this book is to address this first concern.

The second reason that the Bible is not taught in public schools is that for many teachers it is not worth a possible fight. They think that they will end up in court or at least in an uncomfortable board meeting or in the principal or school superintendent's office with parents who

- claim that separation of church and state doesn't allow any Bible instruction
- don't want their sacred text taught as a secular text
- are concerned that the teacher might not have the "right" interpretation of the Bible
- want Bible reading in schools to make a religious point
- (fill in the blank)_____

The problem facing teachers is that teaching the Bible in the public schools is a religious issue, no matter how it is taught. On the one hand, teaching it as literature may diminish the text for some who read it devotionally or as sacred doctrine or theology. On the other hand, teaching it as sacred, prescriptive, or devotional offends those who see the Bible only as an important ancient text that is part of the culture. The problem is that the *who is offended* issue is quickly replaced by the *who is suing whom* for what question. Clarifying the legal issues is the purpose of this chapter.

First, let us address the Constitution. I'm not an attorney, so I'll try a literary reading of the First Amendment before letting the lawyers have their say. (I can feel myself accused already of deconstructing the First Amendment.)

"Congress shall make no law respecting an establishment of religion, or prohibiting the free exercise thereof." The Constitution gives Congress two charges here and puts us on a collision course with ourselves. First it is to make no law respecting religion. This is the "establishment clause," and *respecting* seems to mean "concerning," "supporting," "protecting," or "establishing." Perhaps the Constitution is telling Congress that it just plain can't establish a religion. It may also be the case that establishing a religious practice is, in fact, establishing a religion.

The second clause charges Congress to make no law prohibiting the free exercise of religion. This is the "free exercise clause." This means that Congress can't prohibit people from practicing their religion and at the same time can't make laws respecting religion. There is tension and conflict here. The paradox is, how can the law protect the free practice of religion without making laws respecting or establishing religion?

Nonlawyers are allowed only hypothetical examples. Suppose the practice of a religion includes a generous dose of Bible reading, and students want to do some of this in school. Suppose others, for whatever reason, don't like the idea of students reading or studying the Bible in school. "There ought to be a law letting the students read the Bible," some say. "The students have a right to practice their religion." But wait: If Congress passes a law protecting the Bible readers, is it establishing some kind of religious practice contrary to the Constitution? But wait again: If Congress doesn't protect the Bible readers, has a right to free exercise been violated?

The separation of church and state is obviously more complicated than the issue of teaching the Bible as literature in public schools. The separation established in the Constitution is a metaphor for how we often compartmentalize our lives into secular and sacred. Stephen L.

Carter, in *The Culture of Disbelief*, claims that "the metaphorical separation of church and state originated in an effort to protect religion from the state, not the state from religion" (105). Carter's book is one of the best I've read on the issue of church and state relationships. He brings to the issue the scholarship of a Yale law professor and the good sense of someone who understands the power of belief. The subtitle describes his goal in the book: *How American Law and Politics Trivialize Religious Devotion*. His point is that the school doesn't require protection from religion; religion requires protection from the school.

Fortunately, there are level-headed people working on the problems of religion and the schools, and much of the work is taking place outside the courtroom. The people who are reasoning together include the National Congress of Parents and Teachers, the Freedom Forum First Amendment Center at Vanderbilt University, and the ACLU. Because these groups are working with religious freedom issues, there are now guidelines to help teachers who are teaching the Bible as literature.

Before reviewing the guidelines, let's allow the lawyers to have a historical say. The following section is a review by Shanda Robertson of legal case history involving teaching the Bible as literature in public schools. It is not about all the religious challenges of the schools, just teaching the Bible as literature.

The Law: Case History of Teaching Bible in the Public Schools[6]

Teaching the Bible in the public schools is constitutionally permissible, if taught for its historical and literary value. Although primarily a religious text, the Bible is an important part of this nation's tradition and culture. If the Bible is presented for a secular purpose, without promoting religious instruction, there is no reason it cannot have a place in the public schools.

The First Amendment to the United States Constitution prohibits the government from making any law "respecting an establishment of religion." U.S. CONST. Amend. I. This language is known as the Establishment Clause. Originally only Congressional action was subject to the strictures of the Establishment Clause; however, through the Fourteenth Amendment, states have also become bound by its constraints. *See Everson v. Board of Educ.*, 330 U.S. 1, 5 (1947). Because public schools are institutions of state government, school policies, courses, and texts cannot infringe upon Establishment Clause guarantees.

The criteria for determining if a particular government action violates the Establishment Clause was summarized in the case of *Lemon v. Kurtzman*, 403 U.S. 602 (1971). This case devised a three-factor test for concluding that a statute did not violate the Establishment Clause. "First, the statute must have a secular . . . purpose; second, its principal or primary effect must be one that neither advances nor inhibits religion; finally, the statute must not foster 'an excessive government entanglement with religion.'" *Id*. at 612–13 (citations omitted). Courts have applied this test to a wide range of government activities, including public school policies and curriculum. Although the *Lemon* test has been widely criticized and repeatedly questioned, most courts have applied this three-factor test to public school Bible study programs.

One court attempted to articulate a different standard for evaluating Bible study programs in the public schools. The court in *Crockett v. Sorenson*, 568 F. Supp. 1422 (W.D. Va. 1983), stated that "the appropriate inquiry . . . is simply whether the Bible teaching program constitutes a forbidden religious exercise (i.e., advances religion) or a permissible academic program." *Id*. at 1430. This standard is not a particularly helpful analytical tool because it merely restates the ultimate question. Does the school's Bible study program violate the Establishment Clause? In addition, the *Crockett* court examined the same factors as those traditionally considered by the *Lemon* test to come to its conclusion as to whether a program is "a forbidden religious exercise." Currently the *Lemon* test remains the only established means of assessing the constitutionality of public school Bible courses.

Secular Purpose

It is clearly possible for the Bible to be taught in the public schools for a secular purpose. Although the Bible is primarily a religious text, the Supreme Court has concluded that teaching the Bible as a historical or literary text is a legitimate secular purpose. In fact, the Court has even endorsed teaching the Bible as integral to comprehensive secular education.

In the case of *Abington School District v. Schempp*, 374 U.S. 203 (1963), parents challenged a school district's practice of reading from the Bible without comment and reciting The Lord's Prayer at the commencement of each school day. The United States Supreme Court held that these practices were an unconstitutional establishment of religion. However, the Court declared:

> [I]t might well be said that one's education is not complete without a study of comparative religion or the history of religion and its relationship to the advancement of civilization. It certainly may

be said that the Bible is worthy of study for its literary and historic qualities. Nothing we have said here indicates that such study of the Bible or of religion, when presented objectively as part of a secular program of education, may not be effected consistently with the First Amendment. *Id*. at 225.

Although, generally speaking, the Bible can be taught for a legitimate secular purpose, there are subjects in the Bible that schools may not be allowed to teach. At least one court has held that some biblical text can have no other purpose than religious instruction. In *Wiley v. Franklin*, 474 F. Supp. 525 (E. D. Tenn. 1979), constitutional challenges were raised over a Bible study course taught in the public elementary schools of Chattanooga, Tennessee. The schools' previous Bible course had been declared unconstitutional. A revised curriculum was presented for the court's approval. The court approved of the revisions with the exception of a proposed lesson on the resurrection of Jesus. The court noted that "with the exception of lesson 15 [Reports of the Resurrected Jesus] . . . each lesson is capable of being taught for its secular, literary or historical worth and without religious emphasis." *Id*. at 531. However, the lesson on the resurrection could not, in this court's opinion, have a secular purpose. The court explained, "The account of the resurrection forms the central statement of the Christian religious faith. Its only reasonable interpretation is a religious interpretation. Its only reasonable message is a religious message. It is difficult to conceive how it might be taught as secular literature or secular history." *Id*.

Primary Effect

Any teaching of the Bible in the public schools must not have the primary effect of advancing or inhibiting religion. This means that any course on the Bible must be taught with objectivity and neutrality. "Clearly, however, absolute objectivity is not possible nor required, for as the Court stated in *Lemon*, '[o]ur prior holdings do not call for total separation between church and state; total separation is not possible in an absolute sense'" *Crockett*, 568 F. Supp. at 1429 (quoting *Lemon*, 403 U.S. at 614). Teaching the Bible necessarily requires some touching upon religious themes, but it is not constitutionally permissible for the public school curriculum to be a means of indoctrination.

In *Wiley*, the court stated:

The ultimate test of the constitutionality of any course of instruction founded upon the Bible must depend upon classroom performance. It is that which is taught in the classroom that renders a course so founded constitutionally permissible or constitutionally impermissible. If that which is taught seeks either to disparage or to encourage a commitment to a set of religious beliefs, it is constitutionally impermissible in a public school setting. *Wiley*, 474 F. Supp. at 531.

The case of *Hall v. Board of Commissioners*, 656 F.2d 999 (5th Circ. 1981), is an example of a Bible course that had a primary effect of advancing religion. In *Hall*, a parent claimed that an elective Bible literature course was taught in a manner that advanced the fundamentalist Christian faith. The Fifth Circuit Court of Appeals agreed. The court determined that the textbook "reveal[ed] a fundamentalist Christian approach to the study of the Bible devoid of any discussion of its literary qualities." *Id*. at 1002. The teaching methods used in the classroom were inconsistent with accepted methods of teaching literature. Finally, the court specifically condemned the examinations given because they simply required memorization of biblical passages. *Id*. at 1003.

Wiley v. Franklin, 497 F. Supp. 391 (E.D. Tenn. 1980) [hereinafter referred to as "*Wiley II*"], is a case that shows the breadth of this prohibition against religious influence. After accepting a revised Bible curriculum, new constitutional challenges were raised to the manner in which the course was being taught. The *Wiley II* court monitored ten lessons and concluded that the primary effect of three lessons "would be to convey a religious message rather than to convey a literary or historical message." *Id*. at 396. The court enjoined teaching of the entire course as having the primary effect of promoting religion. The court did not consider the other seven lessons that were monitored, or the course as a whole. The *Wiley II* court appears to have concluded that if any one lesson had a primary religious effect, the entire course was tainted. The court determined that a constitutional violation had occurred, and it could be no defense that this violation was relatively minor. *See id*. at 396 (citing *Schempp*, 374 U.S. at 225).

Religious Entanglement

Public schools offering courses on the Bible must also be careful to avoid religious entanglement. An example of a Bible study program that did not avoid religious entanglement is found in case of *Crockett v. Sorenson*, 568 F. Supp. at 1422. The program at issue in *Crockett* had been in place for forty years. It was instituted and sponsored by local Protestant churches. The curriculum, materials, and teachers were all selected and provided by the churches. The *Crockett* court concluded that despite the secular purpose and objective teaching, the course could not "overcome the perceived aura that the classes are religious in nature." *Id*. at 1430.

A Bible course can become religiously entangled even when control of the program is not in the hands of a particular religious sect. In *Vaughn v. Reed*, 313 F. Supp. 431 (W.D. Va. 1970), a private organization called the Week-Day Religious Education Council taught weekly comparative religion classes in the public schools of Martinsville, Virginia. The court in *Vaughn* called this a religious group and disapproved of the group's control over the course and teachers. Although the court approved of the teacher's qualifications, it concluded that an Establishment Clause violation could be avoided only when the school board had control over the teachers and the program.

Guidelines for Bible Courses in Public Schools

Even though courts have held that a certain Bible study program violates the First Amendment, they have often offered schools the opportunity to implement changes that would make these courses constitutional. Courts have provided guidance for how these programs can be adjusted to suit constitutional requirements. There are five recurring guidelines that can be found in such cases. They are: 1) school board control of teachers and curriculum; 2) teacher qualifications that do not include religious beliefs; 3) objective, secular course materials and classroom presentation; 4) private donations and funding that come without religious "strings"; and 5) student enrollment in the classes as either mandatory or elective. *See Crockett*, 568 F. Supp. at 1431; *Wiley II*, 497 F. Supp. at 393; *Vaughn*, 313 F. Supp. at 433-34.

Courts emphasize the need for secular control of Bible courses in the public schools. The school board should be in charge of hiring appropriately qualified teachers. In addition, school authorities should review and select course materials that focus on the literary and historical aspects of the Bible, and implement appropriate curriculum.

Teachers should be qualified to teach in the public schools. Bible teachers should probably have a background in the secular subjects to which the Bible study relates, such as literature and history. No teacher can be hired to teach the Bible on the basis of religious belief or lack thereof. Schools should be careful to avoid inquiring into the religious sentiments of potential teachers for Bible courses.

Courts also emphasize the necessity for objectivity in a class teaching the Bible. Curriculum, texts, and classroom presentations must scrupulously adhere to the course's secular objectives. Any attempt at indoctrination would be a constitutional violation.

Despite these restrictions, public schools have been allowed to solicit and accept donations from private groups to fund Bible classes. However, these funds must be donated with the strict understanding that there are no conditions attached to the donations, except that the money will be used for the Bible program. The school must not be put in a position in which it will be pressured into supporting religious causes.

Finally, an area of disagreement among courts is whether Bible courses should be mandatory or elective. One court has said that if the course does not violate the Constitution there is no reason to allow students to be excused from attending.

If the course is necessary to the education of one child, it is equally necessary to the education of all students. The controversial nature of a course should not be grounds for dismissing a student from its study. Once the school board determines that a particular course should be taught in the schools, the court sees no justification for allowing a student or his parents to decide that the student will not attend. *Vaughn*, 313 F. Supp. at 433-34.

Another court attacked this position, believing instead that any Bible course must be optional. "I am of the opinion . . . that from a strictly constitutional analysis, requiring a student to participate in a course of Bible study when it runs contrary to his personal religious beliefs would violate the Free Exercise Clause." *Crockett*, 568 F. Supp. at 1431.

Conclusion

It is constitutionally permissible to teach the Bible as literature in the public schools. However, to avoid a violation of the First Amendment's Establishment Clause, any presentation of the Bible in the public schools must have a secular purpose, not have a primary effect of promoting or inhibiting religion, and must avoid religious entanglements. Some of the requirements that courts have put on Bible teaching include secular control of Bible study programs, qualified literature and/or history teachers, objective materials and presentation, and condition-free donations. Courts are divided on whether a course in the Bible should be elective or can be made mandatory. Adherence to these guidelines can shield Bible courses from constitutional litigation.

National Council of Teachers of English and International Reading Association: Standards for the English Language Arts

The legal history establishes precedent and is valuable when discussing the issue with parents and school officials. I have found the history to be quite useful, but most short conversations require only the Supreme Court statement quoted as the epigraph of this book. It is now for the consensus builders to develop guidelines, and at least two groups are trying.

The standards published in 1996 by those who teach English and reading in our schools do not specifically refer to the Bible as a school text. The standards allow latitude for a multitude of texts but do not mention the Bible or other sacred texts specifically.

> The vision guiding these standards is that all students must have the opportunities and resources to develop the language skills they need to pursue life's goals and to participate fully as informed, productive members of society . . . Furthermore, the standards provide ample room for the innovation and creativity essential to teaching and learning. They are not prescriptions for a particular curriculum or instruction. . . .
>
> Students read a wide range of print and nonprint texts to build an understanding of texts, of themselves, and of the cultures of the United States and the world; to acquire new information; to respond to the needs and demands of society and the workplace; and for personal fulfillment. Among these texts are fiction and nonfiction, classic and contemporary works. (NCTE and IRA 3, 27)

One can suppose that "fiction and nonfiction, classic and contemporary works" somehow include sacred texts, but specific mention of the Bible and other religious texts would have offered more support to those teaching the Bible as literature. Even the narrative explaining the standard is not strong on this point:

> Through discussion of what they read and through their own extensive reading, students also learn that any given text can be understood in a variety of ways, depending on the context. African folk narratives or Greek myths, for instance, can be read as delightful, entertaining stories, as representations of mythic archetypes, or as cultural, religious, or philosophical histories of particular regions or people. (27)

The Freedom Forum First Amendment Center at Vanderbilt University

One of the most active groups trying to build consensus on religious liberty in public education is the Freedom Forum First Amendment Center. The Statement of Principles developed by the center is much more inclusive of religious education issues than teaching Bible as literature. In fact, the center goes further than a Bible as literature course or unit. In *Taking Religion Seriously across the Curriculum*, published by the center, Nord and Haynes argue that

> the Court's claim that the Bible and religion must be studied as part of a "secular program of education" should not be taken to mean that the Bible must be read as secular scholars or scientists do (for that would privilege nonreligious over religious approaches and violate the neutrality between religion and nonreligion as required by the Establishment Clause); rather, the purpose of studying the Bible or religion must be educational, not religious. Religion courses cannot be used to proselytize or indoctrinate students. (165)

The point they make is good. Teaching the Bible or religion should serve an educational rather than a religious purpose. Using the word *educational* rather than *secular* helps to clarify the issue. It also takes some of the emotion out of the issue because *secular* is often interpreted as antireligion. I'm not arguing in this book for a strictly secular reading of the Bible or for a religious reading; I'm arguing for an educational reading. We can learn about our world and our religions and ourselves by studying the Bible as literature, and I'm assuming that teaching *about* religion is quite different than teaching religion.

Nord and Haynes may be limiting a literary reading of the Bible:

> It is sometimes suggested that in teaching the Bible as literature rather than Scripture we can stand on common ground, for we need not deal with all those theological interpretations that divide us. This, we believe, is a naive notion. If students are to make educated judgments about the meaning of a text, they must have some sense of the major alternative readings of it. To ignore systematically the profoundly influential theological interpretations, insisting that the only relevant resources for interpreting the text are those provided by secular scholarship, is to take sides in matters of considerable controversy. Perhaps even worse, by excluding the religious interpretations, teachers keep students ignorant of the controversy. (128)

Chapter 6 of this book is my answer to this observation. Perhaps it should be titled *Religious* Perspectives rather than *Cultural* Perspectives.

Although we can argue with the folks at the Freedom Forum about the what it means to read as literature, it would be hard to discount the work the center has done to build consensus on religious issues in the schools. The Forum has drafted Statement of Principles that has been endorsed and jointly sponsored by the following:

American Association of School Administrators

American Center for Law and Justice

American Federation of Teachers

Anti-Defamation League

Association for Supervision and Curriculum Development

Catholic League for Religious and Civil Rights

Carnegie Foundation for the Advancement of Teaching

Central Conference of American Rabbis

Christian Coalition

Christian Educators Association International

Christian Legal Society

Citizens for Excellence in Education

Council on Islamic Education

The Freedom Forum First Amendment Center at Vanderbilt University

National Association of Elementary School Principaals

National Association of Evangelicals

National Association of Secondary School Principals

National Congress of Parents and Teachers

National Council of Churches of Christ in the U.S.A.

National Education Association

National School Boards Association

People for the American Way

Phi Delta Kappa

Union of American Hebrew Congregations

The Statement of Principles developed by the Freedom Forum Center is important for those working to clarify religious issues in the schools. It is available free of charge from The Freedom Forum First Amendment Center at Vanderbilt University, 1207 18th Avenue South, Nashville, TN 37212 (telephone 615-321-9588). Principle 4, Religious

Liberty and Public Schools, is especially important for those teaching
Bible as literature:

> Public schools may not inculcate nor inhibit religion. They must
> be places where religion and religious conviction are treated with
> fairness and respect.

> Public schools uphold the First Amendment when they protect the
> religious liberty right of students of all faiths or none. Schools dem-
> onstrate fairness when they ensure that the curriculum includes
> study *about* religion, where appropriate, as an important part of a
> complete education.

One of the implications of this principle for teachers of Bible as
literature is that it allows teaching about religion in the course of studying the literature of the Bible. Chapter 6 demonstrates this point.

The Center also publishes *A Parent's Guide to Religion in the Public
Schools*, which is free as well. It is a series of questions and answers,
and although it doesn't have the force of law, it is essentially correct
in the answer that most concerns Bible as literature teachers: Is it constitutional to teach about religion in public schools?

> Yes. The Supreme Court has indicated many times that teaching
> about religion, as distinguished from religious indoctrination, is an
> important part of a complete education. The public school's approach
> to religion in the curriculum must be academic, not devotional.

> Study about religion belongs in the curriculum whenever it natu-
> rally arises. On the secondary level, the social studies, literature and
> the arts offer many opportunities for the inclusion of information
> about religions—their ideas and practices. On the elementary level,
> natural opportunities arise in discussions of the family and commu-
> nity life and in instruction about festivals and different cultures.

> *Religion may also be studied in special courses. Some secondary schools,*
> *for example, offer electives in "World Religions," "Bible as/in History or*
> *Literature," and "Religion in America."* [emphasis added].

Religion in the Public Schools: A Joint Statement of Current Law

Published by permission of the ACLU, all rights reserved

One of the most active groups in America on First Amendment
issues is the ACLU. People interested in the Bible and religion in the

public schools have not always perceived the ACLU as friendly. Contrary to this image, the ACLU has published a joint Statement of Current Law, which was cooperatively drafted and adopted by many people interested in the problem. The Joint Statement of Current Law addresses many more religion and school issues than Bible as literature courses. It is available from the ACLU at http://www.aclu.org .The exact address of the document is http://www.aclu.org/issues/ religion/relig7.html.

The Joint Statement of Current Law does not carry the force of law, but I have always looked at the groups who have signed the document and assumed that if I follow the guidelines, I won't get sued by any of the people who were organizational signers of the statement:

> American Civil Liberties Union
> American Ethical Union
> American Humanist Association
> American Jewish Committee
> American Jewish Congress
> American Muslim Council
> Americans for Religious Liberty
> Americans United for Separation of Church and State
> Anti-Defamation League
> Baptist Joint Committee
> B'nai B'rith
> Christian Legal Society
> Christian Science Church
> Church of Scientology International
> Evangelical Lutheran Church in America
> Lutheran Office for Governmental Affairs
> Federation of Reconstructionist Congregations and Havurot
> Friends Committee on National Legislation
> General Conference of Seventh-Day Adventists
> Guru Gobind Singh Foundation
> Interfaith Alliance
> Interfaith Impact for Justice and Peace
> National Association of Evangelicals
> National Council of Churches
> National Council of Jewish Women

National Jewish Community Relations Advisory Council (NJCRAC)

National Ministries, American Baptist Churches, USA

National Sikh Center

North American Council for Muslim Women

People for the American Way

Presbyterian Church (USA)

Reorganized Church of Jesus Christ of Latter-day Saints

Union of American Hebrew Congregations

Unitarian Universalist Association of Congregations

United Church of Christ, Office for Church in Society

The following is from the introduction to the Joint Statement of Current Law:

> The Constitution permits much private religious activity in and about the public schools. Unfortunately, this aspect of constitutional law is not as well known as it should be. Some say that the Supreme Court has declared the public schools "religion-free zones" or that the law is so murky that school officials cannot know what is legally permissible. The former claim is simply wrong. And as to the latter, while there are some difficult issues, much has been settled. It is also unfortunately true that public school officials, due to their busy schedules, may not be as fully aware of this body of law as they could be. As a result, in some school districts some of these rights are not being observed.

Of particular interest to teachers of the Bible as literature are the following sections:

Teaching About Religion

5. Students may be taught about religion, but public schools may not teach religion. As the U.S. Supreme Court has repeatedly said, "[I]t might well be said that one's education is not complete without a study of comparative religion, or the history of religion and its relationship to the advancement of civilization." It would be difficult to teach art, music, literature and most social studies without considering religious influences.

The history of religion, comparative religion, the Bible (or other scripture)-as-literature (either as a separate course or within some other existing course), are all permissible public school subjects. [emphasis added].

It is both permissible and desirable to teach objectively about the role of religion in the history of the United States and other countries. One can teach that the Pilgrims came to this country with a particular religious vision, that Catholics and others have been subject to persecution or that many of those participating in the abolitionist, women's suffrage and civil rights movements had religious motivations.

Student Assignments and Religion

7. Students may express their religious beliefs in the form of reports, homework and artwork, and such expressions are constitutionally protected. Teachers may not reject or correct such submissions simply because they include a religious symbol or address religious themes. Likewise, teachers may not require students to modify, include or excise religious views in their assignments, if germane. These assignments should be judged by ordinary academic standards of substance, relevance, appearance and grammar.

8. Somewhat more problematic from a legal point of view are other public expressions of religious views in the classroom. Unfortunately for school officials, there are traps on either side of this issue, and it is possible that litigation will result no matter what course is taken. It is easier to describe the settled cases than to state clear rules of law. Schools must carefully steer between the claims of student speakers who assert a right to express themselves on religious subjects and the asserted rights of student listeners to be free of unwelcome religious persuasion in a public school classroom.

   a. Religious or anti-religious remarks made in the ordinary course of classroom discussion or student presentations are permissible and constitute a protected right. If in a sex education class a student remarks that abortion should be illegal because God has prohibited it, a teacher should not silence the remark, ridicule it, rule it out of bounds or endorse it, any more than a teacher may silence a student's religiously based comment in favor of choice.

   b. If a class assignment calls for an oral presentation on a subject of the student's choosing, and, for example, the student responds by conducting a religious service, the school has the right—as well as the duty—to prevent itself from being used as a church. Other students are not voluntarily in attendance and cannot be forced to become an unwilling congregation.

c. Teachers may rule out-of-order religious remarks that are ir-
relevant to the subject at hand. In a discussion of Hamlet's sanity,
for example, a student may not interject views on creationism.

The U.S. Department of Education

Although the Statement of Current Law does not have the force
of law, it was the basis for guidelines issued by the Department of
Education in 1995 and reissued in 1998 with an accompanying execu-
tive order of President Clinton. The complete text of the Department
of Education guidelines, along with Education Secretary Richard W.
Riley's letter that accompanied the guidelines is available at http://
www.ed.gov. Although the president's introduction of the Department of Education guidelines does not mention the Bible as literature, it sets the tone for the rest of the document. The president's
preface to the 1998 guidelines follows:

> Schools do more than train children's minds. They also help to
> nurture their souls by reinforcing the values they learn at home
> and in their communities. I believe that one of the best ways we
> can help our schools to do this is by supporting students' rights to
> voluntarily practice their religious beliefs, including prayer in
> schools . . . For more than 200 years, the First Amendment has
> protected our religious freedom and allowed many faiths to flour-
> ish in our homes, in our workplace and in our schools. Clearly
> understood and sensibly applied, it works.

The Department of Education guidelines that most concern the Bible
as literature teachers areas follows:

> Teaching about religion: Public schools may not provide religious
> instruction, but they may teach about religion, including the Bible
> or other scripture: the history of religion, comparative religion, the
> Bible (or other scripture)-as-literature, and the role of religion in
> the history of the United States and other countries all are permis-
> sible public school subjects. Similarly, it is permissible to consider
> religious influences on art, music, literature, and social studies.
> Although public schools may teach about religious holidays, in-
> cluding their religious aspects, and may celebrate the secular as-
> pects of holidays, schools may not observe holidays as religious
> events or promote such observance by students.

Student assignments: Students may express their beliefs about religion in the form of homework, artwork, and other written and oral assignments free of discrimination based on the religious content of their submissions. Such homework and classroom work should be judged by ordinary academic standards of substance and relevance, and against other legitimate pedagogical concerns identified by the school.

The Department of Education guidelines concludes with a list of places from which additional information is available. These places are nongovernmental; they are the places where cool heads seem to prevail as consensus is developed. They are as follows:

Religious Action Center of Reform Judaism
Name: Rabbi David Saperstein
Address: 2027 Massachusetts Ave., NW, Washington, DC 20036
Phone: (202) 387-2800
Fax: (202) 667-9070
E-Mail: rac@uahc.org
Web site: http://www.cdinet.com/RAC/

American Association of School Administrators
Name: Andrew Rotherham
Address: 1801 N. Moore St., Arlington, VA 22209
Phone: (703) 528-0700
Fax: (703) 528-2146
E-mail: arotherham@aasa.org
Website: http://www.aasa.org

American Jewish Congress
Name: Marc Stern
Address: 15 East 84th St., New York, NY 10028
Phone: (212) 360-1545
Fax: (212) 861-7056
E-mail: Marc_S_AJC@aol.com

National PTA
Name: Maribeth Oakes
Address: 1090 Vermont Ave., NW, Suite 1200, Washington, DC 20005
Phone: (202) 289-6790
Fax: (202) 289-6791

E-mail: m_oakes@pta.org
Website: http://www.pta.org

Christian Legal Society
Name: Steven McFarland
Address: 4208 Evergreen Ln., #222, Annandale, VA 22003
Phone: (703) 642-1070
Fax: (703) 642-1075
E-mail: clrf@mindspring.com
Website: http://www.clsnet.com

National Association of Evangelicals
Name: Forest Montgomery
Address: 1023 15th St., NW #500, Washington, DC 20005
Phone: (202) 789-1011
Fax: (202) 842-0392
E-mail: oga@nae.net
Website: http://www.nae.net

National School Boards Association
Name: Laurie Westley
Address: 1680 Duke St., Alexandria, VA 22314
Phone: (703) 838-6703
Fax: (703) 548-5613
E-mail: lwestley@nsba.org
Website: http://www.nsba.org

Freedom Forum
Name: Charles Haynes
Address: 1101 Wilson Blvd, Arlington, VA 22209
Phone: (703) 528-0800
Fax: (703) 284-2879
E-mail: chaines@freedomforum.org
Website: http://www.freedomforum.org

What Does It All Mean?

It is for each teacher to decide what to teach in the context of a
particular school, and there are some guidelines to help teachers avoid
the most obvious legal problems. There are organizations that can

help and the argument is not as shrill as many think. The following is what it means to me in my practice as a teacher:

1. Teaching the Bible as literature in the public school is legal. The Supreme Court has said so: "The Bible is worthy of study for its literary and historic qualities."

2. People don't like surprises. Since discussions are easier when the situation isn't charged with confrontation, principals, parents, and students should be consulted before the class or unit is started. I find that putting my course or unit syllabus into the hands of parents and administrators usually defuses most problems. I go so far as to put my syllabus on my home page on the Internet.

3. I use the guidelines of the Department of Education, the ACLU's Joint Statement of Current Law, and the Statement of Principles from the Freedom Forum First Amendment Center. The Joint Statement seems especially clear. People recognize good sense when they read it.

4. I take seriously the civic ground rules developed at the Freedom Forum:

    a. *Rights.* Religious liberty, or freedom of conscience, is an inalienable right for all. Public education must make every effort to protect the conscience of every parent and student.

    b. *Responsibilities.* As American citizens, we have a civic responsibility to guard that right for every person, including those with whom we deeply disagree.

    c. *Respect.* Not only what we debate but how we debate is critical in a democracy. All parties involved in public schools should agree to debate one another with civility and respect, and should strive to be accurate and fair.[7]

5. I let students use whatever Bible they choose, even it this means using multiple Bible translations in the class. (This point will get more attention in chapter 9).

Notes

6   This legal research was conducted by Shanda Robertson specifically for the author and is reprinted here with her permission. Complete citation in Works Cited.

7   Nord and Haynes note in *Taking Religion Seriously across the Curriculum* that the "three Rs of religious liberty—rights, responsibilities, and respect—are more fully defined in the Williamsburg Charter, an agreement on religious liberty signed by nearly 200 national leaders in 1988. The full text of the charter appears in *Finding Common Ground*.

Chapter 3

What We Should All Know about the Bible: Finding a Common Understanding at the Start

It would be convenient if there were a list of things we should all know about the Bible, but it isn't as easy as that. I tried asking some high school students to make a list. I was a visitor in their English class and told them that I was writing a chapter in a book about teaching the Bible as literature in public schools and needed some help. I asked that they each write a list of half a dozen things that they thought everyone ought to know about the Bible. Some of the students put the list in the form of questions. I suspect that is because they didn't know the answers. Others made very definitive statements about what they thought the Bible taught.

I've included two lists here. The first is almost exactly as it was written by an anonymous student. The second was mostly written by one student, but I have reordered it and included two additional questions frequently asked by other students:

> What are half a dozen or so things that everyone should know about the Bible?
>
> 1. God created heaven and earth.
>
> 2. Adam and Eve were sent out of the Garden of Eden for eating the forbidden fruit. The serpent gave them the apple.
>
> 3. God gave Moses the Ten Commandments.
>
> 4. We should keep the commandments today.
>
> 5. David killed Goliath.

6. Jesus died for us.

7. We should accept Jesus and do what he would do.

This first list is really a confession of faith in the Christian Bible. It also demonstrates obvious confusion with my question. Rather than listing what people should *know about* the Bible, this student lists what he or she thinks people should *learn from* the Bible. It is a cautionary list for teachers, because it indicates how seriously and religiously some students regard the Bible.

The second list was in the form of questions:

1. What is the Bible?

2. What stories are in the Bible?

3. Who wrote the Bible?

4. When was the Bible written?

5. What language did people use to write the Bible?

6. Who translated the Bible into English?

These six questions were frequent enough in the classrooms where I gave my informal survey that they form the basis of this chapter. Teachers interested in a more comprehensive introduction to the Bible may wish to consult Stephen L. Harris, *Understanding the Bible*.

What Is the Bible?

The Bible is not really a book but a library of books. There are many kinds of books in this library. The Bible is one of the few volumes in the world that really has no name. The word *Bible* is not the title of the anthology with many chapters. This word is a transliteration of the Greek *biblia*, which means "book." One might think of the Bible as a collection of books that, to many people, tell one story. According to the *Oxford English Dictionary*, in its earliest usage the meaning was "papyrus," "scroll," "roll," or "book". The first Latin usage is unclear, but Jerome uses *bibliothēca* for the Scriptures, and this name continued in literary use for several centuries.

When people use the word *Bible*, they can mean many things. For some the title is literal: it means "books," and the Bible is just that, a collection of books that were once ancient written records or oral stories set in an area we now refer to as the Middle East. They are the historical texts of ancient Israel. When Christians use the word *Bible*, it is more than just any collection of books to which they refer; it is a sacred collection. It is scripture. In this collection is a record of God's relationship with people on earth since they were created. Part of the record, the Old Testament, is before Jesus Christ came to earth. *Testament* means "covenant," an agreement or promise between God and the people of the earth. The second, smaller part, the New Testament, is the record of Jesus Christ and the beginning of his ministry and the establishment of his church. Christians consider the New Testament to be a new covenant. Together, these testaments teach Christian readers what is required to live properly in this life in order to do what God expects.

The Bible is also a sacred record for Jews. What the Christians call the Old Testament is the only testament, or covenant, for Jewish readers. It is the Hebrew Bible and is a sacred record of how the nation of Israel came to be and how it came to exist in what we now call the Middle East. The ancient children of Israel became God's people, and their country is one established by God as a promised land for His chosen people. For Jews the Hebrew Bible is in three parts. The first five books, or Pentateuch, is the "Law," or Torah. The second section is called "Prophets," and the third section is called "Writings." The Hebrew Bible teaches Jews what they are to do to honor the covenant that God has made with them.

In the Hebrew Bible there are thirty-nine books. In the Protestant Old Testament there are also thirty-nine books, but they are ordered somewhat differently. Catholic Old Testaments have the same thirty-nine books, but in addition, the Catholic Bible adds fifteen more books that are not considered sacred scripture by Protestants or Jews. We commonly call these books the Apocrypha. They are also known as "intertestamental literature" because their stories took place in the era between the end of the Hebrew Bible/Old Testament and the beginning of the New Testament.

To introduce students to the diversity of the Bible with its various translations and versions for Christians and Jews, I like to ask the class a question that is part of the current political discussion: Should the Ten Commandments be posted in the schools of our country? There is usually a good discussion, and the consensus seems to favor posting the commandments, for various reasons. Some students make the theological point that the commandments are still valid today. Others soften the point to say that they are only the beginnings of the laws we know today, or that they are fundamental to our current laws and should be posted for historical reasons.

After the discussion, the next question usually catches students off guard a bit: Which Ten Commandments should we post? Most students assume that the commandments are the same for all Bible believers. I then share an article from the newspaper (sometimes newspapers are more credible than the teacher): "Which—and Whose—Ten Commandments?"

> Both Jews and Christians have Ten Commandments, but there is no agreement on what wording and numbering to follow. The Bible itself contains two versions, one in Exodus 20:1–17 and a slightly different one in Deuteronomy 5:6–21. There are also various English translations from the original Hebrew to choose from.
>
> Moreover, there are five numbering systems because the denominations differ on what to include in the First and Tenth Commandments. Judaism counts "I am the Lord your God, who brought you out of the land of Egypt" as No. 1, while most Christians consider that a preface and list Judaism's No. 2 as their No. 1: "You shall have no other gods before me." Other Christians say that No. 1 consists of both clauses.
>
> Next comes the commandment against idolatry ("graven images"), which Jews combine with the admonition about "no other gods," . . .
>
> As for the next seven commandments—taking the Lord's name in vain, keeping the Sabbath, honoring one's mother and father, killing, adultery, stealing, and bearing false witness—all groups divide up them up identically but apply different numbers.
>
> The Tenth Commandment of Jews and most Protestants is the entire "thou shalt not covet" passage. But Catholics and Lutherans list two "thou shalt not covet" commandments: one against coveting your neighbor's wife, and one against coveting your neighbor's property. ("Which" A2)

The Christian reader doesn't have to look far, even to other Christians and the Ten Commandments, to find that the Bible is not the same book for everyone. There are dozens of translations or versions that make a difference to both religious and academic readers. The Jewish reader who looks closely at the text will also find important differences with Christian translations. The Hebrew prohibits "murder," not "killing." There is a difference because we kill animals, anciently for sacrifice and food and today for food.

The idea of a Bible as one book that can be carried in the hand is fairly new. The idea doesn't seem new to us because we see so many

Bibles in churches, synagogues, motel rooms, libraries, and bookstores, but we only have to go back to 1455, or about 550 years, to find the first Bibles being printed on Gutenberg's press. Even those weren't portable. This may sound like a long time to have had a printed book, but if, as literal readers believe, events in Genesis go back to about 4000 B.C.E,[8] we have had the story of these events for nearly 6000 years. (The Christian year 2000, for instance, was the year 5760 in the Jewish calendar.) We have only had the *printed* story for 550 years, or 9% of the time the narratives have existed. Prior to that the story was copied or transmitted orally. The ability to make exact printed copies has standardized the text somewhat, it is easy to imagine the tremendous variety that would have been possible for the 91 percent of the time that some of the narratives have existed. Of course, Genesis was not actually *written* when it *happened*. Traditional Jews and literal-reading Christians believe Moses wrote it all down at Sinai (dictated by God) which was in 1313 B.C.E. (2448 in the Jewish calendar).

What Stories Are in the Bible?

This may be *the* question for teachers who anticipate teaching the Bible as literature. It is also a question that points to other questions: What writings are included in the Bible besides stories, and what are the various ways to read these writings and stories?

It is tempting to try to list the stories one should know, starting with the beginning of Genesis and concluding (if one is Christian) with the apocalypse of the Revelation. Hirsch, in *The Dictionary of Cultural Literacy*, indicates that "the best-known books of the Old Testament are Genesis, Exodus, the Psalms, the Book of Job, Ecclesiastes, the Song of Solomon, and the Book of Isaiah." The *Dictionary* notes that the main books of the New Testament are "the four Gospels—Matthew, Mark, Luke, and John, which relate the life of Jesus and his teachings—and the Book of Revelation." It concludes, "All educated speakers of American English need to understand what is meant when someone describes a contest as being between David and Goliath, or whether a person who has the 'wisdom of Solomon' is wise or foolish, or whether saying 'My cup runneth over' means the person feels fortunate or unfortunate" (1).

Regarding stories, Hirsch says that it is

> essential for understanding many of the moral and spiritual values of our culture, whatever our religious beliefs. The story of Abraham and Isaac concerns our deepest feelings about the rela-

tions between parents and children. The story of Job is a major
representation in our tradition of being patient during suffering.
The Parables and sayings of Jesus, such as 'Blessed are the meek,
for they shall inherit the earth,' are so often alluded to that they
need to be known by Americans of all faiths. (1)

This text addresses these narratives mentioned by Hirsch, and *The Dictionary of Cultural Literacy* is a good classroom reference for those things we should all know about what is in the Bible.

The question about what stories are in the Bible is a good one but should not allow us to gloss over the fact that there are more than stories in the Bible. There are genealogies, laws, poetry, prayers, drama, and wisdom. Perhaps one of the arguments for teaching the Bible in the public schools is that it seems that almost every literary genre is represented.

Who Wrote the Bible?

We really don't know who wrote the Bible. Many of the books are attributed to people in the Bible, but there is no signed copy of any biblical book. What we do know is that the writers are diverse. Christian writer Josh McDowell accepts the literalness of these attributions and in doing so focuses our attention on the great variety of contributors who wrote over a 1,500-year span. The writers include "kings, peasants, philosophers, fishermen, poets, statesmen, scholars." The texts were written in the wilderness, in a dungeon, on a hillside, in a palace, in prison, and in times of war and peace (16).

The difficulty with the question of who wrote the Bible is that it is a question for both the Hebrew Bible and the New Testament and for virtually every individual book. It is further complicated by the fact that there may be evidence of multiple authors in some books. The most persistent tradition is that the Torah, the first five books of the Hebrew Bible, were written by Moses. This is still the view of most religious Christians and Jews. The New Testament tradition is that the Gospels are named for their authors—e.g., the Gospel According to Matthew. Even though authorship is attributed to these writers, evidence may suggest that the Gospels were composed after the deaths of those given credit as authors. The Epistles were mostly written by Paul. Current scholarship on the New Testament can be found in many resources, including Burton L. Mack, *Who Wrote the New Testament? The Making of the Christian Myth*. Current Hebrew Bible scholarship can be found in Richard Elliott Friedman, *Who Wrote the Bible?*

Over the years I've found that students want to know something about the author(s) and are not satisfied with my vague answers. Sometimes there seems to be little to say. Who actually wrote this book? If there is no original, what is the oldest copy we have? Who wrote the oldest copy? The issue of author is addressed somewhat in class and also in chapter 10 of this book, but it is not the primary focus of a course in the Bible as literature. I give students a start on an answer to these questions by telling them about what is perhaps the oldest fragment of Bible narrative in existence today. It is part of a poem, a poetic prayer for peace similar to a passage in Isaiah. The physical evidence is that it was written for the children near the end of the seventh or the beginning of the sixth century B.C.E. This was before the Babylonian destruction of the first temple, which scholars date as occurring in 586 B.C.E. It was written a thousand years before Mohammed recorded the words of God in the Holy Qur'an; or, if you follow the Christian Bible dating of Bishop Usher, it was written in 1490 B.C.E.

The poem is inscribed on a fragment of silver just less than four inches long and just under an inch wide. This fragment is now in the Israel Museum. Perhaps it was written "with a pen of iron, and with the point of a diamond" as described by Jeremiah (17:1). It was found by Gabriel Barkay in 1980 in a Jewish tomb on a hill facing Jerusalem on its southwest side. The excavation unearthed two rolled fragments in a charnel house excavated from the rock behind the tomb. Graves had been cut into the limestone according to biblical law. Inside these caves, the bodies of the dead were put on shelves, and after a time they would be pushed into the charnel house. The image this recalls is in 2 Kings 22:2: "I will gather thee unto thy fathers, and thou shalt be gathered into thy grave in peace." The passage is recalled because of the gathering and the peace.

The silver fragments were carefully rolled up long before they were found. Originally, they were probably rolled around strings or cords and tied around the necks of dead children. Perhaps they were also worn in life. The Bible is both figurative and literal about words: "bind them about thy neck; write them upon the table of thine heart" (Proverbs 3:3). Some scholars assume that the amulets were worn in life by those laid to rest in the tomb and may have been worn while worshiping at the Temple during the final years before the Babylonian destruction. Perhaps young people wore the tiny scrolls in much the same way that many today wear a crucifix or a Star of David or another religious medallion, like a pendant with the letters WWJD (What Would Jesus Do).

It took two years of testing before a complicated process to unroll the tiny scrolls was finally developed. The open silver scroll was a

wonderful surprise. Here was the first time that the name of God had been found in Jerusalem and in the context of the First Temple period (Romer 94, 95). The message of the silver amulet, perhaps worn by children some 650 years before the Common Era, is in precisely the words of the priestly blessing spoken to Moses, who in turn told Aaron and his sons to bless the children of Israel:

> The LORD bless thee,
> and keep thee:
> The LORD make His face [to] shine upon thee,
> and be gracious unto thee:
> The LORD lift up His countenance upon thee,
> and give thee peace.
> —Numbers 6:24–26[9]

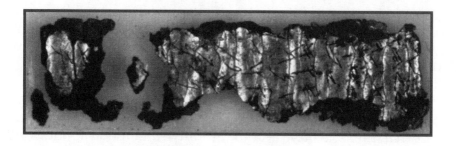

When Was the Bible Written?

The Bible is still being written, if one considers translating and revising to be writing. The latest major translation is the New Revised Standard Version (NRSV). Its copyright date is 1989. This edition can be considered a Bible still being written because it includes notes from the Dead Sea Scrolls, which were first discovered in 1947, with other significant discoveries from 1952 to 1956.

If the question is about when the Bible was first written, the answer isn't as easy, for two reasons. First, most books of the Bible were probably an oral tradition before they were written, so the stories of the Bible are older than any biblical text. Second, there seem to be writings from more than one date mingled together in our modern Bible. The first writing from the oldest text could have been more than 1,500 years ago.

Most biblical criticism scholars date the oldest parts of Genesis to about the tenth century B.C.E. This includes the creation scene in the second chapter of Genesis. The last books of the Hebrew Bible could have been written a couple centuries before the birth of Jesus. This makes the writing of the Hebrew Bible about a thousand-year process.

The editors of the NRSV think that the Song of Deborah in Judges 5 may be the oldest part of the Hebrew Bible. This poem celebrates the victory of the Israelites over the Canaanite general Sisera and is sung by Deborah, a prophet and the judge of Israel at that time. The New Testament, on the other hand, was probably compiled in about a century. Paul's letters could have existed by about 50 C.E., and the latest Christian writings of the Bible about a hundred years later.

What Language Did People Use to Write the Bible?

This is an important question. Sometimes we forget that we are reading literature in translation. Most of the Hebrew Bible was written in Hebrew; some was written in Aramaic, which is closely related to Hebrew. The New Testament was written in Greek, although the "original" text was not spoken in Greek. (Jesus spoke Aramaic.) The title page on the 1611 King James Version (KJV) notes that it has been translated from the "original Greek."

Historically, the first translation of the Hebrew Bible was the Septuagint, which was a Greek translation from the third century B.C.E. The next major translation was of the Christian Bible by the pope's secretary, St. Jerome, near the end of the fourth century C.E. This is a Latin translation and is called the Vulgate. In translating the Bible into Latin, Jerome was more trusting of the text when he could find a Hebrew version. When he could find only Greek versions from which to translate, he indicated that the sources were hidden and called these book Apocrypha, or hidden texts. Today the Catholic Church accepts most of the Apocrypha as part of the Bible, but these books are not included in Protestant Bibles. Most academic Bibles include the Apocrypha.

Who Translated the Bible into English?

It wasn't until after the most important invention of the last thousand years—the printing press with movable type, invented by Johannes Gutenberg in 1455—that the world seemed to become interested in an English Bible translation. It no doubt was encouraged by the Protestant Reformation, fired by Martin Luther, who published a German Bible in 1522.

William Tyndale was the first to translate the Bible into English from Greek and Hebrew. He was also the first to print the Bible in English. It was published in a pocket edition for everyone to own—another first. His first New Testament of 1526 was destroyed, and the revised translation was published in 1534.

> The outlines of Tyndale's life have been generally known: the years at Oxford and in Gloucestershire, the fruitless attempt to get the Bishop of London to support him, the exile to Germany and the Netherlands; the cargoes of Testaments smuggled into England; his arrest in Antwerp, imprisonment and, charged with heresy, burning [1536]. (Daniell 2)

Tyndale's translation has been felt in every English translation since:

> Very many of the treasures which have enriched the lives and language of English speakers since the 1530s were made by Tyndale: a long list of common phrases like "the salt of the earth" or "let there be light" or "the spirit is willing"; the haunting phrasing in parables like the Prodigal Son, "this thy brother was dead, and is alive again: and was lost, and is found"; the gospel stories of Christmas ("there were shepherds abiding in the field") through to the events of the Passion in Jerusalem and the Resurrection; in the Old Testament, the telling of Creation and of Adam and Eve, right through the history told there to Exile in Babylon. All these things came as something new to the men and women of Tyndale's time in the 1520s and 1530s. That was because Tyndale translated them, for the first time, from their original texts in Greek and Hebrew, into English; and then printed them in pocket volumes for everyone to own. Apart from manuscript translations into English from the Latin, made at the time of Chaucer, and linked with the Lollards, the Bible had been only in that Latin translation made a thousand

years before, and few could understand it. Tyndale, before he left England for his life's work, said to a learned man, "If God spare my life, ere many years I will cause a boy that driveth the plough shall know more of the Scripture than thou does." He succeeded. (Daniell 1)

Tyndale is mentioned here because he is the beginning of Bible literature in English translation, which this book proposes we continue to teach in schools. It is for only a little more than 450 years that we have had stories 6,000 years old written down in English. Teachers should also note that this first English translation was a Christian translation faithful to the Protestant Reformation and not to Jewish tradition.

The KJV, or Authorized translation, of the English Bible in 1611 is the most published Bible in our world. It was authorized by King James I and took scholars about seven years to complete. The translation was a scholarly activity conducted by academics of the day, who were translating at a time when language was important. They chose words and phrases carefully and were especially faithful to the earlier work of Tyndale and his successors—the Coverdale Bible of 1535, Matthew's Bible of 1537, the Great Bible of 1539, and the Bishop's Bible of 1568. They were, however, translating for Christian readers. The KJV has persisted until today as perhaps the most literary Bible. It also persisted without much revision until the Revised Version of 1881 and the American Standard Version of the Revised Version, published in the United States in 1901. Since then we have had numerous translations. Most have been efforts to both modernize the language and improve the English translation, but many have particular theological bents.

This brief summary doesn't do justice to the complicated issue of English Bible translations. One only has to type in "Bible" on Amazon.com or in the electronic card catalog in the library to find dozens of choices. Most of the choices are based on religious traditions. Chapter 4 contains some recommendations for parallel Bibles that include specific translations.

Notes

8   B.C.E.,which stands for Before the Common Era, is a more neutral way of saying B.C., which means "Before Christ." Similarly, C.E., Common Era, is used instead of A.D., which stands for Anno Domini and means "Year of Our Lord."

9   Reproduced courtesy of the Israel Museum, where the artifact is on display.

Chapter 4

INTRODUCING THE BIBLE:
FIRST LESSONS AND
RESOURCES FOR THE TEACHER

S ome students will be nervous that the teacher in the public secular school may confront belief by teaching from a sacred text. Some will feel that teaching from their scriptures may diminish the sacred; others, who don't regard the Bible as scripture, may fear that the class is getting too religious. The teacher is walking a fine line by introducing the Bible. There are at least three possible ways to deal with this:

1. Show students that there are many kinds of writing in the Bible and that in school literature courses we mostly study one particular kind. Give examples of five kinds of writing and teach one of those kinds—for example, the short story of left-handed Ehud and fat Eglon. (Judges, chapter 3)

2. Read a fascinating Bible story from the Apocrypha—which, for many students, does not come laden with sanctity because it is not in their Bible. However, it is still clearly biblical. Students will find the story of Susannah, or Daniel and Susannah as it is listed in more modern translations, to be a good one for our modern world. (Teachers will recognize that for many students, the Apocrypha is part of the Bible.)

3. Introduce the Bible by showing how its ideas, allusions, and stories have become part of our secular world. Suggest that Bible stories and allusions good enough to be interesting and

useful to people outside a religious setting are good enough to study in school.

Five Kinds of Writing in the Bible

It helps if students understand that there are at least five kinds of writing in the library we call the Bible and that the Bible as literature is mostly concerned with two of these:

- **Religious Writing.** This writing is sometimes called *doctrine*, *theology*, or *belief*. This is the kind of writing that people read when they want to know what the Bible teaches them to believe and it is usually read in a religious context. Some call it devotional reading. This is the kind of reading people do when they ask questions about grace, faith, redemption, justice and mercy, or other often abstract concepts. It is not the emphasis of literature classes.

  Faith: Chapter 11 of Hebrews is an example of theological discourse. It defines faith and then supports the definition with reference to biblical narrative. This passage is not a poem and tells no story.

  Grace: Ephesians 2:1–10 is a discourse on the relationship of grace and faith.

  Charity/love: Even though 1 Corinthians 13 is poetic, it is not primarily a poem but is a lecture or speech on charity or love. It can be taught as literature.

- **Legal Writing:** The laws are read by those who want to know what they should *do*. Sometimes we call these the *commandments*. These laws sometimes provide a context for our study of literature but they are not the focus of a study of the Bible as literature. Practicing Jews are especially careful readers of the law.

  The laws concerning ritual uncleanness are in chapters 11–15 of Leviticus. The Ten Commandments, Exodus 20, are a familiar example of law.

- **Historical Writing:** This writing is concerned with facts like genealogy, places, events, and data like census records. Sometimes history reads like a story, but it has a goal quite different from that of imaginative literature.

  Genealogy: Genesis 10 is the record of Noah's sons and their families. The genealogy is important to the story but is not the central focus.

History: The two books of Kings have a historical tone. Although some of the narratives read like short stories, chapters 15 and 16 of 2 Kings read more like history texts.

- **Poetic Literature:** This writing is characterized by parallel form and is most obvious in Psalms. It is also characterized by the images it helps us to see.

  Psalm 23 is perhaps the most translated passage in the Hebrew Bible. It is easy to teach simile and metaphor with the images of the psalms. This psalm can be used to introduce poetic qualities. It is discussed more thoroughly in chapter 8.

- **Narrative Literature:** This writing tells a story that speaks to the imagination. One of the characteristics of biblical literature is understatement, which Robert Alter calls "the art of biblical reticence." This literature may be poetic and contain historical, legal, or religious writing, but it is also pleasurable for its own sake because its understatement allows us to see images that we make for ourselves.

The Story of Ehud (Judges 3:12–30)

[12]And the children of Israel did evil again in the sight of the LORD: and the LORD strengthened Eglon the king of Moab against Israel, because they had done evil in the sight of the LORD. [13]And he gathered unto him the children of Ammon and Amalek, and went and smote Israel, and possessed the city of palm trees. [14]So the children of Israel served Eglon the king of Moab eighteen years. [15]But when the children of Israel cried unto the LORD, the LORD raised them up a deliverer, Ehud the son of Gera, a Benjamite, a man left-handed; and by him the children of Israel sent a present unto Eglon the king of Moab. [16]But Ehud made him a dagger which had two edges, of a cubit length; and he did gird it under his raiment upon his right thigh. [17]And he brought the present unto Eglon king of Moab: and Eglon *was* a very fat man. [18]And when he had made an end to offer the present, he sent away the people that bore the present. [19]But he himself turned again from the quarries that *were* by Gilgal, and said, I have a secret errand unto thee, O king, who said, Keep silence. And all that stood by him went out from him. [20]And Ehud

came unto him; and he was sitting in a summer parlour, which he had for himself alone. And Ehud said, I have a message from God unto thee. And he arose out of *his* seat. ²¹And Ehud put forth his left hand, and took the dagger from his right thigh, and thrust it into his belly: ²²And the shaft also went in after the blade; and the fat closed upon the blade, so that he could not draw the dagger out of his belly; and the dirt came out. ²³Then Ehud went forth through the porch, and shut the doors of the parlour upon him, and locked them. ²⁴When he was gone out, his servants came; and when they saw that, behold, the doors of the parlour *were* locked, they said, Surely he covereth his feet in his summer chamber. ²⁵And they tarried till they were ashamed: and, behold, he opened not the doors of the parlour; therefore they took a key, and opened *them*; and, behold, their lord *was* fallen down dead on the earth. ²⁶And Ehud escaped while they tarried, and passed beyond the quarries, and escaped unto Seirath. ²⁷And it came to pass, when he was come, that he blew a trumpet in the mountain of Ephraim, and the children of Israel went down with him from the mount, and he before them. ²⁸And he said unto them, Follow after me: for the LORD hath delivered your enemies the Moabites into your hand. And they went down after him, and took the fords of Jordan toward Moab, and suffered not a man to pass over. ²⁹And they slew of Moab at that time about ten thousand men, all lusty, and all men of valour; and there escaped not a man. ³⁰So Moab was subdued that day under the hand of Israel. And the land had rest fourscore years.[9]

Although the story seems to start as a history, it goes beyond that as it speaks to the imagination. There are points to make about a reticent author and the imagination as students discuss questions about the text.

Of all that could be said about Ehud, the text notes that he is left-handed. The irony is that "Benjamin" means "son of my right hand." Ehud is from the tribe of Benjamin, and the left-handness clarifies the detail about carrying the dagger on his right thigh. What image do we see because of this detail? Would guards be more likely to search Ehud's right or left thigh for a weapon?

We don't know much about Eglon except for the detail that looms largest. "Eglon was a very fat man." What does this lead us to imagine? "Covering his feet" is a euphemism for relieving himself. The "dirt" came out. The shaft went in. This is gross stuff. Are we sure we want to say what we see? The servants are waiting nervously outside the king's summer parlor. What could they be saying?

If the violence of the Ehud story is too much, there are many other short stories that can introduce the literature of the Bible. Parables are particularly interesting, and teachers may consider the story of Susanna or the parable of the prodigal son in Luke 15:11–32. Although many read a religious message from these stories, both actually seem to be more a story of family dynamics.

Susanna: A Short Story for the Modern World

The story of Susanna is short, and it is in the Apocrypha. In some Bible versions it is called "Susanna and the Elders." In the King James Apocrypha it is entitled "The History of Susanna." In other versions it has other names. It is a good place to start, because for many students the Apocrypha doesn't carry the same authority as the Bible. There is a short answer as to what the Apocrypha is in chapter 3, "What We Should All Know about the Bible." This is a story that can be read as a very modern story from an ancient text. It carries a theological message for those reading the story in their own particular religious tradition, but it is easy to read without a message of belief. Most Protestant and Jewish students will have never heard the story before; however, it is in the Catholic Bible.

Because the Apocrypha may not be quickly available, the story is printed here, both from the KJV of 1611 and the NRSV of 1989.[10]

The King James Version of Susanna

[1]There dwelt a man in Babylon, called Joacim: [2]And he took a wife, whose name was Susanna, the daughter of Chelcias, a very fair woman, and one that feared the Lord. [3]Her parents also were righteous, and taught their daughter according to the law of Moses. [4]Now Joacim was a great rich man, and had a fair garden joining unto his house: and to him resorted the Jews; because he was more honourable than all others.

[5]The same year were appointed two of the ancients of the people to be judges, such as the Lord spake of, that wickedness came from Babylon from ancient judges, who seemed to govern the people. [6]These kept much at Joacim's house: and all that had any suits in law came

unto them.

[7]Now when the people departed away at noon, Susanna went into her husband's garden to walk. [8]And the two elders saw her going in every day, and walking; so that their lust was inflamed toward her. [9]And they perverted their own mind, and turned away their eyes, that they might not look unto heaven, nor remember just judgments. [10]And albeit they both were wounded with her love, yet durst not one shew another his grief. [11]For they were ashamed to declare their lust, that they desired to have to do with her. [12]Yet they watched diligently from day to day to see her.

[13]And the one said to the other, Let us now go home: for it is dinner time. [14]So when they were gone out, they parted the one from the other, and turning back again they came to the same place; and after that they had asked one another the cause, they acknowledged their lust: then appointed they a time both together, when they might find her alone.

[15]And it fell out, as they watched a fit time, she went in as before with two maids only, and she was desirous to wash herself in the garden: for it was hot. [16]And there was nobody there save the two elders, that had hid themselves, and watched her. [17]Then she said to her maids, Bring me oil and washing balls, and shut the garden doors, that I may wash me. [18]And they did as she bade them, and shut the garden doors, and went out themselves at privy doors to fetch the things that she had commanded them: but they saw not the elders, because they were hid.

[19]Now when the maids were gone forth, the two elders rose up, and ran unto her, saying, [20]Behold, the garden doors are shut, that no man can see us, and we are in love with thee; therefore consent unto us, and lie with us. [21]If thou wilt not, we will bear witness against thee, that a young man was with thee: and therefore thou didst send away thy maids from thee.

[22]Then Susanna sighed, and said, I am straitened on every side: for if I do this thing, it is death unto me: and if I do it not I cannot escape your hands. [23]It is better for me to fall into your hands, and not do it, than to sin in the sight of the Lord.

[24]With that Susanna cried with a loud voice, and the two elders cried out against her. [25]Then ran the one, and opened the garden door. [26]So when the servants of the house heard the cry in the garden, they rushed in at the privy door, to see what was done unto her. [27]But when the elders had declared their matter, the servants were greatly ashamed: for there was never such a report made of Susanna.

²⁸And it came to pass the next day, when the people were assembled to her husband Joacim, the two elders came also full of mischievous imagination against Susanna to put her to death; ²⁹And said before the people, Send for Susanna, the daughter of Chelcias, Joacim's wife. And so they sent. ³⁰So she came with her father and mother, her children, and all her kindred.

³¹Now Susanna was a very delicate woman, and beauteous to behold. ³²And these wicked men commanded to uncover her face, (for she was covered) that they might be filled with her beauty. ³³Therefore her friends and all that saw her wept.

³⁴Then the two elders stood up in the midst of the people, and laid their hands upon her head. ³⁵And she weeping looked up toward heaven: for her heart trusted in the Lord. ³⁶And the elders said, As we walked in the garden alone, this woman came in with two maids, and shut the garden doors, and sent the maids away. ³⁷Then a young man, who there was hid, came unto her, and lay with her. ³⁸Then we that stood in a corner of the garden, seeing this wickedness, ran unto them. ³⁹And when we saw them together, the man we could not hold; for he was stronger than we, and opened the door, and leaped out. ⁴⁰But having taken this woman, we asked who the young man was, but she would not tell us: these things do we testify.

⁴¹Then the assembly believed them as those that were the elders and judges of the people: so they condemned her to death.

⁴²Then Susanna cried out with a loud voice, and said, O everlasting God, that knowest the secrets, and knowest all things before they be: ⁴³Thou knowest that they have borne false witness against me, and, behold, I must die; whereas I never did such things as these men have maliciously invented against me.

⁴⁴And the Lord heard her voice. ⁴⁵Therefore when she was led to be put to death, the Lord raised up the holy spirit of a young youth whose name was Daniel; ⁴⁶Who cried with a loud voice, I am clear from the blood of this woman.

⁴⁷Then all the people turned them toward him, and said, What mean these words that thou hast spoken? ⁴⁸So he standing in the midst of them said, Are ye such fools, ye sons of Israel, that without examination or knowledge of the truth ye have condemned a daughter of Israel? ⁴⁹Return again to the place of judgment: for they have borne false witness against her.

⁵⁰Wherefore all the people turned again in haste, and the elders said unto him, Come, sit down among us, and shew it us, seeing God hath given thee the honour of an elder. ⁵¹Then said Daniel unto them,

Put these two aside one far from another, and I will examine them.

[52] So when they were put asunder one from another, he called one of them, and said unto him, O thou that art waxen old in wickedness, now thy sins which thou hast committed aforetime are come to light. [53] For thou hast pronounced false judgment and hast condemned the innocent and hast let the guilty go free; albeit the Lord saith, The innocent and righteous shalt thou not slay. [54] Now then, if thou hast seen her, tell me, Under what tree sawest thou them companying together? Who answered, Under a mastick tree. [55] And Daniel said, Very well; thou hast lied against thine own head; for even now the angel of God hath received the sentence of God to cut thee in two.

[56] So he put him aside, and commanded to bring the other, and said unto him, O thou seed of Chanaan, and not of Juda, beauty hath deceived thee, and lust hath perverted thine heart. [57] Thus have ye dealt with the daughters of Israel, and they for fear companied with you: but the daughter of Juda would not abide your wickedness. [58] Now therefore tell me, Under what tree didst thou take them companying together? Who answered, Under an holm tree. [59] Then said Daniel unto him, Well; thou hast also lied against thine own head: for the angel of God waiteth with the sword to cut thee in two, that he may destroy you.

[60] With that all the assembly cried out with a loud voice, and praised God, who saveth them that trust in him. [61] And they arose against the two elders, for Daniel had convicted them of false witness by their own mouth: [62] And according to the law of Moses they did unto them in such sort as they maliciously intended to do to their neighbour: and they put them to death. Thus the innocent blood was saved the same day.

[63] Therefore Chelcias and his wife praised God for their daughter Susanna, with Joacim her husband, and all the kindred, because there was no dishonesty found in her. [64] From that day forth was Daniel had in great reputation in the sight of the people

The New Revised Standard Version of Susanna

[1] There was a man living in Babylon whose name was Joakim. [2] He married the daughter of Hilkiah, named Susanna, a very beautiful woman and one who feared the Lord. [3] Her parents were righteous, and had trained their daughter according to the law of Moses. [4] Joakim was very rich, and had a fine garden adjoining his house; the Jews used to come to him because he was the most honored of them all.

[5] That year two elders from the people were appointed as judges.

Concerning them the Lord had said: "Wickedness came forth from Babylon, from elders who were judges, who were supposed to govern the people." ⁶These men were frequently at Joakim's house, and all who had a case to be tried came to them there.

⁷When the people left at noon, Susanna would go into her husband's garden to walk. ⁸Every day the two elders used to see her, going in and walking about, and they began to lust for her. ⁹They suppressed their consciences and turned away their eyes from looking to Heaven or remembering their duty to administer justice. ¹⁰Both were overwhelmed with passion for her, but they did not tell each other of their distress, ¹¹for they were ashamed to disclose their lustful desire to seduce her. ¹²Day after day they watched eagerly to see her.

¹³One day they said to each other, "Let us go home, for it is time for lunch." So they both left and parted from each other. ¹⁴But turning back, they met again; and when each pressed the other for the reason, they confessed their lust. Then together they arranged for a time when they could find her alone.

¹⁵Once, while they were watching for an opportune day, she went in as before with only two maids, and wished to bathe in the garden, for it was a hot day. ¹⁶No one was there except the two elders, who had hidden themselves and were watching her. ¹⁷She said to her maids, "Bring me olive oil and ointments, and shut the garden doors so that I can bathe." ¹⁸They did as she told them: they shut the doors of the garden and went out by the side doors to bring what they had been commanded; they did not see the elders, because they were hiding.

¹⁹When the maids had gone out, the two elders got up and ran to her. ²⁰They said, "Look, the garden doors are shut, and no one can see us. We are burning with desire for you; so give your consent, and lie with us. ²¹If you refuse, we will testify against you that a young man was with you, and this was why you sent your maids away."

²²Susanna groaned and said, "I am completely trapped. For if I do this, it will mean death for me; if I do not, I cannot escape your hands. ²³I choose not to do it; I will fall into your hands, rather than sin in the sight of the Lord."

²⁴Then Susanna cried out with a loud voice, and the two elders shouted against her. ²⁵And one of them ran and opened the garden doors. ²⁶When the people in the house heard the shouting in the garden, they rushed in at the side door to see what had happened to her. ²⁷And when the elders told their story, the servants felt very much ashamed, for nothing like this had ever been said about Susanna.

²⁸The next day, when the people gathered at the house of her hus-

band Joakim, the two elders came, full of their wicked plot to have Susanna put to death. In the presence of the people they said, ²⁹"Send for Susanna daughter of Hilkiah, the wife of Joakim." ³⁰So they sent for her. And she came with her parents, her children, and all her relatives.

³¹Now Susanna was a woman of great refinement and beautiful in appearance. ³²As she was veiled, the scoundrels ordered her to be unveiled, so that they might feast their eyes on her beauty. ³³Those who were with her and all who saw her were weeping.

³⁴Then the two elders stood up before the people and laid their hands on her head. ³⁵Through her tears she looked up toward Heaven, for her heart trusted in the Lord. ³⁶The elders said, "While we were walking in the garden alone, this woman came in with two maids, shut the garden doors, and dismissed the maids. ³⁷Then a young man, who was hiding there, came to her and lay with her. ³⁸We were in a corner of the garden, and when we saw this wickedness we ran to them. ³⁹Although we saw them embracing, we could not hold the man, because he was stronger than we, and he opened the doors and got away. ⁴⁰We did, however, seize this woman and asked who the young man was, ⁴¹but she would not tell us. These things we testify."

Because they were elders of the people and judges, the assembly believed them and condemned her to death.

⁴²Then Susanna cried out with a loud voice, and said, "O eternal God, you know what is secret and are aware of all things before they come to be; ⁴³you know that these men have given false evidence against me. And now I am to die, though I have done none of the wicked things that they have charged against me!"

⁴⁴The Lord heard her cry. ⁴⁵Just as she was being led off to execution, God stirred up the holy spirit of a young lad named Daniel, ⁴⁶and he shouted with a loud voice, "I want no part in shedding this woman's blood!"

⁴⁷All the people turned to him and asked, "What is this you are saying?" ⁴⁸Taking his stand among them he said, "Are you such fools, O Israelites, as to condemn a daughter of Israel without examination and without learning the facts? ⁴⁹Return to court, for these men have given false evidence against her."

⁵⁰So all the people hurried back. And the rest of the elders said to him, "Come, sit among us and inform us, for God has given you the standing of an elder." ⁵¹Daniel said to them, "Separate them far from each other, and I will examine them."

⁵²When they were separated from each other, he summoned one of them and said to him, "You old relic of wicked days, your sins

have now come home, which you have committed in the past, [53]pronouncing unjust judgments, condemning the innocent and acquitting the guilty, though the Lord said, 'You shall not put an innocent and righteous person to death.' [54]Now then, if you really saw this woman, tell me this: Under what tree did you see them being intimate with each other?" He answered, "Under a mastic tree." [55]And Daniel said, "Very well! This lie has cost you your head, for the angel of God has received the sentence from God and will immediately cut you in two."

[56]Then, putting him to one side, he ordered them to bring the other. And he said to him, "You offspring of Canaan and not of Judah, beauty has beguiled you and lust has perverted your heart. [57]This is how you have been treating the daughters of Israel, and they were intimate with you through fear; but a daughter of Judah would not tolerate your wickedness. [58]Now then, tell me: Under what tree did you catch them being intimate with each other?" He answered, "Under an evergreen oak." [59]Daniel said to him, "Very well! This lie has cost you also your head, for the angel of God is waiting with his sword to split you in two, so as to destroy you both."

[60]Then the whole assembly raised a great shout and blessed God, who saves those who hope in him. [61]And they took action against the two elders, because out of their own mouths Daniel had convicted them of bearing false witness; they did to them as they had wickedly planned to do to their neighbor. [62]Acting in accordance with the law of Moses, they put them to death. Thus innocent blood was spared that day.

[63]Hilkiah and his wife praised God for their daughter Susanna, and so did her husband Joakim and all her relatives, because she was found innocent of a shameful deed. [64]And from that day onward Daniel had a great reputation among the people.

Discussion of Susanna

Students can approach this text like any short story. This usually means starting with some good context and discussion questions. An excellent teacher resource for this is the commentary by Steve Walker, *Seven Ways of Looking at Susanna* (see resource list at the end of this chapter). The story is especially good for illustrating the point about the reticence of biblical literature, and Walker artfully makes this point in his first chapter.

Students will appreciate the contextual information that Walker presents along with some notes about the text. He tells us that there are at least 137 versions of Susanna in drama, fiction, poetry, and painting. In only one genre, drama, there are 16 French versions, 10 Italian, 4 Spanish, 28 German, and 9 English and other. This is a total of 67 dramatic Susannas.

In Christian tradition there are about thirty St. Susannas. They are mostly martyrs to chastity. William Shakespeare named his oldest daughter Susanna. Susanna is clearly in the mainstream of Western culture and makes a good narrative for an introduction to biblical literature. One can't help but think of sexual harassment suits in the modern workplace and school to hear an echo of the Susanna story.

Some questions that have worked in past courses are about the family and social dynamics: (1) Is Susannah a "trophy wife"? (2) Why don't her husband and her parents come to her defense? (3) Why are the people so quick to believe the elders without even giving Susanna a chance to speak? (4) Why is Daniel able to stop the proceeding? (5) Is this a story like modern sexual harassment or rape cases? (6) How is it similar or different?

An attorney in a college class once informed me that this story helps us to understand one of the rules of evidence in modern jurisprudence. It is part of the exclusionary rule, which forbids the introduction of illegally obtained evidence in a criminal trial. Conflicting testimony is illegal and discounts both witnesses. This is still standard procedure in a court of Jewish law.

There is a modern tale in the folklore of the University of Utah that students enjoy in connection with the story of Susanna. I have found no one who can tell me when this happened or to whom, or who can even verify that Utah is the origin of the story. It is modern Susannah-like folklore:

> Two students were so confident of their grades in a chemistry course at the University of Utah that the night before the final exam they drove from Salt Lake City, a dry place (no alcohol), to Wendover, Nevada, a place to party. They got too drunk to drive home in time for the exam and decided to tell the professor that they were late for the exam because of a flat tire.
>
> The professor told them that he would give them a break because they each had an A going into the final exam. He put them in separate rooms and gave them a test that was much different from the one he gave the rest of the class. There were only two questions on their exam. The first was a simple chemistry question that he was sure the students would know. The second question would determine their grade: Which tire?

Biblical Allusions and Knowledge in Our World

A third way of introducing students to the Bible is to share a sample of what people know about the Bible and show recurrent biblical allusions in our modern discourse. There are three possibilities that show biblical knowledge, or more precisely, biblical ignorance.

Jay Leno and Art Linkletter

The *Tonight Show with Jay Leno* featured a six-minute segment on the Bible on November 6, 1997, in celebration of National Bible Week. Leno asked people he met on Melrose Ave here in Los Angeles (probably not the best place for a representative sample of the U.S. population) Bible questions and learned how uninformed many are about the Bible, even though they claim to be religious or informed. One of the best lines occurs when one person identifies the three wise men of the Nativity as the Nina, the Pinta, and the Santa Maria.

Collectively, the teacher and the class will know the correct answers to Leno's questions and will have an introduction to the Bible that demonstrates that the Bible is part of a cultural literary heritage, which, if studied, will continue. The Leno clip is available from Video Monitoring Services of America. Details are given in the section on teacher resources at the end of this chapter.

The wrong answers that Leno gets aren't that far off from a 1950s version of the same idea. Art Linkletter, on his TV show *House Party*, asks kids Bible questions and gets answers every bit as off-the-wall as Leno received.

The clips are not the centerpiece of a literary lesson, just a light introduction that defuses some of the concern about the Bible as text. If Leno and Linkletter can do this, anyone can.

Borrowings from Bartlett

Another way to show the Bible text in our world is to ask students to find biblical allusions. Because the Bible is the most represented work in *Bartlett's Familiar Quotations*, I started with the 440 Old Testament citations and the 230 New Testament citations in the book and did some heavy cutting and slight adding to compile a list, which I give to students to use like a field guide as they look for biblical references. The idea is to find a few of Bartlett's borrowings in our world. Some students tick off a few on the list, others find many, and some add allusions I've missed. If they seek, they will find the allusions in the news and in other TV fare as well as in our daily discourse. It is an assignment that seems to continue all year, as students notice Bible allusions on TV and in the news. The list for students, "Borrowings from Bartlett," is in Appendix A. I suggest editing the list down a bit for the lower grade levels so that it isn't so daunting.

I also suggest a companion list or a separate list that can be compiled from *The Dictionary of Cultural Literacy* (Hirsch and Kett). The difference is that the list from the *Dictionary* includes terms, names, and concepts rather than phrases. Whether or not a list is compiled from the *Dictionary*, it is still a good classroom resource, because the definitions in the Bible section are in terms of the Bible rather than in terms of modern usage. It is a gold mine of biblical allusion.

If the search puts too much importance on the trivial pursuit of biblical phrases, there is another way to demonstrate the way that the Bible has permeated our language. Students can search for allusions to one Bible story. The story of David and Goliath (1 Samuel 17) is a no-fail example. There is always some game that sports commentators promote as a David and Goliath story. Even though sports always work for allusions, the little guy up against the big one can include little computer companies against Bill Gates and Microsoft, the minor party candidate against the political establishment, the small store against the giant chain store, or the owner of an older home in the path of a new freeway. A commercial for the new Chevrolet Malibu shows the car sandwiched in between eighteen-wheel rigs on the freeway and notes that the Malibu was up against the "Goliaths of the highway" and winning, as everyone knows David does. In a quarter century I have never had students who failed to find a David and Goliath example.

Another way to put the language of the Bible in our modern cultural context is to read a short newspaper passage to the class. It is not only the "editorial" ideas of the Bible, such as "Thou shalt" and "Thou shalt not," that have become part of the culture. It is not only the fact that the literary structure of biblical passages often provides a framework for other writers. The very words, especially of the KJV, are part of our language. Because the words are part of our language, they are also part of the way we think.

I first published the Christmas message below in 1991 in the *Deseret News* as a greeting to those who read and respond to my weekly column, "Learning Matters." My goal was to quote the Bible in every sentence. It has since been published numerous times. Notice that every sentence has at least one quotation from or allusion to the Bible.

The allusions are the biblical passages without quotation marks. Many sentences have more than one allusion or quotation and are evidence that the Bible has become part of our cultural DNA and the fabric of the language we use to think.

I often read this passage to a class and raise my hand with each allusion to show the class I'm quoting the Bible. The passage should be read with caution. It takes the language of the Bible out of the context of the Bible. This decontextualization is something we try not to do in a literature class, but at the same time the point being made here is that the words of the Bible have been taken out of the Bible and have become part of the way we think about the world. Our world has decontextualized the Bible much the way this article has.

The context of the article is a discussion about religious displays by government officials in Salt Lake City. The passage is printed with some caution because the issue of public religious displays is not a literary issue. However, the passage does demonstrate that the language of the Bible has become part of the language of everyday discourse.

> City councils must be "at their wits' end" (Psalm 107:27) advising constituents, "Let us reason together" (Isaiah 1:18), as they discuss the annual civic Christmas issue of religious displays.
>
> Opponents of the displays call them worse than "good for nothing" (Matthew 5:13) and tantamount to a government shout "from the housetops" (Matthew 10:27) in support of religion. The opponents suggest that the displays violate the spirit and the letter of the law (Romans 2:29) which is "no respecter of persons" (Acts 10:34) or beliefs.
>
> Some religious groups also oppose secular sponsorship of religion as a "pearl of great price" (Matthew 13:46) that is "cast before swine" (Matthew 7:6). Some even argue that the displays are "graven images" (Exodus 20:4) and regard them with "weeping and wailing" (Esther 4:3).
>
> Those who support religious displays by cities often see the city councils as a "stumbling block" (Leviticus 19:14) on the straight and narrow path (Matthew 7:14). They look for a "scapegoat" (Leviticus 16:8) to blame, such as the ACLU, which they consider a fly in the ointment (Ecclesiastes 10:1) that harps on a twice-told tale (Psalm 90:9). These people see rights going "here a little, and there a little" (Isaiah 38:1). They claim that the handwriting is on the wall (Daniel 5:5) and prophesy the end because "no man can

serve two masters" (Matthew 6:24).

"In the beginning" (Genesis 1:1) it may help if both sides "saw the light" (Genesis 1:4; Acts 9:3) and recognized that the Bible and its words have become "the voice of the people" (1 Samuel 8:7) in this promised land (Genesis 11:4). That is not to say that our land of "milk and honey" (Exodus 14:22) is "holier than thou" (Isaiah 40:15) and a Christian nation.

"The root of the matter" (Job 19:28) is that the language of our culture has some of its roots in the Bible. "The book of life" (Revelation 3:5) has become secular and has "turned the world upside down" (Acts 17:6). In fact, we "labor in vain" (Psalm 127:1) if we try to speak without quoting the Bible. This makes it impossible to separate the wheat from the chaff (Matthew 3:12) or the state from religion or the Bible from our culture. "In the beginning was the Word" (John 1:1), and the word is still with us in everything we say.

Most would agree that we can't "live by bread alone" (Deuteronomy 8:3; Matthew 4:4) and that "the spirit giveth life" (2 Corinthians 3:6). Perhaps this includes a spirit of Christmas as a time to bind up wounds (Psalms 147:3) and try to "see eye to eye" (Isaiah 52:8), even with those with whom we disagree.

The issue of religious displays is, after all, a drop in the bucket (Isaiah 40:15) compared to the problems of brotherly love that we should work on during this season. Perhaps people of all persuasions could pour oil on "troubled waters" (Psalm 46:3) as peacemakers (Matthew 5:9) that the world desperately needs.

It should be as "clear as crystal" (Revelation 22:1) to opponents of civic religious displays as well as to supporters that we will never be "all of one mind" (1 Peter 3:8) and that city councils have "weightier matters of the law" (Matthew 23:23) to deal with for "lo, these many years" (Luke 15:29). Since Christmas is a time for "brotherly love" (Revelation 12:10) perhaps it is also a time to recognize that "the powers that be" (Romans 13:1) can't be "all things to all men" (1 Corinthians 9:22) and enjoy a season of "peace on earth, good will to all" (Luke 2:14) without the traditional annual arguments. "Amen" (Numbers 5:22).

There is still another way to show how the Bible exists in our culture: read the comics. A good place to start is with someone who has done some collecting. Leonard Greenspoon shows part of his comic collection in "The New Testament in the Comics," *Bible Review* 9.6

(October 1991): 40.

Selected Resources for Those Who Wish to Teach the Bible as Literature

Books

Alter, Robert. *The Art of Biblical Narrative*. New York: Basic Books, 1981. (195 pages)

> This book would be listed first even if this list were not alphabetical but instead a reflection of my priority. Alter intends the book "to be a guide to the intelligent reading of biblical narrative." He succeeds by not only making a case for reading the text as literature, but by supporting his case with clear examples.

Alter, Robert. *The Art of Biblical Poetry*. New York: Basic Books, 1985. (228 pages)

> Alter proves again that specific example is the best teacher in this poetic parallel to his first book. The teacher just discovering biblical poetry would do well to consider Ryken's *How to Read the Bible as Literature* before letting Alter make the points clear with his lucid examples.

Alter, Robert. *The World of Biblical Literature*. New York: Basic Books, 1992. (225 pages)

> There are other people who explicate biblical literature besides Alter; however, this collection of essays is a must-read as a capstone experience. It is best enjoyed by the teacher who wants to put a fragmented study of the Bible as literature together.

Alter, Robert, and Frank Kermode. *The Literary Guide to the Bible*. Cambridge: Belknap Press, 1987. (678 pages)

> For most readers, this is not a cover-to-cover read. It is an encyclopedic work of essays by some of the best, and a good resource tool. There is an essay on each major book of the Old and New Testaments. This is an especially good starting point for a teacher trying to explicate a particular biblical narrative.

Bloom, Harold, and David Rosenberg. *The Book of J*. New York: Grove Weidenfeld, 1990. (340 pages)

> Bloom makes exciting commentary on what academic scholars consider to be the oldest documentary source of the Hebrew Bible. The book includes this source, "J," extracted from the rest of the text and allows the reader insights into this theory of what may have been the earliest narratives of the Bible.

Friedman, Richard. *Who Wrote the Bible*? New York: Harper & Row,

1987. (299 pages)

This book offers a nontechnical but insightful analysis of the documentary hypothesis. The analysis takes the form of a search for the author of the Bible. It has been especially helpful to me as I fill out my book request for the bookstore each term. I now know what to put on the line that asks for author.

Frye, Northrop. *The Great Code: The Bible and Literature*. New York: Harvest/HBJ, 1982. (261 pages)

Frye is not an easy read but is a must for the serious student of biblical literature. His goal is to demonstrate the literary influence of the Bible. This is not an introductory text for a teacher just testing the biblical waters. This is for someone who wants to read top-of-the-line criticism.

Gabel, John B., and Charles B. Wheeler. *The Bible as Literature: An Introduction*. New York: Oxford, 1996. (330 pages)

The volume could well be a text for a Bible as Literature course for students with little background in the Bible. It may be that it is more an introduction to the Bible than an introduction to the Bible as literature but it is one of the best general texts in publication.

Hayes, John H., and Carl R. Holladay. *Biblical Exegesis: A Beginner's Handbook*. Atlanta: John Knox, 1987. (159 pages)

Those who admit to not being able to pronounce ĕk′se-jēsĕs will have a friend in this primer. The book does not instruct but is more like a dictionary that defines the different criticisms of the Bible. The book is probably most valuable for its excellent bibliography.

Long, V. Philips. *The Art of Biblical History. Foundations of Contemporary Interpretation*. Vol. 5. Grand Rapids: Zondervan, 1994. (247 pages)

The editor's preface sets the tone. "Dr. Long's clear commitment to biblical historicity will, almost by definition, offend those who believe no one can be considered a scholar who does not find error, myth, or contradiction in the narratives of Scripture. By contrast, his very willingness to ask the hard questions—and thus inevitably to recognize the literary artistry of the narratives—may well put off readers who think there is only one kind of history-writing." For the teacher, this book clarifies, but does not resolve, the relationship between literature and history.

Longman, Tremper III. *Literary Approaches to Biblical Interpretation. Foundations of Contemporary Interpretation*. Vol. 3. Grand Rapids: Academe, 1987. (164 pages)

The entire series, edited by Moises Silva, is worth reading. It is a technical notch above Hayes and Holladay's *Biblical Exegesis: A Beginner's Handbook*, but it is still elementary enough for a starting point.

Potok, Chaim. *Wanderings: Chaim Potok's History of the Jews*. New York: Fawcett Crest, 1978. (576 pages)
> Those who have always regretted not reading the works of Josephus can now escape to a Jewish history spun out by a master storyteller. This book is not about the Bible. It is very readable and a must for those who need the context of the history of the Jews as a backdrop to a literary reading of the Bible.

Romer, John. *Testament: The Bible and History*. New York: Henry Holt and Company, 1988.
> This is the history of the Bible for those who missed the seven-hour TV series also developed by John Romer. It is "the story of the Bible's extraordinary journey from the most ancient East to the heart of the modern West." It is told by an expert in the worlds of art history and archaeology and is especially well illustrated. It is a must for someone who wants a survey of the Bible's history.

Ryken, Leland. *How to Read the Bible as Literature*. Grand Rapids: Academe Books, 1984. (208 pages)
> Although Alter wrote the number one book, Ryken is probably the best place for most people to start. This book is a bit pedestrian but is fundamental in the best sense of the word.

Ryken, Leland. *Words of Delight: A Literary Introduction to the Bible*. Grand Rapids: Baker, 1987. (382 pages)
> Ryken's second book parallels his first but contains actual explications of the texts that are lacking in the first book and are very helpful. The examples make this another candidate as a best place to start.

Ryken, Leland, and Tremper, Longman III eds. *A Complete Literary Guide to the Bible*. Grand Rapids: Zondervan, 1993. (528 pages)
> This encyclopedic work is an excellent collection of essays explicating biblical narrative and poetry. The collection of essays is prefaced with five excellent chapters that introduce the Bible as literature, biblical narrative, and biblical poetry. The work is current and from some of the best close readers of the Bible. It is a good place to start for those new to reading the Bible as literature and those wishing to write on a particular book of the Bible.

Sternberg, Meir. *The Poetics of Biblical Narrative*. Bloomington: Indiana University Press, 1985. (580 pages)
> Robert Alter makes the case for this book. The book "contains some of the most brilliant close readings anyone has done [and] demonstrates in case after case that there is far more that nicely dovetails or complexly interacts in the elements of the received text than has been imagined in the two centuries of biblical scholarship."

Tate, Randolph W. *Biblical Interpretation: An Integrated Approach.* Peabody, MA: Hendrickson, 1991. (226 pages)

> Read this and you too can say, "Yesterday I couldn't pronounce hermeneutics and today I'm doing it." The truth is you were doing it all along. Tate identifies ways to look at the world behind the text, the world within the text, and the world in front of the text. He makes a good summary of what literary criticism purports to do.

Trible, Phyllis. *Texts of Terror: Literary-Feminist Readings of Biblical Narratives.* Philadelphia: Fortress, 1984. (128 pages)

> There are some savvy feminists writing today, and to me Trible seems especially perceptive and articulate. This book explicates four difficult narratives: the stories of Hagar, Tamar, the unnamed woman called "a concubine from Bethlehem" in Judges, and the daughter of Jephthah. In these explications Trible not only help readers understand a feminist perspective, she also helps us to understand some sad stories in the Bible.

Walker, Steven C. *Seven Ways of Looking at Susanna.* Values in Literature Monograph 1. Provo: Brigham Young University, 1984. (115 pages)

> Susanna is a model. Voyeurs and literary critics seek her. The voyeurs clumsily seduce while Walker allows her to model biblical criticism. The value of this work is not only in what it does with Susanna but in what it suggests for other texts. Students who want to write about the Bible would do well to read Susanna first.

Commentary

Albright, William Foxwell, and David Noel Freedman. *The Anchor Bible.* New York: Doubleday. (multiple dates and multiple volumes)

> There of dozens of good multivolume Bible commentaries, and it is impossible to name one of them as the best. *The Anchor Bible* is readable and contains some of the golden nuggets of biblical scholarship.

Dictionaries and Reference Works

There are two multivolume encyclopedic Bible dictionaries that are helpful. The older work, *The Interpreter's Dictionary of the Bible*, is a five-volume work published by Abingdon. The more recent is *The Anchor Bible Dictionary*, a six-volume work published by Doubleday. Both have particular strengths and are excellent reference works. A comprehensive Jewish view is offered in *Encyclopedia Judaica* published by Keter Publishing House. The CD-ROM edition is published by Judaica Multimedia (Israel) Ltd.

Ferguson, George. *Signs & Symbols in Christian Art*. New York: Oxford University, 1961. (183 pages)

> This is a helpful reference volume when looking for symbolic meaning.

Hirsch, E. D. Jr., Joseph F. Kett, and James Trefil. *The Dictionary of Cultural Literacy*. Boston: Houghton Mifflin Company, 1991. (586 pages)

> The twenty-six pages of biblical terms, names, and phrases are worth the cost of the book. It is an excellent classroom reference.

Jeffrey, David Lyle, ed. *A Dictionary of Biblical Tradition in English Literature*. Grand Rapids, Michigan: William B. Eerdmans, 1992. (960)

> This is the book for finding biblical themes in literature. For example, if you want to find a narrative that uses a David and Goliath theme or addresses the same problem as Job, this is the place to look. It was especially helpful when I proposed a college course on biblical themes in literature.

Matthews, Victor H. *Manners and Customs in the Bible*. Peabody, MA: Hendrickson, 1991. (283 pages)

Ryken, Leland, ed. *Dictionary of Biblical Imagery*. Downers Grove, IL: Intervarsity, 1998. (1058 pages)

> Both of these resources are helpful in putting biblical narratives in a cultural context. The latter is a dictionary and the former is written to be read as a text, but good chapter headings and a thorough index make it a good reference work.

Warshaw, Thayer S. *Handbook for Teaching the Bible in Literature Classes*. Nashville: Abingdon, 1978.

> This handbook represents a more traditional and a more comprehensive view of the Bible. It goes beyond teaching the Bible as literature to include the Bible *in* literature and the Bible *and* literature. It is part of the work done by the Indiana University Institute on Teaching the Bible in Literature Courses in the late 1970s and is part of half a dozen good resources published by the Institute. Much of this pioneering work is now out of print.

Bibles

The Complete Parallel Bible with the Apocryphal/Deuterocanonical Books: New Revised Standard Version—Revised English Bible—New American Bible—New Jerusalem Bible. New York: Oxford University Press, 1993.

> My bias is the Authorized, or King James Version, of the Bible. It is what I grew up with, but the problem is that the language is a bit archaic and difficult for students. Another problem is that students feel more com-

fortable with their own Bibles. For this reason I let students use the Bible they prefer and support them with my personal Parallel Bible. Also helpful is the NIV Interlinear Hebrew-English Old Testament (Kohlenburger).

The promotional narrative of the publisher is accurate: "The Complete Parallel Bible presents four of the most highly respected modern-language Bible translations arranged side-by-side for easy comparison. The parallel format brings new insights into the distinct characteristics that distinguish the texts used by Protestant, Catholic, and Orthodox Christians. This unique work highlights the importance of the translation process in defining the priorities and concerns of these different groups, and reveals interesting contrasts in literary styles, verse placement, and canonical content."

The introduction notes that the NRSV and the REB are the most ecumenical translations, "included scholars from Protestant, Anglican, Catholic, Orthodox and Jewish commentaries." (ix) Most English translations of the Bible are Christian or academic in perspective and tone. The Jewish Publication Society offers a good Tanakh student edition for those who wish to use a Jewish Bible in English.

Periodicals

There are hundreds of Bible-related periodicals. Many have a particular theological bent, and none is specific enough to consider the Bible only as literature. The savvy ecclectic reader will enjoy *Bible Review,* or *BR,* which is published bimonthly by the Biblical Archaeology Society. This publication is aimed at an informed but not necessarily scholarly audience. It accepts advertising and is more a magazine than a journal. One reason that this publication is useful is that there is an index to past articles as well as wonderful illustrations. The editors tell me that the index and a full text archive of articles will be on the Web by 2002. Check out http://www.bib-arch.org/br2.html.

The Journal of Biblical Literature is published quarterly by the Society of Biblical Literature. This is the largest organization of Bible scholars, and the journal is the closest we get to some definitive Bible publication. It is a refereed journal, and some of the articles are quite technical. It is an excellent resource.

Videos and Movies

"Bible Questions," *The Tonight Show with Jay Leno*. NBC Network, November 6, 1997 (5 minutes 45 seconds)

Available from Video Monitoring Services of America (VMS), (212) 736-

2010.

"Bible Questions," *The Best of Art Linkletter's Kids Say the Darndest Things.* Vols. 1 and 2. CBS, 1994.
> Produced by the Darndest Partnership/Big Sky Productions, 20434 South Santa Fe Avenue, Long Beach, CA 90810.

Scott, Bernard Brandon. *Hollywood Dreams & Biblical Stories.* Minneapolis: Fortress Press, 1994. (297 pages)
> This is the book to try when looking for a movie. "An accomplished biblical scholar here juxtaposes movies and New Testament themes to uncover the mythic dimensions of each and to explore the primary conflicts in American society."

The Bible as Literature: In the Beginning Was the Word. Video Recording. New York: The Center for Humanities, 1975.
> It's old, but it's good. This two-part video was first a slide presentation but was good enough that the Center for Humanities put it on video. A statement from the teacher's guide best establishes the premise of this production: "The Bible is perhaps the most influential work in history. Its primary function is religious, but it is also important as a work of literature, dealing with themes of universal value. . . . By taking concrete details of life and applying them to profound ideas and feelings, the Bible is able to speak directly to the senses and heart."

Testament: The Bible and History. Princeton: Films for the Humanities, 1988.
> This series is narrated by John Romer. It is essentially the same as his book, which is listed above, but with the addition of an on-location video shot around the world. The series provides an excellent historical perspective of the Bible and is available from Films for the Humanities, Box 2053, Princeton, NJ 08543 (800-257-5126).

Computer Programs

Over the years I have found that asking students to compare translations of particular Bible passages teaches close reading. Students become critical readers when the meaning of a sentence can shift dramatically with the change of one word. These parallel readings are easy to put together with Bible software that shows parallel texts on the computer screen. I like to use the following: Logos Research Systems—information at http://www. logos.com; and Bible Works—information on this program and a dozen others at http://www. wordmicro.com/biblesoftwre.htm. These electronic Bibles include Greek and Hebrew texts.

Comedy

One of the foremost commentators on the Bible today is Bill Cosby. His Noah commentary and his reflections on the origin of childhood brain damage in Genesis are timeless and good for more than a laugh.

Notes

9   The KJV printed here is in the public domain. Teachers may wish to use a translation in modern English such as NEB or NRSV.

10   NRSV is quoted by permission of the National Council of the Churches of Christ in the USA. The story of Susanna is used by permission. All rights reserved. Thomas Nelson Publishers, ©1989.

Chapter 5

THE CREATION NARRATIVE: IN THE BEGINNING

Bible readers use the creation narrative in Genesis to explain history, science, and religion, but in a literature class it is a narrative that captures one of the most important dilemmas of life and one that can be read using at least two established academic approaches. A close reading of the creation story may find very little science or history. It may be that the scientists are asking entirely different questions than religious readers ask. Scientists want to know *how* it all happened. The question for religious readers is *why* the world was created. What of the literary readers? What do they expect to find in the first narrative of the Hebrew Bible?

Stories, whether in the Bible or not, have three basic ingredients, according to Ryken in *How to Read the Bible as Literature*. Reading a story involves paying attention to setting, characters, and plot (35). This is a good first step for students reading the creation narrative in Genesis 1 and 2:

- What is the setting? Where does this story take place? What do we know about this place from the story?

- Who are the characters? Who plays a role other than Adam and Eve?

- What happens?

Because this narrative exemplifies one of the hallmarks of biblical literature, reticence, it offers much for the imagination. It doesn't fill in all the blanks. It is this characteristic that encourages us to see with our imagination as we read. Here is a narrative in which a serpent speaks, fruit is symbolic, and knowledge or knowing has three meanings: "to know," "to understand," and "to have carnal relations with" (Hammond 647).

Literary Interpretation
of the Genesis Narrative

In the *Handbook for Teaching the Bible in Literature Classes*, Warshaw suggests teaching the creative narrative by "translating the work of a literary scholar into classroom material" (35). His example is the work of Kenneth R. R. Gros Louis in chapters 3 and 4 of *Literary Interpretations of Biblical Narratives*. The core of this interpretation is a comparison of Genesis 1 and Genesis 2. The actual dividing line between the two narratives that students compare is Genesis 2:4.

Students are asked to label two columns on paper and label the first column Genesis 1:1–2:3. The second is labeled Genesis 2:4–25. The task is to compare the two chapters, which are printed here from the KJV:

Genesis 1:1–2:3

[1]In the beginning God created the heaven and the earth. [2]And the earth was without form, and void; and darkness *was* upon the face of the deep. And the Spirit of God moved upon the face of the waters.

[3]And God said, Let there be light: and there was light. [4]And God saw the light, that *it was* good: and God divided the light from the darkness. [5]And God called the light Day, and the darkness He called Night. And the evening and the morning were the first day.

[6]And God said, Let there be a firmament in the midst of the waters, and let it divide the waters from the waters. [7]And God made the firmament, and divided the waters which *were* under the firmament from the waters which *were* above the firmament: and it was so. [8]And God called the firmament Heaven. And the evening and the morning were the second day.

[9]And God said, Let the waters under the heaven be gathered together unto one place, and let the dry *land* appear: and it was so. [10]And God called the dry *land* Earth; and the gathering together of the waters called he Seas: and God saw that *it was* good. [11]And God said, Let the earth bring forth grass, the herb yielding seed, *and* the fruit tree yielding fruit after his kind, whose seed *is* in itself, upon the

earth: and it was so. ¹²And the earth brought forth grass, *and* herb yielding seed after his kind, and the tree yielding fruit, whose seed *was* in itself, after his kind: and God saw that *it was* good. ¹³And the evening and the morning were the third day.

¹⁴And God said, Let there be lights in the firmament of the heaven to divide the day from the night; and let them be for signs, and for seasons, and for days, and years: ¹⁵And let them be for lights in the firmament of the heaven to give light upon the earth: and it was so. ¹⁶And God made two great lights; the greater light to rule the day, and the lesser light to rule the night: *he made* the stars also. ¹⁷And God set them in the firmament of the heaven to give light upon the earth, ¹⁸And to rule over the day and over the night, and to divide the light from the darkness: and God saw that *it was* good. ¹⁹And the evening and the morning were the fourth day.

²⁰And God said, Let the waters bring forth abundantly the moving creatures that hath life, and fowl *that* may fly above the earth in the open firmament of heaven. ²¹And God created great whales, and every living creature that moveth, which the waters brought forth abundantly, after their kind, and every winged fowl after his kind: and God saw that *it was* good. ²²And God blessed them, saying, Be fruitful, and multiply, and fill the waters in the seas, and let fowl multiply in the earth. ²³And the evening and the morning were the fifth day.

²⁴And God said, Let the earth bring forth the living creature after his kind, cattle, and creeping thing, and beast of the earth after his kind: and it was so. ²⁵And God made the beast of the earth after his kind, and cattle after their kind, and every thing that creepeth upon the earth after his kind: and God saw that *it was* good.

²⁶And God said, Let us make man in our image, after our likeness: and let them have dominion over the fish of the sea, and over the fowl of the air, and over the cattle, and over all the earth, and over every creeping thing that creepeth upon the earth. ²⁷So God created man in His *own* image, in the image of God created He him; male and female created He them. ²⁸And God blessed them, and God said unto them, Be fruitful, and multiply, and replenish the earth, and subdue it: and have dominion over the fish of the sea, and over the fowl of the air, and over every living thing that moveth upon the earth.

²⁹And God said, Behold, I have given you every herb bearing seed, which *is* upon the face of all the earth, and every tree, in the which *is* the fruit of a tree yielding seed; to you it shall be for meat. ³⁰And to every beast of the earth, and to every fowl of the air, and to every thing that

creepeth upon the earth, wherein *there is* life, *I have given* every green herb for meat: and it was so.

^{31}And God saw every thing that He had made, and, behold, *it was* very good. And the evening and the morning were the sixth day.

^{1}Thus the heavens and the earth were finished, and all the host of them. ^{2}And on the seventh day God ended His work which He had made; and He rested on the seventh day from all His work which He had made. ^{3}And God blessed the seventh day, and sanctified it: because that in it He had rested from all His work which God created and made.

Genesis 2:4–25

^{4}These *are* the generations of the heavens and of the earth when they were created, in the day that the LORD God made the earth and the heavens, ^{5}And every plant of the field before it was in the earth, and every herb of the field before it grew: for the LORD God had not caused it to rain upon the earth, and *there was* not a man to till the ground. ^{6}But there went up a mist from the earth, and watered the whole face of the ground. ^{7}And the LORD God formed man *of* the dust of the ground, and breathed into his nostrils the breath of life; and man became a living soul.

^{8}And the LORD God planted a garden eastward in Eden; and there he put the man whom he had formed. ^{9}And out of the ground made the LORD God to grow every tree that is pleasant to the sight, and good for food; the tree of life also in the midst of the garden, and the tree of knowledge of good and evil. ^{10}And a river went out of Eden to water the garden; and from thence it was parted, and became into four heads. ^{11}The name of the first *is* Pison: that *is* it which compasseth the whole land of Havilah, where *there is* gold; ^{12}And the gold of that land *is* good: there *is* bdellium and the onyx stone. ^{13}And the name of the second river *is* Gihon: the same *is* it that compasseth the whole land of Ethiopia. ^{14}And the name of the third river *is* Hiddekel: that *is* it which goeth toward the east of Assyria. And the fourth river *is* Euphrates. ^{15}And the LORD God took the man, and put him into the garden of Eden to dress it and to keep it.

^{16}And the LORD God commanded the man, saying, Of every tree of the garden thou mayest freely eat: ^{17}But of the tree of the knowledge of good and evil, thou shalt not eat of it: for in the day that thou eatest thereof thou shalt surely die.

^{18}And the LORD God said, *It is* not good that the man should be alone; I will make him a helpmeet for him. ^{19}And out of the ground the LORD God formed every beast of the field, and every fowl of the air; and brought *them* unto Adam to see what he would call them:

and whatsoever Adam called every living creature, that *was* the name thereof. [20]And Adam gave names to all cattle, and to the fowl of the air, and to every beast of the field; but for Adam there was not found a helpmeet for him.

[21]And the LORD God caused a deep sleep to fall upon Adam, and he slept: and he took one of his ribs, and closed up the flesh instead thereof; [22]And the rib, which the LORD God had taken from man, made he a woman, and brought her unto the man. [23]And Adam said, This *is* now bone of my bones, and flesh of my flesh: she shall be called Woman, because she was taken out of Man. [24]Therefore shall a man leave his father and his mother, and shall cleave unto his wife: and they shall be one flesh. [25]And they were both naked, the man and his wife, and were not ashamed.

Discussion

Students are good close readers. They are particularly good at noticing plot differences. They will notice that the creation days are different in the two narratives and that the order of creation is different. After the class spins these out for awhile, I point out some differences noticed by scholars for centuries and used by Louis in his literary analysis:

1. The first version is carefully ordered. On day one, then on day two, and so on, certain things are accomplished. There is a plan that ends with "Let us make man in our image, after our likeness." In the second account things seem to happen in a less orderly fashion. "Man is created before certain other elements of the created universe which are then created with particular emphasis on their relation and importance to man" (Louis 42). Adam then gets involved, as God shows him the animals and Adam names them. This second version is as if an artist, who fashioned the first man of clay and breathed into his nostrils, is more expressive than the orderly creator of version one. Are these right-brained and left-brained versions?

2. Besides all the plot differences, the creator is *God* in the first version (KJV) and *Lord God* in the second. In some translations the first is Elohim and the second is God Yahweh or Lord Jehovah.

3. Louis points out that the first account is structured rather carefully. The creation of light on the first day and God's division of light from the darkness is paralleled on the fourth day by the creation of lights, a greater light and a lesser light. The cre-

ation of the firmament on the second day and God's division of the waters under the firmament from those above the firmament is paralleled on the fifth day by the creation of life *in* the firmament, both in the waters and in the air. The creation of land and vegetation on the third day is paralleled on the sixth day by the creation of life *on* the land (43).

4. The verbs of the first narrative—*created, said, saw, divided, called, made* and so forth—are didactic and orderly and are verbs of a God who commands. The verbs are so strong that there is no metaphor or simile as in the second narrative.

The goal is to teach close reading, and as a result there is an inevitable question about the creation narratives. Why are there two? When students ask this, I ask them a question: Could either narrative stand on its own? Are there really two distinct narratives or is one an explaination of the other? That is, could we get along with just one creation narrative in Genesis? This leads to a good discussion of what each narrative contributes to the other. It is also an opportunity to suggest that there may have been more than one writer here. This is a point that gets additional treatment in chapter 10.

The Great Books Reading and Discussion Program

"The Great Books Reading and Discussion Program is based on the idea that by reading from the great books of our civilization and discussing them with other people—sharing your insights and questions—you can reach a fuller understanding of these works than you could on your own" ("Great" 1). The method of discussion proposed by this nonprofit educational corporation is called "shared inquiry."

Discussion leaders pose "interpretive" questions. These are distinguished from questions of fact and evaluative questions. The most important quality of the interpretive question is that it is a question that really matters, something we care about. "The question should express genuine doubt and curiosity. It calls for a careful assessment of what the author means in a work" ("Great" 14).

The Great Books Program has been successful in promoting the reading of literary classics partly because of the excellent questions that are posed. The program has materials for youth and adults and is firmly established as a secular or educational way of reading. The discussion is good if readers are required to answer from the text itself, not from preconceived ideas or belief. The teacher must continually ask students to cite the text to support their comments. The best answers are those supported by evidence from the reading. "What does the text say?"

The good interpretive question is probably never really answered. "The interpretive question is resolved when participants and leaders thoroughly understand several answers that have been given to the question. But they don't necessarily agree with all of the answers. Participants decide for themselves which answer seems most convincing to them, and they should be able to explain their opinions clearly and support them with evidence from the selection" ("Great" 3).

I have found the nineteen interpretive questions proposed to accompany the Great Books reading from Genesis particularly helpful in class. The questions are long established and are not denominational. After reading Genesis 1–3, teachers can propose the following interpretative question from the Great Books: "Does God demand of people independent moral action or only obedience?" ("Great" 30).

The question is good partly because of the tension in the text. In Genesis 2:16–17 God gives specific instructions to Adam: "And the Lord God commanded man, saying, Of every tree of the garden thou mayest freely eat: But of the tree of the knowledge of good and evil, thou shalt not eat of it: for in the day that thou eatest thereof thou shalt surely die."

In chapter 3 the woman seems to understand what Adam doesn't. "And when the woman saw that the tree was good for food, and that it was pleasant to the eyes, and a tree to be desired to make one wise, she took of the fruit thereof, and did eat, and gave also unto her husband with her; and he did eat." (6) I remind students that Eve got this information from the serpent.

Thus the question is a biblical paradox. Adam has been told not to eat, and Eve sees the advantage of eating. "Does God demand of people independent moral action or only obedience?" Does God want Adam and Eve to make an independent decision, or does God expect them to obey without question?

Another reason this is a good question is that is seems to be one of the basic questions of life. Do I strictly obey the rules or do I exercise independent judgment: Do I pay the British their tax (obey the law) or dump their tea in the harbor (independent moral action)? Do I fight a war I don't believe in (obey the law) or do I hide in Canada (independent moral decision), a dilemma that many men in the United

States faced during the Vietnam War? Do I ride in the back of the bus (obey the law) or risk time in jail by riding where I think I have a right to ride (independent moral action)?

Discussing this as a paradox of life leaves the Bible text behind a bit but is very productive. I remind students that one of the most difficult dilemmas of life is in the first chapters of the Bible.

Chapter 6

CULTURAL PERSPECTIVES: THREE WAYS OF READING ABOUT ABRAHAM AND ISAAC

One of the most difficult challenges in teaching the Bible as literature is helping students understand that biblical narratives are given very different meanings in different religious cultures. It seems that those who grow up reading the Bible assume that it should somehow mean the same thing to every reader, and if there is a disagreement, someone is obviously reading it wrong and needs to be corrected. The less polite term here is *Bible bashing*, prooftext arguments that try to prove doctrinal ideas.

When we talk about different meanings in different cultures we are going beyond the Christian denominationalism with which most of my students are familiar. Cultural templates are much more difficult to deal with than denominational differences, however great, between Catholics and Protestants or between Orthodox and Reform Jews.

Most students understand that we can never view the text precisely through the eyes of the culture that created it. It is too long past or too far removed from our experience. Most can also see that modern denominations can have honest disagreements interpreting biblical texts and still share some common denominator, but the gap between entirely different religious traditions is so wide that it easily invites a "you're wrong, we're right" attitude. A Christian student, even in spite of a best friend who is Jewish, may never really understand what it means to read a biblical text with Jewish eyes and heart.

Ethnocentric genes somehow imprint an "us vs. them" mentality with the consequence that "we" are right and "they" are wrong.

Reading through a cultural template is more than just a matter of interpreting a text. The culture determines the way the text is viewed, and this viewing is much more than a difference in interpretation or translation. A religious or cultural tradition is a template that not only overlays a text, it overlays the world.

The problem is complicated by the fact that much Bible reading is shallow prooftext reading. A small passage, often taken out of context, can account for a single belief or even an entire system of belief for some people. For example, a student once told me that as good Christians his family did not allow a Christmas tree in the house. He said that Christmas trees show vanity. His prooftext was Jeremiah 10:3–4. "For the customs of the people *are* vain: for *one* cutteth a tree out of the forest, the work of the hands of the workman, with the ax. They deck it with silver and with gold; they fasten it with nails and with hammers, that it move not."

The problem with a prooftext like this is that it stops the discussion. How can one argue with the Bible? Notice, for example, how a political discussion can stop in its tracks when someone uses the argument "It says in the Bible that . . ." No one seems to know how to respond at this point. Answering the argument puts us in the position of arguing against the Bible, a position that confronts the religious-cultural template, a position that confronts the "truth" as others know it.

The goal is beyond prooftext reading. The goal is to teach that there are good people with strongly held beliefs in this world who do not share our beliefs, and as a result they read different meanings in the Bible—the whole Bible, not just proofs. The goal is not to change beliefs but to allow students a glance at a biblical text through the template of another culture. A good place to start is where the conflicts seem impossible to resolve because people of different religious cultures just don't seem to understand the text the same and may not even be able to understand each other. This place is the Middle East, specifically Israel.

To say that the problems of the Middle East are confusing is an understatement. Particularly troubling are the fierce emotional sentiments that erupt into violence and seem to wave across the world just when there seems to be some slight progress toward peace. It is hard to understand rioters and terrorists who oppose peaceful progress. It is troubling because we see ourselves in the United States trying to help solve the problems. We invite world leaders to the White House and Camp David to shake hands. We send peacemakers on shuttle assignments from nation to nation looking for common ground. And that may be the problem: the ground is common. It is common to Christian, Jew, and Moslem as each regard it as sacred. It says so in a sacred text.

Although one gets the idea sometimes that the issues are so complex that nobody, not even heads of state, can understand them, it may help those of us who are confused if we had learned something about the Islamic culture and particularly its claim on the entire Middle East. We seem to understand the Jewish claim from the Bible. Abraham received a sacred inheritance from God that became the inheritance of Isaac and of Jacob. We seem to understand the Christian attitude. This is the land of Jesus, the place where he died to save the world.

Perhaps the place to start for a cultural reading is in one of the best-known narratives of the Bible, the story of Abraham and Isaac in Genesis 22:1–19. Abraham is a prophet in Judaism, Christianity, and Islam—the first prophet to declare that there is one God. The biblical passage is a good example of biblical narrative because of its reticence or lack of detail. I usually give it to students doubled-spaced and ask them to write questions between the lines to illustrate the sparsity of detail:

> [1]AND it came to pass after these things, that God did tempt Abraham, and said unto him, Abraham: and he said, Behold, *here* I *am*. [2]And he said, Take now thy son, thine only *son* Isaac, whom thou lovest, and get thee into the land of Moriah; and offer him there for a burnt offering upon one of the mountains which I will tell thee of.
>
> [3]And Abraham rose up early in the morning, and saddled his ass, and took two of his young men with him, and Isaac his son, and clave the wood for the burnt offering, and rose up, and went unto the place of which God had told him. [4]Then on the third day Abraham lifted up his eyes, and saw the place afar off. [5]And Abraham said unto his young men, Abide ye here with the ass; and I and the lad will go yonder and worship, and come again to you. [6]And Abraham took the wood of the burnt offering, and laid *it* upon Isaac his son; and he took the fire in his hand, and a knife; and they went both of them together. [7]And Isaac spake unto Abraham his father, and said, My father: and he said, Here *am* I, my son. And he said, Behold the fire and the wood: but where *is*

the lamb for a burnt offering? [8]And Abraham said, My son, God will provide himself a lamb for a burnt offering: so they went both of them together. [9]And they came to the place which God had told him of; and Abraham built an altar there, and laid the wood in order, and bound Isaac his son, and laid him on the altar upon the wood. [10]And Abraham stretched forth his hand, and took the knife to slay his son.

[11]And the angel of the LORD called unto him out of heaven, and said, Abraham, Abraham: and he said, Here *am* I. [12]And he said, Lay not thine hand upon the lad, neither do thou anything unto him: for now I know that thou fearest God, seeing thou hast not withheld thy son, thine only *son* from me. [13]And Abraham lifted up his eyes, and looked, and behold behind *him* a ram caught in a thicket by his horns: and Abraham went and took the ram, and offered him up for a burnt offering in the stead of his son. [14]And Abraham called the name of that place Jehovahjireh: as it is said *to* this day, In the mount of the LORD it shall be seen.

[15]And the angel of the LORD called unto Abraham out of heaven the second time, [16]And said, By myself have I sworn, saith the LORD, for because thou hast done this thing, and hast not withheld thy son, thine only *son*: [17]That in blessing I will bless thee, and in multiplying I will multiply thy seed as the stars of the heaven, and as the sand which *is* upon the sea shore; and thy seed shall possess the gate of his enemies; [18]And in thy seed shall all the nations of the earth be blessed; because thou hast obeyed my voice. [19]So Abraham returned unto his young men, and they rose up and went together to Beersheba; and Abraham dwelt at Beersheba.

Students are resourceful. I ask them to read between the lines. They are to write questions the text doesn't seem to answer. They ask difficult questions about the narrative:

- Why the "Here I am" statements?
- Does God really "tempt" Abraham or is this in our English translation?
- Where was Sarah? Did she know, or was Abraham sneaking off in the early morning?
- Why a journey of three days? What was said during these three days? (I like to point out one possibility, which a modern screenwriter might do, as three days of silence. There could be inter-

minable flashbacks to Isaac's birth, to Isaac and Ishmael playing, to the sacrifice of a lamb.)

- Isn't Abraham worried about witnesses, the two servants?
- Did Abraham actually hear a voice, or was it a dream or a feel-
ing?
- How old was Isaac? How strong—strong enough to overpower
his old father?
- Was Isaac face down or face up on the altar?

After the questions between the lines are considered, I tell students that there are other places where they can read this story besides the Bible. It is part of the Qur'an, the sacred text of the Moslem
world (sometimes spelled *Koran* in English). The good place to start
in this book of Islamic scripture is with this story, Christians and Jews
are very familiar with it. It is the same story we just read, the story of
Abraham's near-sacrifice of his son, except that in the Moslem version it is Ishmael, not Isaac, who is nearly sacrificed. Christians call
this the binding of Isaac. Jews refer to it as the *akedah*, which also
means "binding."

Before reading the narrative from the Qur'an, it is a good idea to
explain to students what this book is. The following is from a flyer
published by the Islamic Teaching Center. Additional materials are
available from this center at P.O. Box 38, Plainfield, IN 46168. The
flyer is cited here to allow Moslems to speak for themselves, something we don't often do when we want to know about other religions.
There are also many good Web sites with Islamic information.

> The Qur'an is the last revealed word of God and the basic source
> of Islamic teachings and laws. It deals with a variety of subjects
> including the basic beliefs of Islam, morality, worship, knowledge,
> wisdom, God-and-man relationship, and relations among human
> beings. Comprehensive teachings on which sound systems of so-
> cial justice, politics, economics, legislation, jurisprudence, law and
> international relations can be built form an important part of the
> Holy Qur'an.
>
> Though Prophet Muhammad did not receive a formal education,
> the Qur'an, as soon as it was revealed to him in the spoken word,
> was committed to writing by his secretaries. In this way every word
> was written down and preserved during his lifetime by his com-
> panions. The original and complete text of the Qur'an is in Arabic

and translations of its meaning in most known languages are available in major libraries and bookstores.

Hadith, the teachings, sayings and actions of Prophet Muhammad, accurately reported and collected by his devoted companions, explain and elaborate the Qur'anic verses.

The story of Abraham and Ishmael in the Qur'an illustrates a fundamental belief of Islam: inheritance of the land. It is in Sura (chapter) 97:99–113: (The pronoun *We* means God).

> "He [Abraham] said: 'I will go
> To my Lord! He
> Will surely guide me!
>
> O my Lord! grant me
> A righteous (son)!'
>
> So We gave him
> The good news
> Of a boy ready
> To suffer and forbear.
> Then, when (the son)
> Reached (the age of)
> (Serious) work with him,
> He said: 'O my son!
> Now see what is
> Thy view!' (The son) said:
> 'O my father! Do
> As thou art commanded:
> Thou will find me,
> If God so wills one
> Practising Patience and Constancy!'
> So when they had both
> Submitted their wills (to God),
> And he had laid him
> Prostrate on his forehead
> (For Sacrifice),

> We called out to him,
> 'O Abraham!'
> 'Thou hast already fulfilled
> The vision!'—thus indeed
> Do We reward
> Those who do right.
> For this was obviously
> A trial—"

Students can consider a question: What questions that they wrote between the lines of the Bible story seem to be answered in this narrative? A careful reading of this passage reveals some wonderful and subtle plot differences from the account in Genesis 22. They are discrepancies that make a difference for the literary reader. Especially interesting is the obvious compliance by the son in the Qur'an. "So when they had both Submitted their wills (to God)." This is something we only guess from reading the Bible. In addition, the age of the son is alluded to in the Qur'an, and the detail about the son face down on the altar may remove only slightly the sense of terror. The real difference is in the footnote, where the son is said to be Ishmael rather than Isaac.

Note 4101 in the Qur'an says as follows:

> The Jewish tradition, in order to glorify the younger branch of the family, descended from Isaac, ancestor of the Jews, as against the elder branch, descended from Ismail [Qur'an spelling], ancestor of the Arabs, refers this sacrifice to Isaac. Now Isaac was born when Abraham was 100 years old while Ismail was born to Abraham when Abraham was 86 years old. Ismail was therefore 14 years older than Isaac. During his first 14 years Ismail was the only son of Abraham; at no time was Isaac the only son of Abraham. Yet, in speaking of the sacrifice, the Old Testament says (Gen. 22:2) 'And He said, Take now thy son, thine only son Isaac, whom thou lovest, and get thee into the land of Moriah; and offer him there for a burnt offering'

Students want to solve this contradiction. They often ask me if there are any other records that tell us what really happened. A cultural reading is hard to understand. Students want to read the Bible or Qur'an as history at this point, so they ask about "other records." This is a good opportunity to explain that literature isn't necessarily history. Yet the Jews read the Bible as their history and Moslems and Christians alike read it as their history too. The history that happened is not necessarily the history that is recorded or remembered.

Because students ask, I explain that there is one "history" of the event to complement the volumes of commentary. It is certainly not an eyewitness account. No account is from an eyewitness. This "historical" account is from the first century of the C.E. Flavius Josephus was a Jewish historian who, after fighting the Romans in 67 C.E., became complicit with his captors and worked as an interpreter. He was later adopted by Vespasian and given Roman citizenship and a pension. His account helps us to understand the Jewish template through which the story can be read. Josephus was a Pharisee (the scholars who were predecessors of the rabbis). He studied Jewish law. As a Roman citizen he wrote *The Jewish War*, which chronicled the victory of Rome over his country in the first century. He also wrote a collection of twenty books on the history of the Jews. Most scholars seem to agree that his goal in writing the history may have been to gain Roman sympathy for the Jews. Perhaps one irony in his history is that it is used extensively by early Christian writers to defend the Christian faith. It is important that students remember a few things as they read Book 1, chapter 13, of his work *The Antiquity of the Jews*, which is cited below:

1. Josephus was not an eyewitness of the event he is describing. There were no eyewitness writers.

2. The history written by Josephus was written for a political purpose.

3. His work is *a* history, not *the* history. For this reason it is not the answer to the discrepancies between the Bible and the Qur'an.

4. Even though Josephus is not the answer to the conflicts in the two texts, it is an interesting third perspective.

5. The source for the history may have been the Bible.

6. Reading any history is much different than reading literature. Literature is written to speak to the imagination. Literature invites us to write questions between the lines.

7. The term *legitimate* should tip the reader off quickly that Josephus regards Ishmael as someone less than legitimate and thus not a legal heir to the promise given to Abraham. This historian has a point of view.

Josephus: "Concerning Isaac, the Legitimate Son of Abraham"

1. Now Abraham greatly loved Isaac, as being his only begotten, and given to him at the borders of old age, by the favor of God. The child also endeared himself to his parents still more, by the exercise of every virtue, and adhering to his duty to his parents, and being zealous in the worship of God. Abraham also placed his own happiness in this prospect, that, when he should die, he should leave this his son in a safe and secure condition; which accordingly he obtained by the will of God; who, desiring to make an experiment of Abraham's religious disposition towards himself, appeared to him, and enumerated all the blessings he had bestowed on him; how he had made him superior to his enemies; and how his son Isaac, who was the principal part of his present happiness, was derived from him; and God said that he required this son of his as a sacrifice and holy offering. Accordingly he commanded him to carry him to the mountain Moriah, and to build an altar, and offer him for a burnt offering upon it for that this would best manifest his religious disposition towards him, if he preferred what was pleasing to God, before the preservation of his own son.

2. Now Abraham thought that it was not right to disobey God in anything, but that he was obliged to serve him in every circumstance of life, since all creatures that live enjoy their life by his providence, and the kindness he bestows on them. Accordingly he concealed this command of God, and his own intentions about the slaughter of his son, from his wife, as also from everyone of his servants, otherwise he should have been hindered from his obedience to God; and he took Isaac, together with two of his servants, and laying what things were necessary for a sacrifice upon an ass, he went away to the mountain. Now the two servants went along with him two days; but on the third day, as soon as he saw the mountain, he left those servants that were with him till then in the plain, and, having his son alone with him, he came to the mountain. It was that mountain upon which King David [Soloman] afterwards built the temple. Now they had brought with them everything necessary for a sacrifice, excepting the animal that was to be offered only. Now Isaac was twenty-five years old. And as he was building the altar, he asked his father what he was about to offer, since there was no animal there for a sacrifice : to which it was answered, "that God would provide himself an offering, he being able to make a plentiful provision for men out of what they

have not, and to deprive others of what they already have, when they put too much trust therein; that therefore, if God pleased to be present and favorable at this sacrifice, he would provide himself an offering."

3. As soon as the altar was prepared, and Abraham had laid on the wood, and all things were entirely ready, he said to his son, "O son, I poured out a vast number of prayers that I might have you for my son; when you were come into the world, there was nothing that could contribute to your support for which I was not greatly solicitous, nor any thing wherein I thought myself happier than to see you grown up to man's estate, and that I might leave you at my death the successor to my dominion; but since it was by God's will that I became your father, and it is now his will that I relinquish you, bear this consecration to God with a generous mind; for I resign you up to God who has thought fit now to require this testimony of honor to himself, on account of the favors he has conferred on me, in being to me a supporter and defender. Accordingly you, my son, will now die, not in any common way of going out of the world, but sent to God, the Father of all men, beforehand, by your own father, in the nature of a sacrifice. I suppose he thinks you worthy to get clear of this world neither by disease, neither by war, nor by any other severe way, by which death usually comes upon men, but so that he will receive your soul with prayers and holy offices of religion, and will place you near to himself, and you will there be to me a helper and supporter in my old age; on which account I mainly brought you up, and you will thereby procure me God for my Comforter instead of yourself."

4. Now Isaac was of such a generous disposition as became the son of such a father, and was pleased with this discourse; and said "that he was not worthy to be born at first, if he should reject the determination of God and of his father, and should not resign himself up readily to both their pleasures; since it would have been unjust if he had not obeyed, even if his father alone had so resolved." So he went immediately to the altar to be sacrificed. And the deed would have been done if God had not opposed it; for he called loudly to Abraham by his name, and forbade him to slay his son; and said, "It was not out of a desire of human blood that he was commanded to slay his son, nor was he willing that he should be taken away from him whom he had made his father, but to try the temper of his mind, whether he would be obedient to such a command. Since therefore he now was satisfied as to that, his eagerness, and the surprising readiness he showed in this his piety, he was delighted in having bestowed

such blessings upon him; and that he would not be wanting in all sort of concern about him, and in bestowing other children upon him; and that his son should live to a very great age; that he should live a happy life, and bequeath a large principality to his children, who should be good and legitimate." He foretold also that his family should increase into many nations, and that those patriarchs should leave behind them an everlasting name; that they should obtain the possession of the land of Canaan, and be envied by all men. When God had said this, he produced to them a ram, which did not appear before, for the sacrifice. So Abraham and Isaac receiving each other unexpectedly, and having obtained the promises of such great blessings, embraced one another; and when they had sacrificed, they returned to Sarah, and lived happily together, God affording them his assistance in all things they desired.

Three Readings

Now we have Jewish, Christian, and Moslem perspectives, supported by a "historical" narrative. The point is not to argue scripture or theology. The point is that different religious-cultural worlds read the text differently. The following is a summary of the three literary readings in chronological order:

The Jewish Reading

A good resource for the Jewish reading of the Binding of Isaac, or the *akedah* is the *Encyclopaedia Judaica*. This resource is now on CD-ROM. It is also important for teachers to have read the entire biblical narrative of Abraham, Genesis 12–24. This gives a much-needed context to the narrative. The following summary is from these chapters.

In the Jewish reading God has promised Abraham land. He is to be the father of nations. The promise is first given when Abraham has no children. His wife, Sarah, offers her handmaid, Hagar, and Abraham has Ishmael with her. Later, Sarah miraculously has a child in her old age. Now there is a son of the birthright in Jewish tradition, a son of Sarah. The promise of nations is possible.

It is at this point that we read the *akedah*, the biblical narrative above. Abraham is asked to make a sacrifice that could make the promise of God—that he would found a nation—impossible. Yet, Abraham is willing to make this sacrifice. He is stopped by an angel and told that because of his faith he will found nations and that through his posterity all nations of the world will be blessed.

The binding of Isaac has taken place on Mount Moriah, the hill that David chose for the temple and on which Solomon built the temple. This is the holiest Jewish site. It is the place of the Western Wall in today's Israel. It is to Jerusalem that Jewish thought turns every day in Jewish prayer, as well as each year at the end of the Passover seder when Jews say, "Next year in Jerusalem." The biblical narrative of God's promise to Abraham affirms the claim to the land by modern Jews.

The Christian Reading

Christians refer to Isaac as a type of Christ: a Beloved Son whose birth was miraculous, who submitted his will to the Father as a lamb, the Lamb of God. Isaac carried the wood for the sacrifice on his back as Jesus carried his wood, a cross.

As a type of Christ's crucifiction, Isaac's binding is seen as a forecast of a later event, and Christian readers look for parallels in the narrative. There is a three-day journey, and Jesus was in the tomb three days before resurrection. There are two servants, and Jesus was crucified between two thieves.

The Moslem Reading

The Islamic world believes, and the Qur'anic story of this sacrifice illustrates, that the promise given to Abraham of land and inheritance belong to Moslems through the rightful, first son Ishmael. Moslem Palestinians believe that their inheritance has been stolen and that they have absolutely no homeland at all.

The near-sacrifice of Ishmael took place on Mount Moriah. On this hill today in Jerusalem is the Dome of the Rock and the Al-Aqsa Mosque, the second oldest Islamic monument. The rock over which the shrine was built is the third most sacred place to Muslims. The Prophet Muhammad ascended into heaven from the site.

Conclusion

The three readings are complicated by the fact that most of us can't comprehend such an act—a child sacrifice commanded by God. Alan Dershowitz skillfully frames the hard questions in his classes at Harvard Law School and in *The Genesis of Justice*, "Abraham Commits Attempted Murder–and Is Praised:"

No biblical narrative is more dramatic, more poignant, and more confusing than God's command to Abraham that he sacrifice his son Isaac. What kind of a God would ask such a thing of a father? What kind of a father would accede to such a request, even from a God? Why did Abraham, the man who argued so effectively with God over the fate of strangers [on behalf of Sodom, in Genesis 18:23–33], suddenly become silent in the face of so great an injustice toward his own beloved son? Why did God praise Abraham for his willingness to engage in an act of ritual murder? And what are we to learn from a patriarch who follows, without question, immoral superior orders to murder an innocent child? . . . These, and other questions, have been debated by Jews, Christians, and Muslims for generations. (105)

The Artists' Reading

Beyond the political and religious contrasts is a more artistic contrast than what is usually noticed in either the Jewish and Christian readings of Abraham. It is worth the effort to find the October 1993 *Bible Review* for a look at the art of the *akedah* or Binding of Isaac. The article by Robin M. Jensen is entitled "The Binding or Sacrifice of Isaac: How Jews and Christians See Differently." It is from this article that the following teaching idea comes.

In addition to this article, there are many artists' interpretations that make a good class discussion and help students to understand that artists as well as religious cultures see differently. I have found that students who understand that artists see differently are closer to understanding how religious cultures see differently. Particularly interesting to students is the idea that an individual artist may see this narrative in different ways. Showing that an individual artist can see the narrative differently at different times may help students to glimpse how religious cultures can see differently. Rembrandt offers a good example that students enjoy (Riemer 26).

Rembrandt Harmenszoon van Rijn (1606–1669) is the exemplar of 17th century Dutch art. His biblical scenes or portraits are familiar and are often included in family and pulpit Bibles. Rembrandt painted the *Sacrifice of Isaac* and created at least three etchings of Abraham and Isaac. We will compare the painting and one etching. The etching is entitled *Abraham's Sacrifice*.[10] The print of the oil painting is of the *Sacrifice of Isaac*.[11] Students could first be asked about the significance of the titles. Is Abraham the focus of one work and Isaac of the other?

Abraham's Sacrifice

The Sacrifice of Isaac

An interesting detail sets up a good discussion. One of these works was created when Rembrandt was 29 years old; the other is by Rembrandt at 49 years old. The way we view the world can change dramatically in 20 years of living. The question for students is, which picture is which? I must confess that I'm sometimes guilty of giving students a false lead here. I sometimes mention that artists will often do a sketch or etching before undertaking a portrait or larger work, the truth is that this example is the reverse of my sleight-of-comment hint. The oil painting was done in 1635, and the etching was made in 1655.

Students are good at pointing out the obvious differences. In the oil painting, Abraham is surprised at being stopped. He is more determined than he appears in the etching. The Abraham of the etching is older; his eyes are hollow. He is less surprised and perhaps more relieved to be stopped by the angel and wrapped in the angel's arms. Riemer's article offers an excellent description of the two works. Isaac is held down as his eyes are covered in the painting. He is held more gently in the etching, with his eyes shielded from what is about to happen. I always worry about the knife suspended in midair in the painting. Where is it going? Will it miss Isaac?

The real tip as to the age of the author is the way that Abraham holds Isaac and the way that the angel holds Abraham in the etching. Instead of holding Isaac down, as in the painting, Abraham holds Isaac to his stomach. He is in the bosom of Abraham, and Abraham is in the bosom of the angel. Thus the artist has seen differently as the same artist. So surely people of different religious cultures can also see differently.

There is one other teaching resource that I recommend. It tries to answer the central problem of the story: Why would a father be asked to kill a son and why would the father actually try to carry out the request? Lippman Bodoff, in "God Tests Abraham, Abraham Tests God," argues quite persuasively that Abraham may be testing his God even as God is testing him. It is worth reading.

There is one other cultural reading that I add merely as a postscript, because I'm not sure exactly what religious culture is represented by *Xena: Warrior Princess*. The following lets the cover of episode 21, "Altared States," speak for itself:

> The patriarch Anteus believes the one true God has commanded
> him to kill his son Icus. When Gabrielle goes into a trance after

eating Anteus' bread, Xena discovers it's really a ploy by the oldest son, Maell. She defeats Maell as he shouts a "divine" command through a megaphone . . . and another surprise command countermands the order.

I realize that this doesn't mean much to a *Xena: Warrior Princess*–deficient teacher who has been grading papers instead of watching TV. It didn't mean much to me until a colleague recommended that I watch the episode because it was a thinly disguised Abraham-Isaac story. I haven't shown the entire episode in class, but I have shown one particular scene that tries to answer the same hard question as the Bodoff paper. It changes the context enough that the students have a good discussion about obedience to God in the Abraham narrative:

Xena: "We'll stop and rest a while. No sense in killing ourselves—so to speak."

Anteus [Abraham]: "You don't think much of us, do you?"

Xena: "I don't think much of your God—or any god who'd wanna kill a child. But then, I'm not sure He does. It'll ease your breathing. Lean forward. Anteus, I know your mind is hazy right now, but did you ever stop to wonder why he'd ask you to do such a thing?"

Anteus: "Every waking moment of every day since it happened. I keep wondering, Is it me? Have I done something—wrong, and he's punishing me? Or is this some kind of a—a test, to see how far I'll go to prove my faith. Or, is He angry with me because He knows how much I love you [Icus]. Or does His love demand the best, the brightest— You see—it—it never stops."

Xena: "You can stop it. You're still the leader here— You don't have to do this."

Anteus: "You're asking me to deny my God."

Xena: "I am asking you to spare your son!"

Anteus: "And teach him what?! That faith is just for those times when it's convenient to believe? That, that when it gets hard, and, and, and, it hurts to keep faith, y-y-you let go—until it gets easy again? What's the good in sparing his life if I rob him of the very thing that makes it worth living?"

Xena: "You know, I'll stop you."

Anteus: "I know you'll try. God help me, deep down inside, part of me hopes you succeed."

The transcript of this episode is on the academic electronic journal "Woosh" at http://whoosh.org/index.html, along with transcripts of all the episodes. At the very least, this video clip lets students look at another artist's view of the narrative.

Notes

10 *Abraham's Sacrifice* by Rembrandt is reproduced courtesy of the National Gallery of Art, Washington. It is part of the Rosenwald Collection.

11 *Sacrifice of Isaac* by Rembrandt is reproduced courtesy of the Hermitage Museum.

Chapter 7

Teaching Literary Symbols: Finding Literary Meaning

A rose is a rose is a rose, and a tree of life is a tree of life. Trees and roses are symbolic. These symbols are biblical as well as not biblical. With the rose, color matters. The white rose symbolizes purity, and the red rose love. The yellow rose says welcome home, all is forgiven.

The tree of life is not only the tree in the Garden of Eden that is symbolic. It is a tree that represents eternal life, the gospel of Jesus, a resurrection, immortality, truth, wisdom, and understanding. Even though chapter and verse seem to be missing for some of the symbolic tree of life meanings, they are what students tell me it means when I ask about the garden tree of Genesis. The tree of life has outgrown the first garden to become a pervasive symbol, but its original roots are still in Eden. It was there first.

We love the roses of poetry, but there are few roses in the Bible. There are only 131 of them in 129 verses, to be exact, and only one biblical "rose" is a real flower. It is the lone rose of Solomon's Song. "I am the rose of Sharon, and the lily of the valleys" (Song of Solomon 2:1). The Song of Solomon is more correctly titled "Song of Songs" in modern translations. These words are from the bride; she is saying that she is just one among many. The Hebrew word *chatzelet*, here translated as "rose," has also been translated as "tulip," "lily," "crocus," or "wildflower." So much for roses in the Bible. We will let the text take us to other symbols, like the tree.

The tree of life grows ten times in the KJV. Most of the meaning we impose on this symbol is from other texts and contexts. This poem in Proverbs 3:13–18 is entitled "The True Wealth" in the HarperCollins Study Edition of the NRSV. It is not titled in most other versions, but poetic license will let me call it "Tree of Life" and put the KJV in verses for this example of a biblical symbol. I suppose I'm allowed poetic license since the King James translators admitted that they took some.

> Happy *is* the man *that* findeth
> > wisdom,
> > and the man *that* getteth
> > understanding.
> For the merchandise of it *is*
> > better than the merchandise of
> > > silver,
> > and the gain thereof than fine
> > > gold.
> She *is* more precious than rubies:
> > and all the things thou canst desire
> > > are not to be compared unto her.
> Length of days *is* in her right hand;
> > *and* in her left hand riches and honour.
> Her ways *are* ways
> > of pleasantness,
> > and all her paths
> > > peace.
> She *is* a tree of life
> > to them that lay hold upon her:
> and happy *is every one*
> > that retaineth her.

The first question for students: Who is the *she* in the biblical poem? In Judaism the answer to this is "the Torah," and the last few lines above are sung in the synagogue service as the Torah is taken out of the ark for reading. We look for her qualities:

- better than silver
- to gain her is better than fine gold
- more precious than rubies

- her ways are pleasant
- her paths are peace
- she is a tree of life

The original search in the poem was for wisdom and understanding. The search ends with *she*, who is a tree of life. Glancing back at the tree of life in Genesis, the reader notices that the tree of life is different from the forbidden tree (the tree of the knowledge of good and evil). It was after taking the forbidden fruit that God sent Adam and Eve out of the garden so they would not take from the tree of life, "and eat, and live forever" (Genesis 3:22).

The tree of life, represented by feminine personal pronouns in this poem (*she* and *her*), is wisdom and understanding. The tree of life is as much a symbol as the rose. In the Garden of Eden there is also a tree that represents the knowledge of good and evil. Is this a tree that represents wisdom?

With a little help, most students recognize the tree of life as a symbol, so after a brief glance at roses and trees, this chapter takes a more extended look at a very slippery symbol, the serpent. The fish symbol persists as an important religious symbol today and will be the next example. We will then answer Kermit the Frog's question: "Why are there so many songs about rainbows?" After that, students will learn to give meaning to hair. Gold, frankincense, and myrrh are gifts that are symbolic of the best and are included in Appendix B as supplementary material.

Teachers will recognize that there may be a danger in this kind of symbol searching. It allows students to look outside a particular narrative or poem for meaning. This is the nature of the search and the nature of symbols. The problem with the kind of search is that it can be confused with doctrinal searches, which look for proof wherever it may be found in the Bible with no regard for context. The search for symbolic meaning is extratextual. That is how symbols and allusions work.

Teachers will also recognize that the serpent, the fish, and the gifts of the magi are laden with religious connotation. Since teachers may be reluctant to teach the symbolic gifts because of the close association with the Nativity and Christmas celebrations, this information is in Appendix B as a supplementary resource. The rainbow is not so overladen with sanctity for most students and is a no-fail lesson for me. Hair is not usually a religious issue, but one exception that I've frequently encountered is with Native Americans. Long hair is an important religious symbol to them, and talking about hair in class has given them an opportunity to explain this and the rest of us an opportunity to better understand it. For me, the rainbow and hair lessons are no-fail lessons on symbols, and teachers may want to check them out first.

The intent of the discussion of serpent, fish, rainbows, hair, and gifts is to give teachers background and examples that they can edit for their own purposes. The serpent is especially complex and may be beyond the scope of many classes, but the rainbow can be used as a lesson as it is, complete with the poetry of William Wordsworth and the music of Kermit the Frog and the Rolling Stones. The hair symbol provides a good student activity for learning about the symbolic.

The Serpent Deceives, the Serpent Heals: The Serpent Symbol in the Bible

> And the LORD God said unto the serpent, Because thou hast done this, thou art cursed above all cattle, and above every beast of the field; upon thy belly shalt thou go, and dust shalt thou eat all the days of thy life. (Genesis 3:14)

> And Moses made a serpent of brass, and put it upon a pole, and it came to pass, that if a serpent had bitten any man, when he beheld the serpent of brass, he lived. (Numbers 21:9)

It isn't enough that *bad* sometimes becomes *good*; now the word *bad* actually means *good*, and the badder the better. "Totally bad" is totally good. There isn't even a "nym" (i.e., synonym, homonym, antonym, oppositonym) to define this phenomenon or perhaps phenomenym.

Bible readers encounter this problem. The first time we read the word *terrible* is in Exodus 34:10. The context is the covenant with Israel after the tablets that Moses destroyed are replaced. "And He said, Behold, I make a covenant: before all thy people I will do marvels, such as have not been done in all the earth, nor in any nation: and all the people among which thou art shall see the work of the LORD: for it is a terrible thing that I will do with thee."

Here the Hebrew word translated as "terrible" is *norah*, which in its verb form means "to fear," "to revere," "to be in awe of." This use and definition seems to hold, with the exception of Job, until the book of Isaiah. Then, in Isaiah, Jeremiah, and Ezekiel, the same "terrible" in English is used for the Hebrew word *aertz*, which is fearful, or tyrannical. This translation problem is even more complex because there are five other Hebrew words translated as *terrible*, *terribleness*, *terribly*, *terrified, terrifiest, terrify, terror,* and *terrors.* (See *Strong's Exhaustive Concordance of the Bible.* Other good resources include Ferguson's *Signs & Symbols in Christian Art* and Ryken et al.'s *Dictionary of Biblical Imagery.* all are listed in Works Cited.) After one gets through with *terrible,* there is *dreadful,* which seems to have followed the same path and has become a oppositonym. It makes one wonder if awful has become *awesome* or "awe-ful"! The translation problem is difficult enough for those who read the Bible as theology, complete with prooftexts to support already established beliefs, and often hang onto specific words to advance truth claims. It is equally difficult for the reader of the Bible as literature who views this collection and responds that "the Old and New Testaments are the Great Code of Art." These are the words of William Blake, quoted by Northrop Frye. The text challenges, not only because of shifts in word meanings, but because of shifts in the meanings of some of the most important symbols, like the serpent.

The "subtle" snake under goes a metamorphosis of idea and image as it transforms from sinister serpent to savior. Perhaps it is the ability of the serpent to shed its skin that allows this shift in meaning. It may be perhaps that no symbol is inherently evil or inherently good, that only the context makes it so. Northrup Frye seems to take this view in *The Great Code:*

> The forbidden tree has a cursed serpent crawling limply away from it on its belly, so the tree of life, if the same imagery applied, would have an erect serpent of wisdom and knowledge climbing up through its branches, as in the Indian symbolic system known as Kundalini Yoga. This is not given in Genesis, but we should keep in mind the fact that no image is inherently good or bad, apocalyptic or demonic: which it is, depends on the context. Because of its role in the Eden story, the serpent is usually a sinister image in the biblical tradition; but it could also be a symbol of genuine wisdom (Matthew 10:16) or of healing (Numbers 21:9), just as it was in Greek mythology. In fact King Hezekiah's fear of serpent worship (2 Kings 18:4) may be reflected in the "subtle" treachery assigned the serpent in Genesis (148).

Whether Frye is correct in saying context is the key, the serpent clearly changes. It goes from a subtle but loathsome creature in Genesis, destined to crawl all its days on its belly, to a brazen symbol on a staff that will heal those of the Exodus who look on it. In the beginning it is cursed to eat the same ingredient (dust) from which man was created, but then that is lifted up to become a type of savior that heals (John 3:14). This transition from a devourer to a savior is dramatic, especially when one considers the brazen serpent as a type of Christ. Perhaps if the serpent is viewed as a God symbol, then God is an Old Testament devourer and a New Testament savior. Remember that the Old Testament is the Hebrew Bible and the New Testament a Christian addition. Jews and Christians read the serpent differently.

The figurative use of the serpent is not limited to the garden of Eden. As the snake becomes a savior symbol, Buttrick's *The Interpreter's Dictionary of the Bible* notes that it represents evil people (Psalm 58:4), the Assyrians, Babylonians, and Israel's enemies (Isaiah 14:29, Jeremiah 8:17, Deuteronomy 32:33). It also represents danger in general (Psalm 91:13), and the effects of wine (Proverbs 23:32).

The midpoint of the metamorphosis from sin to redemption is the bad and the good of the serpents in the miracles that occur before the Exodus. The rod or staff is a temporary serpent for Moses in Exodus 4:3 and 7:15; for Aaron in Exodus 7:9–10; and for the Egyptians in Exodus 7:12. What makes this a midpoint in the transition is that "Aaron's rod swallowed up their rods" (7:12). This very rod or serpent then turns the river to blood and eventually divides the Red Sea. Some serpents must be more powerful than others, and the implication is that some are good and some are bad. Some serpents can make water into blood and divide seas. Could the serpent-staff be seen as foreshadowing the blood of Jesus in the New Testament, in the Christian view? Is blood another interesting symbol for students to follow?

It is interesting to look beyond the Bible at a serpent of Roman mythology. It is from this tradition that the symbol is retained in the physician's caduceus. A snake is entwined about the wand of Mercury, who is the messenger of the gods. It protects Mercury on his travels. Mercury is associated with magic and science, and his caduceus has since come to symbolize medicine. Although the caduceus comes from the Romans, the Greek messenger of the gods, Hermes, also carries a staff entwined with snakes.

Viewing this symbol in its cultural context in the Near East is helpful because it reinforces the idea the serpent can be both evil and good:

> It is abundantly clear from a wide range of evidence that the snake
> was a symbol of deity and of fertility powers in the ancient Near
> East. In Egypt, where the veneration of serpents in one form or
> another was common (some serpents being good, and others harm-
> ful), the ancient serpent-goddess of Lower Egypt was the benefi-
> cent Buto or Wazit. In the form of a uraeus or cobra she became the
> symbol of royalty, and she was later attached to the royal crown as
> protectress of the king. On the other hand, the most important of all
> Egyptian demons (or evil gods) was Apophis, the supreme oppo-
> nent of Re, and he also was represented by a serpent (Buttrick 290).

The serpent continues to be venerated by the Israelites after the experience with Moses in the wilderness. One of Hezekiah's reforms in 2 Kings 18:4 was that "he broke in pieces the brazen serpent that Moses had made: for unto those days the children of Israel did burn incense to it." The veneration of the brazen serpent had become idolatrous; a temporary symbolic reminder had itself become a graven image.

This does not spoil the image of the serpent as redeemer for Christians. What it does is to define correct worship. Perhaps the veneration of a redeemer can itself be destructive if the symbol itself is worshiped. Even though the serpent seems to progress from the representation of subtle sin to a representation of a redeemer, the point needs to be made that in the eschatology of Revelation the identification is definitely with the Devil (Revelation 12:9–15, 20:2). The symbol of the struggle in Eden is to be cast forever into the lake of fire and brimstone (Revelation 20:10). The redeeming serpent worshiped as a graven image suffers an eschatological destruction. The serpent is subtle and crafty when the symbol of redemption can be worshiped in such a way as to cause destruction. Perhaps the conclusion then is not of a progressive symbol but of a cyclical one, such as when the snake bites its own tail and worshipers descend a serpentine slide.

A definitive statement on serpents was made by Jesus. It could have been an allusion to Jacob's blessing of Dan in Genesis 49:17. Weak and small Dan could advance its cause with the cunning of a serpent. Although weak, the followers of Jesus and those who read the Bible as literature are sent forth as sheep in the midst of wolves. Teachers must be, as he told his apostles, as "wise as serpents, and harmless as doves" (Matthew 10:16)—especially in the meaning we give to literary symbols as we teach the Bible as symbolic literature. After all, the meaning can change.

The Fish as a Religious Symbol

Phonetic spelling can be very confusing. It is one of the hazards of the English language, according to George Bernard Shaw, who allegedly used this example: *Ghoti* spells "fish." Just sound it out. Use the *gh* from "cough," the *o* in "women," and the *ti* in "action."

There is another way to spell *fish* that some see almost every day without recognizing it. The fact that we don't recognize it may demonstrate the argument for looking closely at biblical symbols. This way of spelling fish is often seen on the back of a car and is usually inscribed inside a line drawing of a fish. It is part of our culture and the religious tradition of many who live in our community.

Perhaps two brief references to the Bible will put the fish in some context. The first is a tongue-in-cheek question: Did fish die in the Flood? The second is more serious. Why was the writer of the Gospel of John so specific in chapter 21 as to mention that there were 153 fish pulled up in the nets of the fishermen? The idea behind the second question is that the fish of John 21 may be symbolic of something other than fish.

The earliest theory is St. Jerome's. His claim was that the ancients knew that there were 153 kinds of fish in the world. Biologists today would dispute this idea; they currently recognize about 22,000 species of fishes, and only 790 of them are fresh water species. The 153 fish caught in John 21 included every possible kind of fish for the Bible translators. It may have been the writer's way of saying that the message of the fish was for everyone. The 153 fish are symbolic.

This leads to the point of the fish we see in line drawings. It is often written in Greek as Ichthys or I.CH.TH.Y.S. Most reference books about the symbolism in Christian art will include the fact that the fish that often appears in art stands for Christ himself, just as the fish we see in the line drawing stands for Christ.

In fact, one writer who tries to link the world's religions claims that there is more to the symbolic fish. The name Jesus is a Greek version of the name Joshua. The Joshua of the Hebrew Bible is called "the son of Nun" (Joshua 1:1). W. Robertson Smith, in *Kinship and Marriage in Early Arabia*, makes the point that Joshua's patronymic may be based on that of the Syrian god Dagon, also named Ichthys. He notes that the Hebrew letter Nun means "fish." The point is that fish becomes an important Christian symbol.

The association of the fish with Jesus is a cryptogram based on the Greek spelling of *fish*. The initial letters of the formula Iesous Christos

Theou Yios Soter (Jesus Christ, Son of God, Savior) reads I.CH.TH.Y.S., the Greek for "fish." The line drawing of the fish often contains the Greek letters that spell fish, ἰχθὺς.

Understanding the fish of the Bible and of early Christian tradition helps to explain the fish symbol on the back of some cars. The drivers of these cars are making a symbolic statement. We can now also read more meaning into the Sermon on the Mount:

> Ask, and it shall be given you;
> seek, and ye shall find:
> knock, and it shall be
> opened unto you:
>
> For every one that asketh receiveth;
> and he that seeketh findeth;
> and to him that knocketh
> it shall be opened.
>
> Or what man is there of you whom if his son ask bread,
> will he give him a stone?
> Or if he ask a fish,
> will he give him a serpent? (Matthew 7:7-10)

Students will find this "modern" fish symbol below to be an interesting postscript or point of departure for the further discussion of symbols. What does this symbol say? Has science replaced religion or Jesus? Has this fish with feet made progress over the earlier fish? Do we worship science represented by this fish? Has the fish evolved from its biblical meaning?

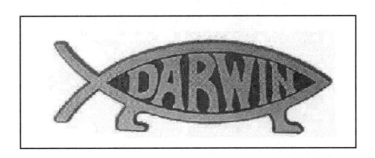

Rainbow Connections

Why are there so many songs about rainbows
And what's on the other side?

Kermit the Frog asks a good question. He's pretty observant for a frog. There's the old song from Oz: "Somewhere over the rainbow, way up high." Then there is the more recent cut by the Rolling Stones on *VooDoo Lounge*. "Yeah, you're blinded by rainbows, watching the wind blow . . . blinded by rainbows and faces in windows." There are so many songs about rainbows.

Dorothy's tune is a sentimental search for something beyond Kansas. Or is she looking back from Oz? It probably doesn't matter, since the whole thing was a dream, anyway. "There's a land that I dreamed of once in a lullaby." For all I can tell, since most of Mick Jagger's words were replaced by question marks in the version I downloaded from the Internet, his song is not so lofty in spite of biblical allusions. This is only an educated guess, because even the most savvy students could not understand the lyrics when I played the music in class. Perhaps these careful listeners were "Blinded by Rainbows" as the title indicates.

The Rolling Stones' cut "Blinded by Rainbows"[12] does seem to find Jesus and doubts that others have. It offers some biblical symbolism that we don't get in *The Wizard of Oz* lyrics of Edgar Y. Harburg, even with their reference to "way up high" and a "land that I dream of." The Stones' song isn't so idyllic, either.

Did you ever feel the pain
that he felt upon the cross?

. . .

Yeah, you're blinded by rainbows,
Watching the wind blow,
Blinded by rainbows,
Do you dream at night;
Do you scream at night?
Do you smell the fear;
is your conscience clear?
Do you kick and sweat,
and your clothes are wet;

> do you see the light;
> is the end in sight?
> See the face of Christ,
> and the paradise? doubt it . . .

Has Mick Jagger read his Bible? With so many nights in hotel rooms around the world and thanks to the Gideon Society, he has probably read the book of books cover to cover. How else can one account for the lyrics?

But Kermit's question about why so many songs about rainbows still stands. The promise in his song pulls us on a search for connections:

> Someday we'll find it,
> the rainbow connection,
> The lover, the dreamers, and me.

The key here is that he is looking for connections, a rainbow connection. Kermit's search is not just a quest for the pot of gold at the end of prism-refracted light. That's what we do in literature. We find allusion from one rainbow to the next, connections. At the end of one is the golden key to the next. Often the allusions take us to our literary roots, maybe even to the Bible.

I think the Bible may be where William Wordsworth, if not Mick Jagger, was headed with his rainbow. Wordsworth (1700–1850) seems to have made connections in "My Heart Leaps Up":

> My heart leaps up when I behold
>   A rainbow in the sky:
> So was it when my life began;
> So is it now I am a man;
> So be it when I shall grow old,
>   Or let me die!
>
> The Child is father of the Man:
> And I could wish my days to be
> Bound each to each by natural piety. (34)

The connection makes the heart leap as much as the sight of the rainbow does. "The Child is father of the Man" in the perpetual link of humanity in which the heart of the father turns to children, and the heart of the children to their fathers (Malachi 4:6). There is a connection, but is it a rainbow connection? Wordsworth's rainbow reminds the reader only of genealogical connections, unless the look back to literary roots in the Bible goes back to the first rainbow.

Students will no doubt remember the biblical Flood, when it rained forty days and forty nights (Genesis 9). "There were giants on the earth in those days" (Genesis 6:4). There was also a promise by God after the deluge that it wouldn't happen again.

> [8]And God spake unto Noah, and to his sons with him, saying, [9]And I, behold, I establish my covenant with you, and with your seed after you: [*This is obviously a connection—the child is father of the man.*] [10]And with every living creature that is with you, of the fowl, of the cattle, and of every beast of the earth with you; from all that go out of the ark, to every beast of the earth. [11]And I will establish my covenant with you; neither shall all flesh be cut off any more by the waters of a flood; neither shall there any more be a flood to destroy the earth. [12]And God said, This is the token of the covenant which I make between me and you and every living creature that is with you, for perpetual generations: [13]I do set my bow in the cloud, and it shall be for a token of a covenant between me and the earth. [14]And it shall come to pass, when I bring a cloud over the earth, that the bow shall be seen in the cloud: [15]And I will remember my covenant, which is between me and you and every living creature of all flesh; and the waters shall no more become a flood to destroy all flesh. [16]And the bow shall be in the cloud; and I will look upon it, that I may remember the everlasting covenant between God and every living creature of all flesh that is upon the earth. [17]And God said unto Noah, This is the token of the covenant, which I have established between me and all flesh that is upon the earth.

The passage is redundant enough to be clear. The rainbow is the symbol of a connection. It is called a "token" in the Genesis passage. God promises that the earth will never be flooded again and leaves humanity a reminder of the promise for perpetual generations. This promise is not lost on James Baldwin in *The Fire Next Time*. "If we do not now dare everything, the fulfillment of that prophecy, re-created from the Bible in song by a slave, is upon us: God gave Noah the rainbow sign, No more water, the fire next time!"

The rainbow promise connects all humanity. It "is the token of the covenant which I make between me and you and every living creature that is with you, for perpetual generations." It connects as surely as Wordsworth's rainbow, where days of children who are fathers of men are "bound each to each in natural piety."

For a biblical allusion, however, the rainbow stops a bit short in the book of books. We lose sight of it until Ezekiel's vision (Chapter 1) before the prophet's call:

> [26]And above the firmament that was over their heads was the likeness of a throne, as the appearance of a sapphire stone: and upon the likeness of the throne was the likeness as the appearance of a man above upon it. [27]And I saw as the colour of amber, as the appearance of fire round about within it, from the appearance of his loins even upward, and from the appearance of his loins even downward, I saw as it were the appearance of fire, and it had brightness round about. [28]As the appearance of the bow that is in the cloud in the day of rain, so was the appearance of this brightness round about. This was the appearance of the likeness of the glory of the LORD. And when I was it, I fell upon my face, and I heard a voice of one that spake.

Ezekiel's fall on his face in the presence of a rainbow is questioned by the Rabbis, as bowing is to be done only to God. However, Ezekiel is bowing to "the appearance of the likeness of the glory of the LORD." The rabbis suggest that a "bow" to a "bow" may imply that the rainbow is worshiped. There is, however, a blessing given in the Talmud, to be recited on seeing a rainbow (Babylonian Talmud, *Berakoth* 59a).

The passage referring to a rainbow in Revelation is a bit problematical, according to modern commentators. *The Anchor Bible* commentary by Massyngberde Ford makes the point:

> The Greek work, *isis*, may mean "rainbow," "halo," or "radiance." However, *isis* is not used for rainbow in Greek versions of Genesis 9:13 or Ezekiel 1:28; the word used is *toxon*. In the Genesis narrative the rainbow appears to be Yahweh's war-bow just as flashes of lightning are seen as His arrows; cf. Psalms 7:17, Hab[akkuk] 3:11. The covenant with Noah in Genesis means that Yahweh sets aside His bow and hangs it up in the clouds as a sign that His anger has subsided. When men gaze upon this rainbow, they feel

assured that the storm has passed and no flood will come again;
cf. Sirach 43:11, 50:7. (71)

This commentary doesn't seem to let the bow unite humanity in a covenant that inspires a leaping heart. Instead we see Yahweh's bow and feel thankful that God won't extract the same kind punishment next time we are evil, or we feel fearful that something worse could happen.

The rabbis looked closely at this symbol. More from Ford's *Anchor* commentary:

> It was said to be one of the ten things created on the eve of the sabbath at twilight, *Pesachim* 54a; that it was a revelation of God's glory on earth, cf. *Gen*[esis] *R*[abbah] 35:3; and that, just as one should not look upon a high official, one should not gaze upon the rainbow, *Hagigah* 16a . . . On the other hand, some saw the rainbow as a sign of judgment. In *Gen*[esis] *R*[abbah] 35:2, it is said that the generation of Rabbi Hezekiah and the men of the Great Synagogue founded by Ezra to act as the official guardians of the Law did not need the sign of the rainbow because they were completely righteous. However, to others the rainbow was given as a sign of censure and reminded one of the wickedness of the earth (71).

God's bow, censure, or promise makes the heart leap up, and, as the rabbis suggest, a prayer is appropriate, a blessing that makes a rainbow connection for generations: "Blessed are You, Lord our God, King of the universe, who remembers the covenant and is faithful in His covenant and fulfills His word" (*Berakoth* 59a).

For me the liturgical work *Ecclesiasticus,* in the Apocrypha, offers a heart-leaping response to the rainbow symbol: "Look at the rainbow, and praise its Maker; it shines with a supreme beauty, rounding the sky with its gleaming arc, a bow bent by the hands of the Most High" (43:11–12).

For those whose heart still leaps—*zokheir habrit.* Blessed is God who remembers the covenant (with Noah). The rainbow is also found in literature—the voice of God from "Noah's Flood," a Mystery Play last produced in 1575:

> Where cloudes in the welkin been,
> That ilke bow shall be seen,
> In tokening that my wrath and teen
>   Shall never thus wroken be.

The string is turned towards you
And towards me is bent the bow,
That such weather shall never show;
   And this beheet I thee. (390–39)

It is complex but it works with students if I provide context as we go:

- I show them Wordsworth's poem and ask about the hard line first. What does it mean to say that the child is father of the man?

- We then read the text in Genesis about the rainbow. What does it represent in the Bible?

- Next is Kermit's song. What kind of connections could Kermit mean?

- Mick Jagger's tune is a difficult translation. What could the rainbow of the song represent?

- The clincher: Does the Bible help us understand the rainbow symbol of Wordsworth, Kermit, and Jagger?

- Has the rainbow of the Bible found its way into popular culture?

Hair: A Student Search for the Symbolic

It helps if at least one student is having a bad hair day. Or maybe the teacher can set a good example and have bad hair. It also helps if students know that the search for the symbolic isn't whimsical or arbitrary. We don't just start looking for hair in the Bible because we have "hat hair" or "bed head." Something in some text takes us on a search.

In this case the text is the story of a muscular judge, Samson. His story is in Judges 13–16. Before he is even born, we get a hint about his hair when his mother is told that "no razor shall come on his head: for the child shall be a Nazarite unto God from the womb" (Judges 13:5).

One of the characteristics of biblical narrative is understatement. Details are sparse and allow for imaginative reading. Of all the things an author could tell us about this Samson, only one must be important at this point. He will be a Nazirite, a person who has taken a vow not to cut his hair, drink wine, or eat grapes (Numbers 6). We learn much more latter, but imagine a modern writer leaving us with this sketchy detail. There must be something very important about the hair, for why else could not cutting it constitute some kind of religious vow?

Before reading the story, students like to discuss hair problems:

1. Do hairstyles stereotype people?

2. Do students in our school choose hairstyles that identify them with certain groups?

3. Could a politician with spiked orange hair like an English punk rocker get elected to office in our city? What if the hair were all that our politician had in common with the rocker? Maybe hair is only a matter of style to both politician and punk rocker?

4. Why do some old women have blue hair?

5. Why do some old bald men do a comb-over on their shiny pate? Don't they know that a slim handful of hair pulled over the top doesn't really cover it?

6. Why would someone spend hundreds of dollars for a wig or hair-growing medicine or a hair transplant? How important is hair?

7. What does hair mean, anyway? Is it a symbol of something?

Students know that hair is symbolic. Scott Iwasaki, *Deseret News* music critic, put it this way:

> Throughout my junior high and high school days, I kept my hair long. I guess it was a Samson thing. It gave me strength . . . in the form of confidence. I didn't think people would take me seriously if I had short hair. (I thought I looked geeky). And I just couldn't get used to the image of myself playing drums in a thrash-metal bar band, headbanging with a crew cut (10).

After this brief introduction I ask students to read the story and note passages about hair and Nazirites. They find that the story could be used for many other purposes besides teaching about symbols. Samson is an archetypal bad guy we like. He is like Jesse James, Butch Cassidy, Robin Hood, and Dennis Rodman. Teachers who want to teach this should refer to Appendix C, "Samson as Archetype." The material is based on work by O. B. Davis, who also suggests the use of Samson as a foil for Moses. This doesn't quite work because Samson and Moses aren't in the same narrative. Samson is in Judges and Moses is in Exodus. Even with this problem, Samson the judge makes it easy to teach about literary foil, and I've included the material in Appendix D.

Students searching for hair and Nazirite should find the following:

> KJV, Judges 13:5: For, lo, thou shalt conceive, and bear a son; and no razor shall come on his head: for the child shall be a Nazarite unto God from the womb: and he shall begin to deliver Israel out of the hand of the Philistines.

> KJV, Judges 13:7: But he said unto me, Behold, thou shalt conceive, and bear a son; and now drink no wine nor strong drink, neither eat any unclean *thing*: for the child shall be a Nazarite to God from the womb to the day of his death.

> KJV, Judges 16:17: That he told her all his heart, and said unto her, There hath not come a razor upon mine head; for I *have been* a Nazarite unto God from my mother's womb: if I be shaven, then my strength will go from me, and I shall become weak, and be like any *other* man.

The next question for students is about what this means. They will probably need some information here. They will want to know what a Nazirite is. There is good information in biblical sources (e.g., Numbers 6) or in *Encyclopaedia Judaica*. The following is from the latter:

1. The Nazirite may not contaminate himself by touching a dead body.
2. He must abstain from strong drink (intoxicants).
3. He must not cut his hair.

Students will notice that Samson breaks all three vows. The teacher may suggest that the hair is symbolic of all the vows he was supposed to keep. It is a visible sign of a Nazirite.

> The uncut hair of the Nazirite is his distinction . . . Its importance is indicated by the root of the term *Nazirite*, which refers at times to the hair. . . . Since hair continues to grow throughout life (and apparently for a time after death), it was considered by the ancients to be the seat of man's vitality and life-force, and in ritual it often served as his substitute.

The information in *Signs and Symbols in Christian Art* may also help with the discussion: "Loose, flowing hair is a symbol of penitence. . . . Long hair worn by men may sometimes symbolize strength, an allusion to the story of Samson" (Ferguson 47).

After students understand the vows of the Nazirite and the biblical symbolism of hair, they will enjoy a clip of the Turner movie production *Samson and Delilah*. My preference is not to show the complete movie, for two reasons. It leaves the text far behind, and viewing the entire long film tends to pass the point of hair as a symbol and clutter the lesson.

There are two scenes that help to teach the symbolism of hair. The first is at 27 minutes, 30 seconds in Part 1 and runs for 2 minutes, 20 seconds.

In this scene Delilah is discussing Samson with one of the Philistines. It is before she has actually met Samson, but, she is obviously infatuated with him. Two activities seem to overlay the discussion. First, she plays with her hair while she talks. At this point she does not know that hair is a symbol of Samson's strength. The director is giving us a transparent but artful forecast of something Delilah will learn later.

Also overlaying the scene and discussion of Samson's strength is a dance at the court of the king. The dancers are doing some sort of Maypole-type dance with a man. They wrap him in hair and eventually carry him out on their shoulders. Entangled and entrapped in hair the dancer is defenseless and at the mercy of the other dancers.

The second scene is when Samson gets his haircut. In this interpretation he is awake when Delilah does the deed. The scene begins at 41 minutes, 4 seconds in Part 2, with Samson confessing to Delilah the source of his strength. I don't recommend starting the video ahead of the scene because the haircut culminates nine days of mutual seduction. The strength of the scene is that the viewer seems to understand why Samson would tell his secret after previous bad experiences with the lying seductress. Another strength of this particular scene is that the haircut takes place when Samson is awake. Delilah blindsides Samson with the scissors after explaining that she could have done the deed while he slept.

The questions for students after the scene are about the strength of hair as a symbol: If his hair is so important and represents what he is, why is Samson willing to tell this secret to someone proven so untrustworthy? Has this symbolic meaning of hair continued into our present culture?

After this introduction to a biblical symbol, students are more aware of the clothes, foods, and everyday artifacts that can carry symbolic meaning in biblical literature. They also notice the insects, animals, birds, and flowers. There is meaning in *staff* and *bread* and *blood* and even *serpent*, *fish*, and *gold*.

Students may then be ready for a closer look as "Samson as Archetype", Appendix C, and "Samson as Foil", Appendix D.

Chapter 8

TEACHING BIBLICAL POETRY IN BOTH TESTAMENTS: WRITING PSALMS AND PROVERBS

After an introduction to biblical poetry, students write psalms and proverbs using some of the poetic structures and de vices they have discovered. The results are fun. I often bind the student work together as the class book of Psalms and Proverbs. They can also be posted on the class website or simply enjoyed in a class poetry reading.

Imagine translating a poem into a second language. Suppose that the poem rhymes and has a poetic meter in the first language. It may be possible to preserve either rhyme or meter in the translation, but preserving both is unlikely. A nonbiblical example of a poetic translation problem will help the class to understand.

The haiku is a Japanese poetic form that includes three lines. Consisting, respectively, of five, seven, and five syllables. The first and third lines rhyme (Perrine 722).

Following are two Japanese haiku from *Literature: Structure, Sound, and Sense*. The translators of the version on the left are Earl Miner and Babette Deutsch, who try to preserve the syllable count. The translations on the right by Harold G. Henderson preserve the poetic structure by making the first and third lines rhyme.

The lightning flashes!	A lightning gleam:
And slashing through the darkness,	Into darkness travels
A night-heron's screech.	A night heron's scream.

Matsuo Bash (1644–1694)

The falling flower	Fallen flowers rise
I saw drift back to the branch	Back to the branch—I watch:
Was a butterfly.	Oh . . . butterflies!
	Moritake (1452–1540)

The amazing feature of biblical poetry and other poetry in sacred texts is that, unlike the translations of the haiku, the essential qualities are translatable.

Parallelism

This point is made about translation because the essence of biblical Hebrew poetry and other ancient sacred poetry is translatable thought rhyme. This includes poetry in the Qur'an, Ugaritic texts, Sumero-Akkadian literature, ancient Greek and Latin literatures, the Book of Mormon and the New Testament. There is a good review of ancient poetry in Welch's *Chiasmus in Antiquity*. The value of this work is the rather complete index to *chiasmus* in the Hebrew canon. It only seems appropriate that the poetry probably most translated into many languages, sacred poetry, retains its most important poetic quality in translation. This quality is called parallelism.

This idea was first explicated by Bishop Robert Lowth in 1753 in his *Lectures on the Sacred Poetry of the Hebrews*. Gabel and Wheeler in *The Bible as Literature* put it this way: "The key to Hebrew poetry . . . is that it is a structure of thought rather than of external form and that a Hebrew poem is composed by balancing a series of sense units against one another according to certain simple principles of relationship" (37).

The parallel though rhyme can be easily demonstrated in class by asking students to hold an arm out straight and with one eye closed point to a small object like a light switch, thermostat, or tennis ball on a front desk. After the students have the object in their sight, ask them to keep their pointing arm still and change eyes. When they look with the other eye, it will appear as if their aim is off. Blinking from eye to eye will make it look as if the aim changes for each eye, when in fact the aim stays the same. The reason is that each eye is taking a slightly different picture from a slightly different angle.

When we look with both eyes open, the two different pictures are merged into one picture. This is obvious in the one-eye pointing exercise. Our brain puts the two pictures together and we get depth perception. If we had only one eye we would lose our sense of depth perception, our three-dimensional view of the world. Depth perception is what we get from sacred literature that allows two looks at the same idea. This and other examples in this chapter is from the KJV: "The Heavens declare the glory of God/And the firmament showeth his handiwork" (Psalm 19:1). "Heavens" and "firmament" are synonyms (nouns). "Declare" and "showeth" are synonyms (verbs). "Glory of God" and "handiwork" are close synonyms.

The idea is that both lines (the technical term is *hemistichs*), look at the same idea, from slightly different angles. The lines don't rhyme and do not share the same meter. The lines don't express exactly the same idea or they would be redundant. The pleasure in these parallel lines is in the shifting relationships between lines. In this case the lines are synonymous. This first type of parallelism, *synonymous parallelism* is the easiest to teach and to write.

Perhaps an additional example is helpful: "Wash me thoroughly from mine iniquity/And cleanse me from my sin" (Psalm 51:2). "Wash me thoroughly" and "cleanse me" are synonyms. "Mine iniquity" and "my sin" are synonyms.

Both subjects and predicates are synonymous, and both are looks at the same idea from a slightly different angle. The lines are synonymously parallel. Students may remember more easily if they are told to think *restatement* when looking for synonymous parallelism.

Some linguists reinforce the idea that each view from the literary binocular is slightly different by suggesting that there are no true or absolute synonyms. No matter how close the meaning of two words, they are not actually synonyms unless they can each be inserted at the same point in a text without changing the meaning even slightly.

Two more examples may be helpful.

> He maketh the deep to boil like a pot:
> he maketh the sea like a pot of ointment.
> —Job 41:31

> He that sitteth in the heavens shall laugh:
> the Lord shall have them in derision.
> —Psalm 2:4

Another kind of parallelism is called *anthithetical*. In this, the second line or thought *contrasts* with the first by presenting an opposite thought. "A virtuous woman is a crown to her husband/But she that maketh ashamed is as rottenness in his bones" (Proverbs 12:4). It is isn't as easy as looking for antonyms, but students seem to intuitively see the idea that a "virtuous woman" is in some ways the other side of "she that maketh ashamed," and that "a crown to her husband" is opposite of "rottenness in his bones."

"Chariots" and "horses" certainly aren't opposite, but they are different. The one pulls and the other is pulled. "Some trust in chariots/And some in horses" (Psalm 20:7).

Another example may make the search for anthithetical parallelism more intuitive:

> He asked for water,
> And she gave him milk.
> —Judges 5:25

> For the LORD knoweth the way of the righteous:
> but the way of the ungodly shall perish.
> —Psalm 1:6

> My son, keep thy father's commandment,
> and forsake not the law of thy mother.
> —Proverbs 6:20

Some writers distinguish two other kinds of parallelism, *climactic parallelism* and *synthetic parallelism* (Ryken, *How to Read* 104). The two are so similar that I teach them both as synthetic parallelism. The key word for students to remember is *completion*. The second line or thought restates and then completes the first. The idea seems to grow with the addition of a parallel line: "The Lord reigneth/Let the earth rejoice" (Psalm 97:1).

Notice how the ideas seem to grow in the following passage as it moves to completion:

> When I consider thy heavens, the work of thy fingers,
> the moon and the stars, which thou hast ordained;
> What is man, that thou art mindful of him?
> and the son of man, that thou visitest him?
> For thou hast made him a little lower than the angels,

and hast crowned him with glory and honour.
Thou madest him to have dominion over the works of thy
hands;
thou hast put all *things* under his feet:
All sheep and oxen, yea, and the beasts of the field;
The fowl of the air, and the fish of the sea,
and whatsoever passeth through the paths of the seas.

—Psalm 8:3-8

he leadeth me in the paths of righteousness
for his name's sake.

—Psalm 23:3

Scheindlin, in the *Book of Job*, suggests that Job 28:20–26 is a good anthology of types of parallelism (28).

After students understand parallelism, I often give them an extended piece of biblical poetry and ask them to work in small groups to try and discover which lines are parallel and in what ways. The following is the first paragraph of Psalm 102 from the KJV and is an example often used by Steve Walker of Brigham Young University:

Mark lines that are synonymous (restatement) with an S.
Mark lines that are antithetical (contrast) with an A.
Mark lines that are synthetic (completion) with a C.
  Hear my prayer, O LORD,
  and let my cry come unto thee.
  Hide not thy face from me
  in the day *when* I am in trouble;
  incline thine ear unto me:
  in the day *when* I call
  answer me speedily.
  For my days are consumed like smoke,
  and my bones are burned as an hearth.
  My heart is smitten, and withered like grass;
  so that I forget to eat my bread.
  By reason of the voice of my groaning my bones cleave to my
  skin.
  I am like a pelican of the wilderness:

I am like an owl of the desert.

I watch, and am as a sparrow alone upon the house top.

Mine enemies reproach me all the day;

and they that are mad against me are sworn against me.

For I have eaten ashes like bread,

and mingled my drink with weeping,

Because of thine indignation and thy wrath:

or thou hast lifted me up, and cast me down.

My days *are* like a shadow that declineth;

and I am withered like grass.

—Psalm 102: 1–11

The students will notice that not all parallel lines in this psalm are next to each other. There are different patterns in Hebrew poetry, and there is a particular pattern in some poetic passages, the chiasm.

Since this idea of looking poetically from two slightly different angles may be a characteristic of sacred literature besides the Bible, I like to show students a nonbiblical example. It is a reminder that we could study many sacred literatures and find poetic qualities. The first verses of the Qur'an are a good example. These verses were written as parallel lines/thoughts:

1 Glory to God Most High, full of Grace and Mercy;

2 He created All, including Man.

3 To Man He gave a special place in His Creation.

4 He honoured man to be His Agent,

5 And to that end, endowed him with understanding,

6 Purified his affections, and gave him spiritual insight;

7 So that man should understand Nature,

8 Understand himself,

9 And know God through His wondrous Signs,

10 And glorify Him in Truth, reverence, and unity.

I'm not so presumptuous to suggest how a Moslem reads this in Arabic (the language of the Qur'an). This is an issue, according to the student who gave me a copy of his holy book. He was careful to remind me that I wasn't really reading the Qur'an because I couldn't read the language, the rhymed Arabic. He made it clear that I could only read a translation and that the English translation is not the

Qur'an. He reminded me that *Qur'an* means "recitation" or "something to be recited" and is really meant to be recited, not read.

With these cautions in mind, I notice parallel poetry. To me, lines 3 and 4 are synonymously parallel. "His Agent" and a "special place" are two looks at the same idea. Lines 5 and 6 also offer synonymous options, and to "understand Nature" and "understand himself" seem like synthetic ideas.

Chiasmus

After students understand some of the principles of parallel lines, the teacher can explain the most common and elegant pattern, chiasmus. The form is named for the Greek letter chi, χ. The chi has become a religious symbol because it is the first letter of Christos, a Greek word that means "the anointed." The poetic explanation of the term requires a return to the discussion of eyes.

Each eye takes a picture from a slightly different angle. The image is projected on the retina, a one-cell thick layer called *rods* and *cones*. The nerves from the retina separate so that some nerves from each eye go to each side of the brain, but most of the nerves from the right eye go to the left side of the brain, and most of the nerves from the left eye go to the right side of the brain. The point at which the nerves cross is called the *optic chiasm*. The idea is that we see depth the same way some poets write for depth.

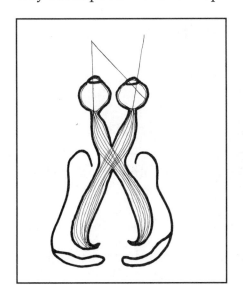

The poetic form is like the reflection on a still mountain in the lake in the early morning before the breeze comes up. This idea occurred to me as I looked across a lake in the high Uinta Mountains of Utah during one of those wonderful moments of insight. The reflection and the mountain converged at the base, or on the shoreline. The summit of the mountain and the summit of the reflection are parallel ideas. The lake is never perfectly still, so the real image and the reflected image are always a little different, but on a still day it is hard to tell which image is which. The dual view offers depth.

The structure of the chiasm is A/B/C/D/C¹/B¹/A¹, and it does look like a reflection of itself and the shape of a chi, χ:

A

  B

    C

      D

    C¹

  B¹

 A¹

There are two easy examples in the first two verses of Psalm 76:

1. In Judah is God known: his name is great in Israel.
   A In Judah
     B God is known
     B¹ his name is great
   A¹ in Israel

2. In Salem also is his tabernacle, and his dwelling place in Zion.
   A In Salem also
     B is his tabernacle,
     B¹ and his dwelling place
   A¹ In Zion

It gets a bit more complex in Jeremiah 2:27:

A but in the time of their trouble they will say,
 B Arise, and save us.
  C But where *are* thy gods that thou hast made thee?
 B¹ let them arise, if they can save thee
A¹ in the time of thy trouble.

An extended example is included in a good introductory text, *Introduction to Biblical Interpretation* by Klein, Blomberg, and Hubbard (238). The example is also found in Jeremiah 2:5–9:

⁵ Thus saith the LORD, What iniquity have your fathers found in me,

that they are gone far from me and have walked after vanity, and are become vain:

⁶ Neither said they, Where is the LORD that brought us up out of the land of Egypt, that led us through the wilderness, through a land of deserts and of pits, through a land of drought, and of the shadow of death, through a land that no man passed through, and where no man dwelt?

⁷ And I brought you into a plentiful country, to eat the fruit thereof and the goodness thereof; but when ye entered, ye defiled my land, and made mine heritage an abomination.

⁸ The priests said not, Where is the LORD? And they that handle the law knew me not: the pastors also transgressed against me, and the prophets prophesied by Baal, and walked after things that do not profit.

⁹ Wherefore I will yet plead with you, saith the LORD, and with your children's children will I plead.

Bold Italics have been added below to make the structure look more obvious"

Thus saith the LORD,
A   What iniquity have your *fathers* found in me,
     that they are gone far from me
         B   and have walked after vanity, and are become vain:
              C   *Neither said they,*
                   Where is the Lord
                       D   that brought us up out of the *land* of Egypt,
                            that led us through the wilderness,
                                through a land of deserts and of pits,
                                through a land of drought,
                                and of the shadow of death,
                                through a *land* that no man passed
                                    through,and where no man dwelt?
                       E   And I brought you into a plentiful
                            country,
                                to eat the fruit thereof
                                and the goodness thereof;

> D¹   but when ye entered, ye defiled my **land**,
>   and made mine heritage an abomination.
>
>   C¹   *The priests said not,*
>   *Where is the LORD?*
>   And they that handle the law knew me not:
>   the pastors also transgressed against me,
>
> B¹ and the prophets prophesied by Baal,
>   and walked after things that do not profit.
>
> A¹ Wherefore I will yet plead with you,
>   saith the Lord,
>   and with your **children's children** will I plead.

This poetic form gets far more complicated than can be taught in the public schools, with some commentators finding chiasmas in long narratives and entire books of the Bible. I find that students are a bit awed by the simplicity of parallel poetry and the simple chiasm, and they offer good psalms of their own if given a little more information about another poetic form in the Bible.

The Lament

As part of the discussion of Psalms and poetry, I point out to students the most common psalm, the lament. This is to prepare them for a psalm writing assignment. About 45% of the biblical psalms are in the lament form. This means that they roughly follow the following typical stages:

1. The psalm addresses or invokes God. Christians often use the term *invocation* for prayers at the beginning of church meetings.

2. Some problem or persecution is described.

3. The poem or the narrator then asserts faith.

4. It then asks for help, and sometimes it offers a vow.

5. The lament thanks God for helping. This is comparable to a "benediction," a term often used to indicate a concluding prayer in Christianity.

What is described here is the threefold structure of Jewish prayer: praise, petition, and thanks (in that order). If students are interested in writing this kind of psalm, I suggest two parallel lines for each idea.

Since the form can be considered a prayer, I allow students to secularize the assignment if they wish by asking them to follow the form below using parallel lines. There is no legal reason the students can't write a prayer as an educational activity. It is devotional writing and reading that is not allowed in the school. If teachers are uncomfortable with prayer writing, this more secular from can be used to:

A
A¹   address anyone who can help with a trouble or problem

B
B¹   identify the problem

C
C¹   say that a solution to the problem will come

D
D¹   suggest a solution to the problem and include a promise

E
E¹   say thanks for the help

The following is a typical secular response to this assignment. (Notice the nice alliteration in some lines and notice that the parallelism seems to be natural.)

A   Oh teacher who knows the equations
A¹ Who carefully calculates the constants,
B   My mind works with words.
B¹ Nebulous numbers numb the noggin.
C   I know I can calculate with the best,
C¹ But passing the present principles would be perfect.
D   Could knowledge be poured on my open mind
D¹ Like the Nye Science Guy pouring down from the sky?
E   Thanks be to theorems, formula, and functions
E¹ For Pythagoras, Euclid, and Eienstein.

In order to further appreciate the Psalms and other biblical poetry, it is important to know that the essence of biblical Hebrew poetry is not the formal pattern of a lament or a praise, or a prayer of thanksgiving. The most common property of biblical poetry is parallelism. It is to Hebrew poetry what rhyme and meter are to English poetry.

Psalm 23

It would be a serious omission to not teach the most translated passage in the Hebrew Bible. Warshaw suggests an established scholarly approach, which is expanded a bit here (42–44). The early history of Psalm 23 is found in Appendix E. It is a good study of how the metaphors of the psalm are the translations that hold over the years.

The following translation is from the KJV of 1611 which is the culminating translation in the literary history of Appendix E. The KJV is put in the verse form of the NRSV to make it easier to teach poetic principles:

¹ The LORD *is* my shepherd; I shall not want.
    ²He maketh me to lie down in green pastures:
he leadeth me beside the still waters.
    ³He restoreth my soul:
he leadeth me in the paths of righteousness for his name's sake.

⁴Yea, though I walk through the valley of the shadow of death,
    I will fear no evil:
for thou *art* with me;
    thy rod and thy staff they comfort me.

⁵Thou preparest a table before me
    in the presence of mine enemies:
thou anointest my head with oil;
    my cup runneth over.
⁶Surely goodness and mercy shall follow me
    all the days of my life:
and I will dwell in the house of the LORD
    for ever.

The search for poetic symbols and metaphor of Psalm 23 include the following:

Shepherd:	In this context a shepherd leads sheep rather than driving them.
Green Pastures:	These are scarce in the land of this psalm and would be very valuable.
Still Waters:	This could be an oasis which is idyllic compared to a rushing wash that floods during storms.
Darkness or Valley of the Shadow of Death:	The rough ravines and dry landscape seem to invite death.

Staff/rod:	The shepherd sometimes has a staff to ward off wild animals or a crook for guiding sheep. In this poem the rod and staff are comforting.
Enemies:	One would have to be confident to eat in the presence of enemies.
Cup Runneth Over:	This metaphor describes abundant blessing and joy.
Anointed with Oil:	The head of an honored guest was anointed with oil. This is also the ritual for inducting a King.
Goodness and Mercy All the Days:	It is like dwelling in the tabernacle (house of the LORD) forever.

The following is Warshaw's commentary:

> Warshaw divides the poem into three stanzas. They are verses 1-3, verses 4-5, and verse 6. He suggests that these three divisions represent the psychic progress of the speaker in the psalm. In the first stanza the speaker is complacent, like an untroubled lamb.

> Warshaw starts the second part after verse 5 but the NRSV translators break after verse 4. In this part the images are things that threaten and the speaker addresses the Lord as thou. "Midway in this second stanza the sheep becomes a person, who now eats at a table rather than in a pasture. The trust remains, but . . . the speaker can look away from the Lord as he (or she) expresses confidence. He passes from innocence to experience, to use Blake's categories" (43).

> The last stanza returns to the first with a "serene confidence" as we see the development. "The speaker's trust has undergone a change. So has the imagery. In the first stanza the Lord provided physical sustenance and guidance for the here and now. In part two, the Lord protected the speaker from threats of death and enemies, over whom he exulted. In the third stanza, the speaker's trust is spiritualized and projected beyond the present" (43).

> Warshat notes one scholar who "sees *the house of the Lord* and *for ever* as eternal life in God's celestial abode" (43) Although this is an interesting reading it is probably through a more modern Christian template since it doesn't seem to be completely consistent with ideas of immortality expressed from a Jewish perspective in the Hebrew Bible.

The fact that the Lord appears at the start and finish of the poem indicates an "inclusio" to Warshaw. Finding such a devise invites the reader to pay attention to the progress of the idea throughout the poem. "For the speaker, the Lord is the beginning and the end" (44).

When literary analysis of a poem uncovers the use of technical devices that subtly reinforce, and are justified by, its meaning, we must acknowledge the poem's literary artistry. This kind of analysis is one of the main reading skills the teacher of English would like his or her students to learn. Surely Psalm 23 is as valid a piece of literature for such a lesson as any other" (44).

1 Corinthians 13

One of the most poetic passages of the New Testament is the hymn of 1 Corinthians 13. Warshaw suggests that the poetic hymn can also be taught in Bible as literature courses using the work of modern Bible scholars (44–48). The following is again from the KJV but I have taken the liberty of defining verses, something not done in most modern translations even though the poetic form seems so intuitive and obviously natural. I also replaced the word *charity* with *love*, as do most modern translations. In Greek the word is *agape* and is intended in Christianity to define the highest kind of love that is directed first toward God and then to oneself and others or neighbors. This use of the word *charity* has changed, and *love* makes a less confusing modern translation. The Oxford English Dictionary notes that the use of charity as the highest love is obsolete.

[1] Though I speak with the tongues of men and of angels,
    and have not [love],
        I am become *as* sounding brass, or a tinkling cymbal.

[2] And though I have *the gift of* prophecy,
and understand all mysteries, and all knowledge;
and though I have all faith, so that I could remove mountains,
    and have not [love],
        I am nothing.

[3] And though I bestow all my goods to feed *the poor*,
and though I give my body to be burned,
    and have not [love],
        it profiteth me nothing.

⁴ [love] suffereth long, *and* is kind;
    [love] envieth not;
    [love] vaunteth not itself, is not puffed up,

⁵ Doth not behave itself unseemly,
    seeketh not her own, is not easily provoked,
        thinketh no evil;

⁶ Rejoiceth not in iniquity,
    but rejoiceth in the truth;

⁷ Beareth all things,
    believeth all things,
hopeth all things,
    endureth all things.

⁸ [love] never faileth:
    but whether *there be* prophecies,
        they shall fail;
    whether *there be* tongues,
        they shall cease;
    whether *there be* knowledge,
        it shall vanish away.

⁹ For we know in part,
    and we prophesy in part.

¹⁰ But when that which is perfect is come,
    then that which is in part shall be done away.

¹¹ When I was a child,
    I spake as a child,
    I understood as a child,
    I thought as a child:
but when I became a man,
    I put away childish things.

¹² For now we see through a glass, darkly;
    but then face to face:
now I know in part;
    but then shall I know even as also I am known.

¹³ And now abideth faith, hope, [love],
    these three;
but the greatest of these *is* [love].

The first question I ask students about this passage is if my editorial replacement of the word *charity* with *love* makes a difference. We go to dictionaries and Bible dictionaries for a look and then discuss. The next question is a natural follow-up. Should I replace other archaic words? Would this change the tone or the meaning? Do we have any right to change the words of Paul? This is an important new genre in the Bible, a letter or an epistle. It was written to the Christians in Corinth. The earliest translations are Greek. In changing it from a rather archaic English translation to a modern English translation, has something of its historical value been changed? Reading the same passage from other translations is a good exercise that promotes close reading.

Besides the translation question, there are interesting formal issues. This familiar passage comes between two chapters about spiritual gifts and then seems to discount these gifts by saying that there is something, *agape*, much more important than the gifts. This is the point of the last verse of chapter 12, which serves as a preface to chapter 13: "But covet earnestly the best gifts: and yet show I unto you a more excellent way."

Warshaw divides this passage into three stanzas for analysis: verses 1–3, 4–7, and 8–13 (45–47). This makes analysis easier because each stanza offers a different message. The first contrasts love with gifts. The second defines the basic virtue of love. The third stanza is a synthesis. It "contrasts three gifts of the spirit with three virtues" (46).

The concluding question for students may be whether love is as good as Paul writes?

Proverbs

Proverbs are part of a genre we call wisdom literature. I tell students that the hottest-selling literature today is wisdom literature, and after we start a list, they get the idea and add to it with a vengeance:

Chicken Soup for the Whatever

Think and Grow Rich

How to Win Friends and Influence People

All I Needed to Know I Learned in Kindergarten

Seven Habits of Highly Annoying People

The One Minute Manager

After we get the list going and clarify my sarcastic editorial work on book titles, we add sayings from greeting cards, poster aphorisms, graffiti, e-mail lists, and babble. Students bring examples to class so I can make the point that for early Christian commentators, wisdom was more important than knowledge. I ask this as a question. Is wisdom more important than knowledge? What is the difference? Even the top ten lists sometimes seem proverbial or wise and are understood by the unknowledgeable.

Before we start writing proverbs, I suggest that perhaps some biblical proverbs have a poetic form. Showing Proverb 31:10–31 in Hebrew helps to make the point:

10 אֵשֶׁת־חַיִל מִי יִמְצָא וְרָחֹק מִפְּנִינִים מִכְרָהּ׃

11 בָּטַח בָּהּ לֵב בַּעְלָהּ וְשָׁלָל לֹא יֶחְסָר׃

12 גְּמָלַתְהוּ טוֹב וְלֹא־רָע כֹּל יְמֵי חַיֶּיהָ׃

13 דָּרְשָׁה צֶמֶר וּפִשְׁתִּים וַתַּעַשׂ בְּחֵפֶץ כַּפֶּיהָ׃

14 הָיְתָה כָּאֳנִיּוֹת סוֹחֵר מִמֶּרְחָק תָּבִיא לַחְמָהּ׃

15 וַתָּקָם בְּעוֹד לַיְלָה וַתִּתֵּן טֶרֶף לְבֵיתָהּ וְחֹק לְנַעֲרֹתֶיהָ׃

16 זָמְמָה שָׂדֶה וַתִּקָּחֵהוּ מִפְּרִי כַפֶּיהָ (נָטַע) [נָטְעָה] כָּרֶם׃

17 חָגְרָה בְעוֹז מָתְנֶיהָ וַתְּאַמֵּץ זְרוֹעֹתֶיהָ׃

18 טָעֲמָה כִּי־טוֹב סַחְרָהּ לֹא־יִכְבֶּה (בַלַּיִל) [בַלַּיְלָה] נֵרָהּ׃

19 יָדֶיהָ שִׁלְּחָה בַכִּישׁוֹר וְכַפֶּיהָ תָּמְכוּ פָלֶךְ׃

20 כַּפָּהּ פָּרְשָׂה לֶעָנִי וְיָדֶיהָ שִׁלְּחָה לָאֶבְיוֹן׃

21 לֹא־תִירָא לְבֵיתָהּ מִשָּׁלֶג כִּי כָל־בֵּיתָהּ לָבֻשׁ שָׁנִים׃

22 מַרְבַדִּים עָשְׂתָה־לָּהּ שֵׁשׁ וְאַרְגָּמָן לְבוּשָׁהּ׃

23 נוֹדָע בַּשְּׁעָרִים בַּעְלָהּ בְּשִׁבְתּוֹ עִם־זִקְנֵי־אָרֶץ׃

24 סָדִין עָשְׂתָה וַתִּמְכֹּר וַחֲגוֹר נָתְנָה לַכְּנַעֲנִי׃

25 עֹז־וְהָדָר לְבוּשָׁהּ וַתִּשְׂחַק לְיוֹם אַחֲרוֹן׃

26 פִּיהָ פָּתְחָה בְחָכְמָה וְתוֹרַת־חֶסֶד עַל־לְשׁוֹנָהּ׃

27 צוֹפִיָּה הֲלִיכוֹת בֵּיתָהּ וְלֶחֶם עַצְלוּת לֹא תֹאכֵל׃

28 קָמוּ בָנֶיהָ וַיְאַשְּׁרוּהָ בַּעְלָהּ וַיְהַלְלָהּ׃

29 רַבּוֹת בָּנוֹת עָשׂוּ חָיִל וְאַתְּ עָלִית עַל־כֻּלָּנָה׃

30 שֶׁקֶר הַחֵן וְהֶבֶל הַיֹּפִי אִשָּׁה יִרְאַת־יְהוָה הִיא תִתְהַלָּל׃

31 תְּנוּ־לָהּ מִפְּרִי יָדֶיהָ וִיהַלְלוּהָ בַשְּׁעָרִים מַעֲשֶׂיהָ׃

This particular section (Pr. 31: 10–31), is a song, "Woman of Valor," that Sabbath-observant Jews sing before dinner on Friday night in honor of the woman of the household.

I ask students if they see anything poetic about this page, and since "it's Hebrew to them" they don't see much. But is there any pattern or form? I point out that there seems to be a gap in the center of each line, and it looks like a blank line weaves its way vertically through the text. They are looking at the divisions between parallel thoughts. I then talk about the Hebrew alphabet. English borrowed the word *alphabet* from the first two Hebrews letters, Aleph and Bet, א and ב. The first line of the proverb begins with Aleph, the second with Bet, and the proverb continues with each letter of the Hebrew alphabet in order. This is called an acrostic. It is similar to the poetic form we use when we write a poem with each line starting the letter of some name:

> M is for the many things she gives me.
>
> O is that she's only growing old.
>
> T is for the tears she said to save me.
>
> H is for her heart as pure as gold . . .

And so on, until the students tell me how "cheesy" this is, even for MOTHER.

The assignment is to bring a family proverb to share with the class. I'm always interested in the short lessons-in-a-sentence that seem to be the private possession of a family. When I went out to work with my dad and forgot a tool and had to return to the house, he'd tell me, "What you don't have in the head you got to have in the feet."

The proverb depended on who sent us to get apples stored in the basement for the winter. Mom would tell us to bring up the apples that were starting to go soft, so we could eat them before they went bad. Dad said, "If you get the best apples you can find, then we're always eating the best." This is wisdom literature.

When we whined, coaxed, or threatened, Mom would say, "You can catch more bees with honey than you can with vinegar." And when we worried about what others would think, Dad would say, "You wouldn't worry about what others thought of you if you knew how little they did."

Students get the idea and bring proverbial family literature to class that makes us all smile. Then I ask that they write their own proverbs and suggest the following guidelines.

1. The proverb should suggest something that you want everyone to do or believe and give a good reason for doing or believing.

2. The proverb's meaning should not require explanation. That is, it should stand on its own. It may generate discussion, but the two lines of advice should make sense without explanation.

3. The proverb should provoke more agreement than argument.

4. Two sentences is the maximum. One compound sentence is okay.

Proverbs aren't always that easy: "For in much wisdom *is* much grief/and he that increaseth knowledge increaseth sorrow" (Ecclesiastes 1:18) Students find a lot to talk about in the proverb. What is sorrowful about knowing? Does knowing give us additional responsibility? In knowing do we realize how much we don't know? I try to suggest that it isn't like what my proverbial brother used to say:

> The more you study, the more you learn.
> The more you learn, the more you forget.
> The more you forget, the less you know.
> So why study?

Chapter 9

TEACHING CRITICAL THINKING:
IT IMPROVES IN THE TRANSLATION

Bible scholars frequently compare Bible translations. The value of these comparisons is an argument for allowing and encouraging multiple Bible translations in the classroom. We all read through different templates, anyway; why not allow our templates to choose a translation? The translation comparisons in the classroom teach critical thinking or close reading.

The reader requires the same confession that I make to students; I'm not a biblical language scholar. I don't read Hebrew or Greek, and neither do many teachers who choose to compare Bible translations. I read biblical literature in translation and teach the Bible as literature in an English department. Since most of my work has been in a public college, the learning objective for these comparisons is primarily secular. This makes me a parasite, according to C. S. Lewis. Students have a question after they hear this confession: "Isn't it important to know the language so you can determine if the text is translated correctly?"

Well, yes and no. Yes, it is important to know the intent of the author; it is also impossible. No, the Bible is literature in translation and we each read it according to a very personal template that includes our particular language. . . .

And no again: even an English teacher is entitled to read and teach translated literature without reading the "original" language. Most Americans probably haven't read *War and Peace* in its original language. We read foreign language novels and poetry, and even the literature of early England without knowing the original language. Few in the world can read the language of the earliest English literature or even the Middle English of *The Canterbury Tales*.

This idea can be introduced in class with a 28-minute video, *History of the English Language*. The video compares modern, early modern, Middle English, and Old English translations of the story of Solomon's wisdom. This is the story of a child custody dispute between two prostitutes in 1 Kings 3:16–28. It is a bit of a surprise for students to hear English that they can't understand and glimpse a bit of the history of our language with a Bible story. The video is well worth showing. It is available from Films for the Humanities and Sciences in Princeton, NJ or can be ordered at http://www. films.com. The video introduces students to the idea of reading biblical narrative in the context of the time the narrative was translated. It is a much different reading than "sound-bite" Bible study, which is like trying to understand the corpus of Shakespeare by reading *Bartlett's Familiar Quotations*.

The variant translations of biblical texts offer a way to teach critical thinking in English composition courses as well as in literature courses. This critical thinking is what many would call close reading, and Bible texts from various translations help to teach this skill. The goal is modest. I want students to read carefully as they have a personal dialog with the narrative.

It may be appropriate for an additional confession, perhaps a confession of my faith. Teaching Bible as literature has taught me that sometimes I must say something about what I believe because of the reverence that students have for the text. They don't require any confession in my literature courses for my belief in Hardy or Joyce or Shaw. Nobody has to believe literature, but the Bible is different literature. It is sacred to many students, and they want to know what the teacher believes. People haven't died for Macbeth, but they have for the Bible.

So my confession of faith is that we all bring something to the text, and the text brings something to us. We will bring more and find more if we read closely, critically, and suspend judgment. The idea of critical reading is a graduation from sound-bite reading. It is progress for students to consider that the Sound bites have contexts that seem different in various translations. Teachers probably require no examples of sound-bite belief, but I continue to be amazed. I've had students tell me that eating leftovers is contrary to the Bible (Leviticus

7:15) and that Christmas trees are vain (Jeremiah 10:3–4). We hear more serious arguments about blood transfusions, capital punishment, abortion, homosexuality, and a host of other social issues. What most of these arguments seem to have in common is reliance on a particular prooftext.

Part of the problem of using the Bible as prooftext is that the argument often centers on translation. It is on this point that I start teaching critical reading by comparing translations. The difference between these literary comparisons and those done by people looking for *the* truth is that the comparisons are not threatening; they are literary.

Teachers can point out to students that some words on almost any page of the KJV Old Testament are in italics. The words are in italics to identify translation problems, and perhaps teachers can cite an example where italics matter as a start to careful reading. "And there was again a battle in Gob with the Philistines, where Elhanan the son of Jaare-oregim, a Bethlehemite, slew *the brother of* Goliath the Gittite, the staff of whose spear *was* like a weaver's beam" (2 Samuel 21:19). In at least five modern translations, "the brother of" is omitted. The italics in the KJV indicate that the translators had to add these words to give David the credit for killing Goliath. The translators may have been on pretty safe ground here because their "correction" makes the passage agree with both tradition and 1 Chronicles 20:5. It is best to keep and open mind. Perhaps the Hebrew text is correct and the two passages are not *supposed* to agree.

A note from the Bible Dictionary bound with many old editions of the KJV explains the use of italics:

> In the King James Version italics identify words that are necessary in English to round out and complete the sense of a phrase, but were not present in the Hebrew or Greek text of the manuscript used. Such additions were necessary because in some instances the manuscript was inadequate, and the translators felt obliged to clarify it in the translation. In other instances italics were necessary in cases where the grammatical construction of English called for the use of words that were not needed to make the same thought in Hebrew or Greek. Italics thus represent the willingness of the translators to identify these areas. (708)

There is something else interesting in the KJV Bible dictionary's explanation of the use of italics. It refers to Hebrew and Greek manuscripts. A similar reference is made on the title page of the New Testament, where it notes that the testament has been translated from the original Greek.

Teachers can point out to students that the text may have been first written in Greek but was not first spoken in Greek. Was Greek the language of Jesus and his disciples? Was Greek the language of the synagogue where the early apostles preached? The point is that what is claimed as the "original Greek" could itself a be a translation of the original spoken words. Since the New Testament was probably an oral text long before it was a written text, the original language was probably not Greek.

The note from the dictionary makes another point. There are grammar challenges in translation. We are used to thinking with English verbs. This means that we think in a three-dimensional time system of past, present, and future. This way of thinking is an artifact that can't be separated from our language. The challenge is what to do when we read or translate a different way of thinking based on a different language. There is an "absence of tenses (in our sense) in Hebrew verbs" as Kugel notes in his analysis of Psalm 23 (193–194). The Hebrew verb system allows for the *complete* and the *incomplete*. It is more two dimensional. The Hebrew "invites the reader . . . to fill in the blanks, at least mentally" (193).

There are also the unique idioms of a language. A nonbiblical example may illustrate. Once when we had some Japanese guests for dinner, one of the kids in my family made an off-the-cuff comment about something that would make their dad "hit the ceiling."

> "What means hit the ceiling?"
>
> "It means he'll come unglued!"
>
> "And what means that?"
>
> "He'll blow his stack . . . he'll flip out . . . he'll go into orbit . . . he'll
> have a cow . . . blow a gasket . . . pop a cork."

None of these translations seemed particularly helpful to our international guests at the time, and they still aren't. Students like to suggest other options for me to consider, and when they do I wonder if idiomatic English is leaving me behind. Students know that the old idioms are long gone when I share a biblical example.

In Judges 3:24 the servants of Ehud are wondering why he is so long in his parlor: "Surely he covereth his feet in his summer chamber."

And what means "covereth his feet"?

I'll get right to the point. He was defecating.

"I'm sorry I asked." But since you did, this narrative is often a good place for students to start reading the Bible as literature.

There are other language points students ought to know before becoming close readers. In the second chapter of Genesis, the common word *da'at*, a cognate form of the verb *yada*, has three meanings: to know, to understand, and to have carnal relations with. Is it any wonder that translation is difficult? Gerald Hammond makes a good point in his essay on English translations in *The Literary Guide to the Bible*. Hammond takes an uncommon word, *khiydah*, and finds eight different contexts. In these contexts there are five different translations of the same word in the KJV. Reading these passages with the class offers an opportunity to ask about context. Is each translation good in its particular context?

Ezekiel 17:2, Judges 14:12-17 = *riddle*

Proverbs 1:6, Psalms 49:5, 78:2 = *dark saying*

Habakkuk 2:6 = *taunting proverb*

Daniel 8:23 = *dark sentence*

1 Kings 10:1 = *hard question*

Each translation does make a literary difference. A *riddle* may or may not be a *dark saying*. A *taunting proverb* is surely something different than a *hard question*. No teacher asks taunting proverbs on a midterm examination. It could result in a fifteen-yard penalty. The different translations of *khiydah* may or may not make a theological difference to those who may read the Bible as prooftext, but the literary difference can be profound. It is in fact the less dramatic and subtle differences that make the literature interesting. It is the subtle difference between a *dark saying* and a *dark sentence* that often speak to our imagination, more than the dramatic difference between a *taunting proverb* and a *hard question*.

Consider Judges 1:11–15. It is a very short story where translation makes a significant difference. This difference has been pointed out by Beverly Beem of Walla Walla College in an unpublished manuscript, *The Wisdom of Achsah: A Reading of Judges 1:11–15*. Students enjoy this very short story, and it is a good example of the difference a translation can make.

KJV (King James Version);

> And from thence he went against the inhabitants of Debir: and the
> name of Debir before was Kirjath-sepher: And Caleb said, He that

smiteth Kirjath-sepher, and taketh it, to him will I give Achsah my daughter to wife. And Othniel the son of Kenaz, Caleb's younger brother, took it: and he gave him Achsah his daughter to wife. And it came to pass, when she came to him, that she moved him to ask of her father a field; and she lighted from off her ass; and Caleb said unto her, What wilt thou: And she said unto him, Give me a blessing: for thou hast given me a south land; give me also springs of water. And Caleb gave her the upper springs and the nether springs.

RSV (Revised Standard Version);

From there they went against the inhabitants of Debir (the name of Debir was formerly Kiriath-sepher.) Then Caleb said, "Whoever attacks Kiriath-sepher and takes it, I will give him my daughter Achsah as wife." And Othneil son of Kenaz, Caleb's younger brother, took it; and he gave him his daughter Achsah as wife. When she came to him, she urged him to ask her father for a field. As she dismounted from her donkey, Caleb said to her, "What do you wish?" She said to him, "Give me a present; since you have set me in the land of the Negeb, give me also Gulloth-mayim." So Caleb gave her Upper Gulloth and Lower Gulloth.

NRSV (New Revised Standard Version);

From there they went against the inhabitants of Debir (the name of Debir was formerly Kiriath-sepher). Then Caleb said, "Whoever attacks Kiriath-sepher and takes it, I will give him my daughter Achsah as wife." And Othniel son of Kenaz, Caleb's younger brother, took it; and he gave him his daughter Achsah as wife. When she came to him, she urged him to ask her father for a field. As she dismounted from her donkey, Caleb said to her, "What do you wish?" She said to him, "Give me a present; since you have set me in the land of the Negeb, give me also Gulloth-mayim." So Caleb gave her Upper Gulloth and Lower Gulloth.

REB (Revised English Bible)

From there they marched against the inhabitants of Debir, formerly called Kiriath-sepher. Caleb said, "I shall give my daughter Achsah in marriage to the man who attacks and captures Kiriath-sepher." Othniel, son of Caleb's younger brother Kenaz, captured it, and

Caleb gave him his daughter Achsah. When she became his wife, Othniel induced her to ask her father for a piece of land. She dismounted from her donkey, and Caleb asked her, "What do you want?" She replied, "Grant me this favour: you have put me in the arid Negeb; you must give me pools of water as well." So Caleb gave her the upper pool and the lower pool.

NAB (New American Bible)

From there they marched against the inhabitants of Debir, which was formerly called Kiriath-sepher. And Caleb said, "I will give my daughter Achsah in marriage to the one who attacks Kiriath-sepher and captures it." Othniel, son of Caleb's younger brother Kenaz, captured it; so Caleb gave him his daughter Achsah in marriage. On the day of her marriage to Othniel she induced him to ask her father for some land. Then, as she alighted from the ass, Caleb asked her, "What is troubling you?" "Give me an additional gift," she answered. "Since you have assigned land in Negeb to me, give me also pools of water." So Caleb gave her the upper and the lower pool.

NJB (New Jerusalem Bible);

From there, he marched on the inhabitants of Debir–the name of Debir in olden days was Kiriath-Sepher. Caleb said, "To the man who conquers and captures Kiriath-Sepher, I shall give my daughter Achsah as wife." The man who captured it was Othniel son of Kenaz, younger brother of Caleb, who gave him his daughter Achsah as wife. When she arrived, he urged her to ask her father for arable land, but when she alighted from the donkey and Caleb asked her, "What is the matter?" she said to him, "Grant me a blessing! As the land you have given me is the Negeb, give me springs of water, too!" So Caleb gave her what she wanted: the upper springs and the lower springs.

NEB (New English Bible);

From there they marched against the inhabitants of Debir formerly called Kiriath-sepher. Caleb said, "Whoever attacks Kiriath-sepher and captures it, to him I will give my daughter Achsah in marriage." Othniel, son of Caleb's younger brother Kenaz, captured it, and Caleb gave him his daughter Achsah. When she came to him,

> he incited her to ask her father for a piece of land. As she sat on the
> ass, she broke wind, and Caleb said, "What do you mean by that?"
> She replied, "I want to ask a favor of you. You have put me in this
> dry Negeb; you must give me pools of water as well." So Caleb
> gave her the upper pool and the lower pool.

There are a half dozen other versions, but the point is made. Even
though translations don't seem to change most of the facts of the story,
the tone is surely changed. It starts as a fairytale: whoever captures
the city gets the king's daughter. It ends after a daughter asks for, and
is granted, a larger dowry with better water.

Perhaps a question for students will make the literary point. Whose
idea is it to ask for a better dowry that would include water?

KJV   - "she moved him to ask of her father a field"

RSV   - "she urged him to ask her father for a field"

NRSV - "she urged him to ask her father for a field"

REB   - "Othniel induced her to ask her father for a piece of land"

NAB   - "she induced him to ask her father for some land"

NJB   - "he urged her to ask her father for arable land"

NEB   - "he incited her to ask her father for a piece of land"

If a literary author is developing a character who initiates an action,
this a very important issue. The force of the verb is also important. *She*
moved, urged, and induced. *He* induced, urged, and incited. Each option develops a different character. *Incited* certainly seems the stron-
gest in modern usage, "and he incited her." The weakest suggestion is
probably when she *moved* him.

For character development, nothing speaks louder than the words
used by Achsah asking her father for more dowry. Certainly the tone of
request borne on broken wind makes Achsah more feisty in one translation. It is a translation difference that makes a literary difference. One
would be hard-pressed to claim that the translation difference makes
any doctrinal difference.

It may make the point to look at a poetic difference. The following
is the Hebrew text of a familiar passage from the *Biblia Hebraica
Stuttgartensia*, commonly known as the Stuttgart Bible: (I point out to
students that the text goes from right to left, perhaps the original way
of writing. Who writes "backwards"?) The passage is Genesis 1:4.

כִּי־טוֹב   הָאוֹר   אֶת   אֱלֹהִים   וַיַּרְא

good that   the-light   ***   God   and-he-saw

I explain to students that the dots and dashes are the Hebrew vowel sounds. The oldest Hebrew texts show no vowel sounds. The reader had to know the sounds without visual cues. It wasn't until about 900 C. E. that a commonly accepted way of indicating vowel sounds came into use. I ask students to write their names without vowels and then try to pronounce them, and they see the translation difficulty. The word that is translated with three asterisks is the sign of the definite article. It indicates that we are reading about *the* light, not just any light.

I am certainly not the first to notice the differences in this passage. There is a very good analysis using this example in Hammond's essay. Let's turn the text in our familiar left to right direction and add the literal translation:

Vayar	*elohim*	*et-ha'or*	*ki-tov*
and-he-saw	God	the light	that-good

KJV - "And God saw the light, that *it was* good."

NRSV - "And God saw that the light was good;"

REB - "and God saw the light was good,"

NAB - "God saw how good the light was."

NJB - "God saw that light was good,"

NEB - "and God saw that the light was good."

When I ask students if there are differences, subtle or obvious, in the translations, they usually tell me that the KJV seems more poetic. They also notice the KJV italics. They notice a certain familiar rhythm on each side of the comma. They also notice that the King James translation seems to make God the principal actor. Somehow He sees to it that light is good. In other versions He seems to notice that it is good. The NJB has the most passive God, who notices that "light was good." The NAB translators seem to assume that there must be degrees of goodness by writing "God saw how good the light was." Students often wonder aloud if there is somewhat good light, good light, and awesome light. I've had some students read close enough to suggest that the phrase is gender neutral—a point of departure for another day.

I also like to give students an example of a new "improved" translation. The Dead Sea Scrolls, first discovered in 1947, is an ancient library of 800 volumes and fragments. These 2,000-year-old manuscripts and scraps were discovered in caves along the Dead Sea at Qumran. When asked at a symposium sponsored by the Smithsonian Institution in 1990 if any writing from the scrolls was now part of the Bible, James A. Sanders, professor of intertestamental and biblical studies at the School of Theology at Claremont, California, gave this answer:

> If you look in your Bible [NRSV] in the marginal notes at the bottom (sometimes they are in italics) you see noted how other authorities or other manuscripts read, and Q is used to indicate a Qumran reading. It indicates what has been learned from the scrolls. One thing is this Hannah story I was just talking about. The NRSV melds the two versions in the old manner and at the very end of that, the NRSV says that Hannah left the child at the Temple. Now, what is the basis for that statement: It is a lacuna [an empty space or missing part, a gap in the text.] in 4QSam that ends with a suffix, "him." Professor Cross conjectured that what was in the lacuna was, "She left him there," and so the NRSV reads. No other Bible has that. That is an example. You also have a place elsewhere, I think somewhere in Kings, where you have three or four verses that are quite, quite different in the scrolls from what they are in the Masoretic text and the NRSV uses the Qumran version. There are a number of instances where NRSV readings are significantly influenced by the scrolls (73).

The passage referred to here is the last verse in 1 Samuel 1. I point out numerous Q references and footnotes in 1 Samuel. It is interesting to note that the NRSV quoted by Sanders shares a genealogical lineage with the KJV. The Preface of *The New Oxford Annotated Bible: New Revised Standard Version*, makes the lengthy historical point in one sentence: "The New Revised Standard Version of the Bible is an authorized revision of the Revised Standard Version, published in 1952, which was a revision of the American Standard Version, published in 1901, which, in turn embodied earlier revisions of the King James Version, published in 1611" (ix).

Perhaps one more translation example will help. It is a famous passage for Christians from the Nativity narrative in Luke, chapter 2, and familiar to most students. It is a passage cited on Christmas cards and seems to sum up a prayer of all who wish for peace in our world. The passage cites a promise of peace (Luke 2:14):

KJV - "Glory to God in the highest, and on earth peace, good will toward men."

NRSV - "Glory to God in the highest heaven, and earth peace among those whom he favors!"

REB - "Glory to God in the highest heaven, and on earth peace to all in whom he delights."

NAB - "Glory to God in the highest and on earth peace to those on whom his favor rests."

NASB - "Glory to God in the highest, And on earth peace among men with whom He is pleased."

RNT - "Glory to God in the highest; and on earth peace to men of good will."

NIV - "Glory to God in the highest, And on earth peace to men on whom his favor rests."

The question my students usually ask after a close reading is, for whom is this peace intended? Is peace for everyone, or just those of goodwill? There is also another issue here that can be discussed with students. What would it do to the text as a literary work to "correct" the sexist language by changing *men* to *people*?

At this point it is good to remind ourselves of the differences between revision and translation. Last time I counted, there were twenty-six English Bibles. That is how many versions are used to compile the good one-volume resource for teachers, *The Word: The Bible from 26 Translations* (Vaughn). An easier Parallel Bible to use is *The Complete Parallel Bible* published by the Oxford University Press. It is also less expensive and includes the NRSV, REB, NAB, and NJB in parallel columns. The NRSV and REB are the most ecumenical, with a translation committee comprising Christians and Jews.

Many versions are not translations from ancient or any other manuscripts. They are revisions. Some are revised to clarify particular doctrine. Others try to put the Bible in modern language. In the preface to a 1993 edition, *Black Bible Chronicles*, Andrew Young makes this argument:

> The *Black Bible Chronicles* is an attempt to put the most important message of life into the language of the streets. This is in keeping with the very origins of the Bible. The New Testament was originally written in Koine Greek, the street language of the people. Subsequently, Martin Luther and others translated the Bible into the language of the people of their day. The *Black Bible Chronicles* stands in this tradition, bringing the Word to our younger generation in contemporary language.
>
> This book seeks to reach many of our young people for whom the traditional language of faith has lost the power to bring them in touch with their God. The *Black Bible Chronicles* attempts to express a faith which addresses the deepest longings of our younger generation for hope, love, and an encouraging vision of the future (McCary v–vi).

The notation on the title page of *Black Bible Chronicles* indicates that P. K. McCary is "interpreter." It is significant that this is not a translation. The results are interesting and students enjoy them. The passage from Genesis that was compared above reads: "And the Almighty liked what He saw and let the light hang out a while before it was dark again" (2).

The MTV-type video version of some Bible stories is a "translation," according to the American Bible Society:

> "Out of the Tombs," based on Mark 5.1–20, represents a new venture in Scripture translations—a translation into images as well as words. Prepared with young people in mind, the video uses a very contemporary style of photography, editing, and storytelling. It aims to create the same feelings and emotions in a modern audience as were experienced by those who first heard the words of Mark's Gospel." (video cover)

Translation does make a difference for the literary reader, but the difference isn't in doctrine, liturgy, or dogma. The difference the translation makes is in the images we see. Literature is writing that speaks to our imagination. The best analogy may be to the visual arts or to music. Because there are no words to express some ideas and emotions, artists paint and composers write music. However, some people who have nearly inexpressible ideas can't paint or compose music. They write literature. They write stories and poems that speak to us in images, as music and pictures do.

When I read that God divided the light from the darkness, I see an image that is mine alone. I can't explain my image of the great division. It is in the literature that speaks to my imagination. Because it is somehow in the literature and in me, I see it as an image. The passage doesn't say how, or it would be a didactic textbook, perhaps scientific. It doesn't say why, or it would be theology. It just is. The light was divided from the darkness and God saw that it was good. I see it because it's literature.

Because students may also have personal images of biblical narratives, I allow them to bring whatever translation they wish to class. If students don't have a favorite translation, I suggest The KJV for literary readers with a good vocabulary. Students who need a modern language translation will enjoy *The Oxford Study Bible*, which uses the REB and has excellent literary footnotes. This is available in paperback. The NRSV continues the lineage of the KJV with more modern language, as does good choice published as *The New Oxford Annotated Bible*. If recent is better, the NRSV is a good choice.

Whatever choice is made, don't make the mistake of laughingly suggesting that students rent a cheap motelroom and "borrow" the Gideon Bible (a KJV). I did this at Snow College and was given a present the following week by the Snow College Forensics Team. They had a speech meet on the weekend and stayed at the Salt Lake Marriott. They returned with a gift stack of Gideon Bibles and a serious question: "Is it a sin to steal a Bible?" The students returned the Bibles to the Marriott.

Over the years I have found that asking students to compare translations of particular Bible passages teaches close reading. Students become critical readers when the meaning of a sentence can shift dramatically with the change of one word. Following are some parallel passages that teachers are welcome to use. As a side note, these are easy to put together with Bible software that shows parallel texts on the computer monitor that includes Hebrew and Greek. I like to use the following: Logos Research Systems (http://www.logos.com) and Bible Works (http://www.wordmicro.com/biblesoftwre.htm).

There are many searchable Bible versions on the Internet. Most, like Bible Gateway—which offers a site that will search the Bible in nine languages and multiple versions—promote devotional reading from a Christian perspective (http://bible.gospelcom.net/bible?). English Bible Versions (http://www.mcn.net/~wleman/english.htm) seems to be more objective than many of the sites that argue for the validity of one version over another.

The best academic site is a subscription service of Chadwyck-Healey (http://www.chadwyck.com). This service, "Literature Online," offers The Bible in English (990–1970), 20 different versions of the English Bible from the tenth to the twentieth century, including 12 complete Christian Bibles, 5 New Testament texts, 2 versions of the Gospels only, and William Tyndale's translations of the Pentateuch, Jonah, and the New Testament.

Both the Logos and Bible Works noted above include Greek and Hebrew Bible texts that are researchable. The Jewish Publication Society (http://www.jewishpub.org/Store/Shop/bible) has an extensive catalog of Hebrew Bibles.

This next one is easy for students. They should easily notice the difference between an "offended brother," a "reluctant brother," and an ally. They will notice that there is no quarreling in one translation and that castles, citadels, fortresses, and keeps are all different and the same. Thanks to Steve Walker of Brigham Young University for this reference.

Proverbs 18:19

King James Version   KJV (1611)
    A brother offended *is harder to be won* than a strong city:
    and *their* contentions *are* like the bars of a castle.

American Standard Version   ASV (1901)
    A brother offended *is harder to be won* than a strong city;
    And *such* contentions are like the bars of a castle.

Revised Standard Version   RSV (1951)
    A brother helped is like a strong city,
    but quarreling is like the bars of a castle.

New American Standard Bible   NASB (1971)
    A brother offended *is harder to be won* than a strong city,
    And contentions are like the bars of a castle.

New International Version   NIV (1978)
    An offended brother is more unyielding than a fortified city,
    and disputes are like the barred gates of a citadel.

New Jerusalem Bible   NJB (1985)
A brother offended is worse than a fortified city,
and quarrels are like the locks of a keep.

New American Bible   NAB (1986)
A brother is a better defense than a strong city,
and a friend is like the bars of a castle.

New Revised Standard Version   NRSV (1989)
An ally offended is stronger than a city;
such quarreling is like the bars of a castle.

Revised English Bible   REB (1989)
A reluctant brother is more unyielding than a fortress,
and quarrels are as stubborn as the bars of a fortress.

Other interesting comparisons include:

Job 19:25-27   The story of Job seems to hang on this passage. It is Job's answer to the question he has about when bad things happen to good people. The problem is that there is no certain translation.

1 Corinthians 13   This poetic passage on charity, or is it love, is a frequently quoted and oft-debated passage where translation makes a difference.

Psalm 8   This psalm is interesting because of the shifts from translation to translation as some try to "correct" sexist language. Also interesting is that some try to name specific animals and some use more general terms. It is interesting to see how these editorial translation shifts also shift the meaning of the Psalm.

Appendix E shows the literary history of Psalm 23 and is the most interesting for students. It is also the most literary example. The pre-KJV sources were compiled for the psalm by Charles C. Butterworth in 1941 in *The Literary Lineage of the King James Bible, 1340–1611*. The lineage since 1611 (publication of the KJV) was compiled by this author. Psalm 23 is the most translated passage in the Bible and is a case

study of how the Bible changes with translation. What is most apparent in looking at the changes is that the translations that persist are
metaphor and of superior literary quality. One could argue that it
improves as literature in the translation.

Chapter 10

TEACHING ABOUT BIBLE SOURCES: LOOKING FOR THE AUTHOR

And all thy children

shall be taught of the LORD;

and great shall be the peace

of thy children.

—Isaiah 54:13

The passage in Isaiah is a short poem whose poetic qualities can be taught. It could be that some lines are parallel, and the poem reads A, B, C, A^1. It is a poem from the Bible that we read in our schools as poetic literature. There is no metaphor or symbol in this poem. It is a prayer from biblical literature that challenges the way we read the Bible, and part of the challenge is in the search for the author. Is this poem really from someone named Isaiah?

If the same poem were in William Shakespeare or James Joyce, we would easily put it in the mouth of the character speaking it and assume it is from the pen of an author we know. If someone looked for a prayer to quote, this one might be found in *Bartlett's Familiar Quotations*, and Shakespeare or Joyce and the fictional character would get some credit.

To show how strong belief in an author is I offer the following citation from the Articles of Affirmation and Denial adopted in 1982 by the International Council on Biblical Inerrancy:

(1) the normative authority of Holy Scripture is the authority of God Himself;

(2) the Bible expresses God's truth in propositional statements, and . . . biblical truth is both objective and absolute;

(3) since God is the author of all truth, all truths, biblical and extrabiblical, are consistent and cohere, and . . . the Bible speaks truth when it touches on matters pertaining to nature, history, or anything else;

(4) Genesis 1–11 is factual, as is the rest of the book.

This statement makes God the implied author of the Bible, but despite this belief in biblical inerrancy, we don't have a single copy of an original Bible text, including the poem in Isaiah. There is no way to determine if what we call the Bible is as it was originally written. There are no signed copies of any Bible text. No author has copyrighted the text.

The fact that there is no "original" text or signed copy may not be as serious for the literary reader as it first seems. There are hundreds of ancient copies of the texts. Some are still being found. In the collection we call the Dead Sea Scrolls, every book of the Bible but Esther is represented, and the beginning of this discovery was 1947, with some scrolls found as late as 1960. Even though copies of the text seem to abound, the question of an artful author remains. Did an author intend a literary reading of the text with crafty writing? I'm sure a reading of the Jewish poem can be literary. It is a poem. It has poetic structure and other poetic qualities that are discussed in chapter 8.

So the question remains: What does it mean to read the Bible as literature? Does reading it as literature offer an enhanced perspective, or does it conflict with the very essence of the book? What makes these questions questions is the issue of authorship. Who wrote the Bible? If written by God, aren't we being presumptuous to regard God as an author who uses literary devices like metaphor and symbol and poetic forms? If written by a literary author, does the Bible become less and in fact become a good book instead of the Good Book?

The following section is verbatim from *Davita's Harp*, a novel by Chaim Potok. Perhaps the words of a writer of stories can help us to understand the ways to read the Bible and the important problem of author.

from *Davita's Harp* by Chaim Potok[13]

We were studying the Book of Genesis, the stories of the Patriarchs and Matriarchs. That was the winter of early 1941, when German planes were daily bombing England, and Franklin D. Roosevelt was inaugurated for his third term as President of the United States.

I loved the stories in Genesis. Mr. Margolis taught slowly and with some impatience. We were studying the Hebrew text along with the commentary of Rashi, a great French rabbi who lived in the period of the First Crusade. Always I got myself ready for class by studying the text in advance, even when Mr. Margolis did not assign it. I had learned that method of study from David, who always prepared in advance whatever page of Talmud would be studied next by his class.

We were in the twelfth chapter of Genesis. God tells Abraham— Abram was his name at the time—to leave his country and the place of his birth and his father's house for a distant land. Abraham journeys with his household to the land of Canaan. There he travels as far as a site called Shechem. And the text says, "The Canaanites were then in the land."

Mr. Margolis wanted to know if there was any problem in that verse with the Hebrew word, then.

He stood behind his desk, tall and dark, one finger in a pocket of his vest, waiting.

No one said anything.

Eyes stared at the Hebrew word. Who paid attention to a small word like that? Then. "The Canaanites were then in the land." I had gone over the text before class but had not thought to stop on the meaning of that word.

Then. At the time. That's what it meant. At the time when Abraham came to Shechem there were Canaanites in the land. But why did we have to be told that? Obviously there were Canaanites in the land. It was called the land of Canaan.

"I want you to think about it," Mr. Margolis said.

I raised my hand.

"Ilana."

"Rashi says the Canaanites were conquering the land from the children of Shem."

"Very good, Ilana."

"But if the Canaanites were conquering the land from the children of Shem, why was it called the land of Canaan?"

He stood tall and dark behind his desk, fingering his pocket watch, and looked at me. "What should it have been called, Ilana?"

"The land of Shem."

"The land of Shem." He looked down at the open Bible on his desk and scanned the Rashi. The top of his skullcap formed a dark shiny satin moon as it caught and reflected the winter sunlight that came through the windows. Steam hissed softly in the silver-painted radiators. There were cracks in the pale green walls and flaking paint on the white ceiling. The room was overheated. *Oz.* Then. What could that little word mean? Clearly the then of the story was the time of Abraham. But, again, why did we have to be reminded that there were Canaanites in the land of Canaan? Perhaps—perhaps—

Something hung elusively on the edge of thought, but I could not grasp it and it was gone.

Mr. Margolis looked up from the Bible on his desk and gave the class a thin smile. "Ilana asks a good question. Why was it not called the land of Shem if, according to Rashi, the Canaanites were not actually living there but were conquering it?"

Along the periphery of my vision I saw Ruthie raise her hand.

"Ruth?"

"Maybe the Canaanites were living in it a long time already and were still trying to conquer the rest of it."

Mr. Margolis's thin smile widened. "Very good, Ruth. Very good. The Canaanites had no doubt been living in it a long time already. Like America. It was called America even while Americans were still conquering the west. Very good, Ruthie."

Ruthie, her face suddenly a shade of high color that accentuated her freckles, looked astonished at having stumbled upon the answer wanted by Mr. Margolis.

I talked about the verse during supper with my father, and he said Ruthie's explanation made sense to him. David said there couldn't be any other explanation. My mother sat at the table looking very tired and said nothing. Her early risings to get to the synagogue, her half-days at work, her journeys to the synagogue for the afternoon and evening service—all had put her in a state of permanent fatigue.

Later I lay in my bed reading a novel my mother had taken out for me from the Brooklyn Public Library on Eastern Parkway. On the other side of the hallway, David was softly studying Talmud in his room, the chanting reaching me through the walls that separated us. I thought again of the word and looked up from the novel at the harp that hung on the back of the door. It lay in shadows cast by the bed lamp. Suppose Jakob Daw had used that word in a sentence in one of his stories. What would it mean? I tried to imagine it in his story about the bird who went wandering through the world in search of the source of the world's music. Suppose it left its land, its flock, its nest, and found a land of tall hills and fertile valleys. And suppose Jakob Daw had then said, There were Canaanites then in the land. What would that mean? It would mean—it would mean that at the time Jakob Daw was telling me the story—or was writing the story—there weren't any Canaanites in the land. And if it was important for my understanding of the story that I know of the existence of Canaanites in the past, he would have to remind me of it. And he would do that by saying or writing, There were Canaanites *then* in the land.

What was that? Had a wooden ball lifted of itself and fallen upon a string of the harp? Had the birds stirred? I was in a dream, of course. I had drifted off to sleep for a moment and had been in a dream. I put the book on the night table, removed my glasses, and snapped off the light.

The last thing I thought I heard as I slid into sleep was the faint singing of the harp blending with the quiet music of the Talmud that came from David's room.

The next day I raised my hand in Mr. Margolis's class and waited to be called.

"Yes, Ilana."

"May I go back to yesterday and give another explanation of *oz*?"

"Of course."

We had been on a difficult verse. I could sense the class relaxing all around me. My mouth was dry, my heart beat loudly.

"*Oz* can mean that at the time this story was written down, there were no longer any Canaanites in the land; and the writer of the story is reminding the reader that at the time the story took place there *were* Canaanites, because Canaanites are important to the story."

Mr. Margolis stood very still behind his desk, gazing at me. He asked me to repeat my explanation.

I repeated it, slowly, my heart thumping wildly. Why was he looking at me like that?

He said, solemnly, "You mean to say, Ilana, that a writer wrote this story?"

"Yes."

"And who was this writer?"

"I don't know."

"You don't know. And when did he write this story?"

"When there were no longer any Canaanites in the land."

"There were always Canaanites in the land, Ilana."

"When there were no longer any Canaanites near Shechem."

The room was strangely hushed, as if all had long ceased breathing.

"Ilana," Mr. Margolis said, after a pause that seemed endless, "we do not study the Torah this way here."

I sat very still, my heart thundering.

"God wrote the Torah," Mr. Margolis said. "Not a writer. God. It's the holy word of God. Do you understand?"

I had never seen him so dark and stern. He seemed to be growing in darkness before my eyes.

"If people wrote the Torah, why should we bother with it? Why should we sacrifice ourselves for it? Why should we read it in shul every Shabbos and yom-tov? Why should we be willing to die for it? God spoke every single word of the Torah to Moses, who wrote it all down, every word. Even his own death Moses described, with tears running down his face."

He paused for a moment and took a breath, then went on. "The Torah is not stories, Ilana. The Torah is not a piece of make-believe. It is not like Shakespeare or like—what is his name?—James Joyce or like your good friend Jakob Daw. The Torah is God's stories. God's! The truth of God. The eternal truth given to us by the Master of the Universe. Rashi has the correct understanding of the verse. And that is the way we will learn it here. I want you to think about that, Ilana. I want you to remember that. All right? Very good. Now let us continue reading."

I sat in a pall of confusion and shame and heard nothing of what went on for all the rest of the day in that class.

My father had an English commentary in his library in the living room. I went to it that evening after supper. The commentary was by a modern English rabbi named J. H. Hertz. I found the verse and read the commentary:

> the Canaanite was then in the land—i.e., was already in the land. 'Before the age of Abraham, the Canaanites had already settled in the lowlands of Palestine—Canaan, be it noted, signified Lowlands' (Sayce). The interpretation of this verse as meaning that the Canaanites were *at that time* in the land, but were no longer so at the time when Genesis was written (an interpretation which misled even Ibn Ezra), is quite impossible. The Canaanites formed part of the population down to the days of the later kings.

I read it again.

Ibn Ezra, I knew, was one of the greatest of the Jewish commentators of the Middle Ages. He had been born in Spain and wandered throughout Europe. I had ventured a guess—and had come up with Ibn Ezra's answer! I wondered how Ibn Ezra would have responded to Mr. Margolis's questions. Would Ibn Ezra have sacrificed himself for the Torah? I couldn't understand why Mr. Margolis seemed fearful of there being more than one way to understand the meaning of the Torah. Was he afraid he would lose control over our thinking? Why did he need to control the way we thought? Did he believe that God wrote stories with only one kind of meaning? It seemed to me that a story that had only one kind of meaning was not very interesting or worth remembering for too long.

The harp sounded muted that evening as I came into my room and sat down at my desk to my homework. I looked at it, wondering if something was wrong with its strings. Across the hallway from me David softly sang his Talmudic music. In the living room my parents were listening to a symphony on the phonograph. Outside an icy wind moaned in the trees, rustling bare branches in a sad music of its own.

This same passage, Genesis 12:6, is mentioned as a difficult legal problem by Alan Dershowitz in *The Genesis of Justice* (14):

> Ibn Ezra wonders about the historical accuracy of that statement, offers a possible interpretation, and then hedges his bet: "Should this interpretation be incorrect, then there is a secret meaning to the text." He cautions, "Let one who understands it remain silent." A commentator on Ibn Ezra suggests a reason for the rather cryptic warning: Ibn Ezra realizes the clause about the Canaanites is an anachronism but is loath to engender doubt among his readers. The solution: silence! (14)

Dershowitz then offers legal understatement. "The question of who wrote the Bible has been hotly debated by academics for more than a century" (14).

It is more than a problem of finding an author. Today's theorists find four authors of the Hexateuch. For students the search can start in the first chapter of Genesis. A lesson on the creation narrative of Genesis is in chapter 5. Besides the creation narrative, the Flood narrative is a good place to ask a question about authors.

In the Flood narrative of Genesis, two of every kind of animal a destined for a ride in the ark. "And of every living thing of all flesh, two of every *sort* shall thou bring into the ark, to keep *them* alive with thee: they shall be male and female. Of fowls after their kind, and of cattle after their kind, of every creeping thing of the earth after his hind, two of every *sort* shall come unto the, to keep *them* alive" (6:19).

In the next chapter, Genesis 7:2–3, the instructions to Noah are different: "Of every clean beast thou shalt take to thee by sevens, the male and his female: and of beasts that *are* not clean by two, male and his female. Of fowls also of the air by sevens, the male and the female; to keep seed alive upon the face of all the earth."

Students notice that the reason for two is "to keep them alive," and the reason for seven pair is "to keep seed alive." Sounds like the same reason, but the number of animals is different. Students are good at proposing ways to reconcile this difference. I like to offer them another alternative called the Documentary Hypothesis. I emphasize that the purpose here is to think about who the possible author behind a text could be.

This Documentary Hypothesis proposes four literary sources in the following chronological sequence: the J for Jehovist or Yahwist, the E for Elohist, D for Deuteronomist, and P for Priestly. The hypothesis was first proposed by Julius Wellhausen near the end of the nineteenth century. Although the hypothesis falls in and out of favor, it is still a way of reading the text. This *source criticism* proposes a priestly redactor (R) or editor who combined P with JED using P as the framework for the first five books of the Bible. Here is what the initials of these authors mean:

J is the oldest source, probably the 10th or 9th centuries. The translation of this source uses Jehovah or Yahweh for the name of God. In 1990 Harold Bloom and David Rosenberg published just these oldest writings as *The Book of J*. Bloom's commentary notes that the work is probably the product of the Jerusalem court during the age of David or Solomon and is associated with the southern kingdom, Judah. Bloom also introduces a new idea by suggesting that the J writer was a woman. Most of this source seems to end with the death of Moses, and Bloom recommends that those who believe Moses to be the writer of the first five books of the Bible think of "J" as the "voice of Moses."

E is the most fragmentary of the four sources and uses the Hebrew word *Elohim* for God. It is dated to the 9th and 8th centuries and associated with the northern kingdom.

The D source, of which the Book of Deuteronomy is the best example, was probably written after the end of the monarchy in 587 B.C.E. and has the benefit of hindsight as it retells the problems of the kings and blames their troubles on their failure to keep the commandments.

The P source is the most disputed. Some suggest that P was mainly an editor who compiled the other sources. Wellhausen dates it after 500 B.C.E. This source is characterized by interest in ritual, sacrifice, and priestly practices.

The first Genesis creation passage is generally considered to be from the P source, the second from the J writer. The two-by-two flood passage is from the P source and the two-by-seven from J.

There are many good resources for those who want to sort out the documents. It is a project beyond most high school classes, but the resources are good for a teacher who likes to teach students to look for the voice of the author in literature. The first is hard to find, published in 1900. It is *The Hexateuch According to the Revised Version*, edited by Carpenter and Harford-Battersby. The second is *Sources of the Pentateuch: Texts, Introductions, Annotations* by Campbell and O'Brien. The second resource is a more modern argument, while the first is a copy of the text sorted out into particular sources.

Why do we even want to look at source criticism of the Bible? Why would it matter that there may be four sources in the first five books, three Isaiahs, Gospel writers who use each other's text as a primary source, writers who just put oral tradition into writing, and some writers who plagiarize? We look for authors to help us understand how we look at texts. Robert J. Nash makes the point in *Faith, Hype, and Clarity: Teaching about Religion in American Schools and Colleges*:

> Each of us (students, authors, and instructor) is a complex container of meanings. As we encounter each other for the first time in a class, we must realize that each of us embodies a particular *pre-text* (we hold prior religious/metaphysical assumptions), a *context* (we inhabit particular social, political, religious, and educational worlds), an inter-text (we draw upon prior textual influences in our lives, including formative readings, persons, and events), *proof-texts* (we reiterate pivotal passages, quotations, and assertions from cherished authors and others in order to prove our points), and a *post-text* (we are always in the process of "writing" our personal [religious] narrative, enlarging, deepening, and enriching the religious language we already possess). (50)

To make the point of teaching Bible as literature for education purposes, I'd change Nash's *religious* in the last line to *literary*. We find meaning in literary texts we encounter, not only through the text we read but the pre-texts, contexts, and proof-texts we bring to the experience. Searching for the author helps us to recognize these variant personal texts.

Nash uses an extended example in his class:

> Take the gospel of John in the New Testament. *This gospel is actually 5 different texts.* Text 1 is the gospel John thought he was writing. This is the *author's text.* Text 2 is the gospel each one of you thinks John wrote. This is the *individual reader's text.* Text 3 is the gospel that John actually wrote. This is the *objective text.* Text 4 is the gospel that each one of you is "writing" as you interpret this gospel from your own cultural and historical context. This is the *hermeneutical text-in-process.* And text 5 is the gospel you and I might be able to agree on as the gospel that John intended to write. This is the *consensus text.*

> None of us can ever know with any degree of certainty the truth of text 1, because we do not know what was in John's mind while he was writing. Neither can we ever fully capture text 3, because there is no such thing as an "immaculate reception" of a text, absolutely devoid of a reader's, or writer's, presuppositions. In fact, to speak of an "objective" text makes no sense at all, because without "subjects" to read and interpret the text, the text has no inherent meaning. The only texts worth studying, then, are text 2, text 4, and text 5; and while text 5 is certainly worth pursuing, universal consensus on *all* meanings in any text is virtually un-achievable. Thus, we are left only with text 2 and text 4 as texts to analyze, and because these texts are always subject to very personal reading and commentaries, then, in a real sense, when we study the gospel of John, we are really studying ourselves (52).

A clear search for an Old Testament author is *Who Wrote the Bible?* by Richard Elliott Friedman. For a similar treatment of the New Testament, I recommend *Who Wrote the New Testament? The Making of the Christian Myth* by Burton L. Mack.

Note

13 Excerpt (326–332) from *Davita's Harp* by Chaim Potok (copyright 1985) is reprinted by permission of Alfred A. Knopf, a Division of Random House Inc.

Chapter 11

TEACHING PARABLES AS SHORT STORIES: STORIES THAT STILL SPEAK

P arables are not easy, but they are fun. Students with a Christian biblical background seem to come to the class so grounded in the parables that they think they know what the stories mean even before we read them. This can be difficult because it forestalls a variety of literary readings. For others the stories of the parables are new and clear enough, but the meanings aren't quite so easy. In the end, parables lead to the best discussions when those who already "know" lighten up and those who are new to these tales read closely.

The parables are a genre that require close examination because they seem to tell us what we should be doing in difficult situations. In this respect they are close cousins of fables or folktales. However, they aren't as easy as fables, which seem to offer a clear moral of the story as a postscript. One of the reasons parables aren't always easy is because most Christians interpret the parables as allegories. This point is made by Craig L. Blomberg in *Interpreting the Parables*, which is a good teaching resource.

Teachers should know that there doesn't seem to be scholarly consensus on this issue. Some scholars claim that the parables are allegorical because of the reading template brought to them by early Christians. Perhaps the most common ground is to agree that many can read them allegorically and, at the least, that they are laden with simile and metaphor and seem to argue their points from analogy. Ryken, in *How to Read the Bible as Literature*, says, "The most obvious feature of the parables is that they are realistic stories, simple in construction and didactic ("aiming to teach") in purpose, that convey religious truth and in which the details often have a significance beyond their literal narrative meaning" (202).

I've found that a good place to start is with a parable none of the students have read. It is one of thousands in the talmudic tradition and illustrates the fact that parables aren't that easy and are fascinating to discuss. Teachers interested in talmudic parables will enjoy Blufield and Shook's *Saving the World Entire and 100 Other Beloved Parables from the Talmud*.

Before reading a "new" parable I suggest that each parable seems to have at least two elements. First, most parables present a problem to be solved or a question to be answered: Who is a neighbor? What do I do to feel less anxious? Who will get to heaven? Second, the parable will answer the problem, but not always in a way that is crystal clear: thus we see who it was that was "neighbor" to him who fell among thieves.

I've seen two versions of the following rabbinic parable that are not in the Bible. The first time I saw it was in a Bible as literature course. I've tried, unsuccessfully, to find a talmudic reference, but it is cited in *Ways of Reading the Bible* by Wadsworth. Both versions are a bit different, so the following allows some very slight editorial work on my part. I added no new information to what I first read from the transparency projected on the screen:

> Bar Ma'jan died unexpectedly and was given a splendid funeral. At the same time a poor scholar died, but nobody followed his body to the grave, since the whole city was escorting Bar Ma'jan's body. How could the justice of God permit this? *This is one of the important elements of the parable, a problem to solve or question to answer.* Now the answer. Bar Ma'jan, though not a pious man, had done one splendid good deed. He had invited the city councillors to a banquet, and they, to insult him, refused to come. So in a rage he gave orders that the poor should come and eat the food, in order that it not be wasted. (Wadsworth 198)

English teachers are good at this part. What does this story mean?

1. Is it better to be a poor scholar who hasn't done anything but merit the title *scholar* than a nonreligious person who has done one good deed?

2. Good scholarship is often unrecognized? (One student asked in class why anyone would want to recognize a bad student. I

suppose "poor scholar" could equal "bad student" to some readers.)

We may have the cart before the funeral cortege for Bar Ma'jan here. There are some things the class will want to talk about before they discuss what it all means:

1. What about this good deed? What motivated it? Does motivation matter when it comes to good deeds?

2. What about the reward for the good deed? Is it that great to have a big funeral? (Mark Twain, Will Rogers or Yogi Berra said that you always want to go to people's funerals, otherwise they won't come to yours.)

3. What do we really know about this scholar? Is most of what we know what we bring to the text or what we think when we hear the words "poor scholar?"

There is a second rabbinic parable I sometimes use that is more difficult and more interesting to me. It is from the Midrash, *Leviticus Rabbah* and is cited in jasper and Prickett, *The Bible and Literature: A Reader*:

> Simeon, the son of Rabbi [Judah], prepared a [wedding] banquet for his son. He went and invited all the sages, but he forgot to invite Bar Kappara, who thereupon went and wrote on the door of R. Simeon's house: After rejoicing is death. So what value is there to rejoicing?
>
> Who did this to me? R. Simeon asked. Is there anyone we did not invite?
>
> One of his men told him: Bar Kappara. You forgot to invite Bar Kappara.
>
> R. Simeon said: To invite him now would be unseemly. So he went and made a second banquet, and he invited Bar Kappara as well. But at every course that brought before the guests Bar Kappara recited three hundred fox-fables, and the guests didn't even taste the dishes before they grew cold. The dishes were removed from the tables just as they had been brought in.
>
> R. Simeon asked his servant: Why are all the dishes coming back untouched?
>
> The servant replied: There is an old man sitting there. At every course he tells fables until the dishes grow cold, and no one eats.

> R. Simeon went up to Bar Kappara: What did I do to make you
> ruin my banquet?
>
> Bar Kappara answered: What do I need your banquet for? Didn't
> Solomon say, "What real value is there for a man in all the gains he
> makes beneath the sun?" (Ecclesiastes 1:3)? And what is written
> after that verse? "One generation goes, another comes, but the earth
> remains the same for ever" (1:4). (229–230)

After a discussion of at least one of these unfamiliar parables, I
suggest that a parable can be written so that some listeners will understand while others will not. This suggests that understanding is
in the meanings that each of us brings to the story. This idea is in the
explanation that Jesus gave for using parables (Luke 8:10-13):

> [10]And the disciples came, and said unto him, Why speakest thou
> unto them in parables? [11]He answered and said unto them, Because
> it is given unto you to know the mysteries of the kingdom of heaven,
> but to them it is not given. [12]For whosoever hath, to him shall be
> given, and he shall have more abundance: but whosoever hath not,
> from him shall be taken away even that he hath. [13]Therefore speak I
> to them in parables: because they seeing see not; and hearing they
> hear not, neither do they understand.

So only some will understand, according to this biblical text. Let's
see how we do as a class with a simple question about one parable.
First students need to know that the word "talent" doesn't necessarily refer to something we are good at doing. *Talent* can refer to money
or can be a symbol for that which is precious or important or valuable; it can also be something we are good at doing. Think of the
money first. Suppose you had money and wanted to make money.
Which is easier, to double two million dollars or to double five million dollars? The class never seems to come to complete consensus.
Some argue that doubling two and doubling five take the same skill.
Others note that the interest on five million is more money per year
than on two million and that you can often get a higher rate of interest on a larger amount. They quote the old saw that it takes money to
make money, and they obviously understand the principle of compound interest. Having never been in a situation to discover this for
myself, I leave the question open and have the class read a parable in
Matthew 25:14–30.

> [14]For *the kingdom of heaven is* as a man traveling into a far country,
> *who* called his own servants, and delivered unto them his goods.

[15]And unto one he gave five talents, to another two, and to another one; to every man according to his several ability; and straightway took his journey. [16]Then he that had received the five talents went and traded with the same, and made *them* other five talents. [17]And likewise he that *had received* two, he also gained other two. [18]But he that had received one went and digged in the earth, and hid his lord's money. [19]After a long time the lord of those servants cometh, and reckoneth with them. [20]And so he that had received five talents came and brought other five talents, saying, Lord, thou deliveredst unto me five talents: behold, I have gained beside them five talents more. [21]His lord said unto him, Well done, *thou* good and faithful servant: thou hast been faithful over a few things, I will make thee ruler over many things: enter thou into the joy of thy lord. [22]He also that had received two talents came and said, Lord, thou deliveredst unto me two talents: behold, I have gained two other talents beside them. [23]His lord said unto him, Well done, good and faithful servant; thou hast been faithful over a few things, I will make thee ruler over many things: enter thou into the joy of thy lord. [24]Then he which had received the one talent came and said, Lord, I knew thee that thou art an hard man, reaping where thou hast not sown, and gathering where thou hast not strawed: [25]And I was afraid, and went and hid thy talent in the earth: lo, *there* thou hast *that is* thine. [26]His lord answered and said unto him, *Thou* wicked and slothful servant, thou knewest that I reap where I sowed not, and gather where I have not strawed: [27]Thou oughtest therefore to have put my money to the exchangers, and *then* at my coming I should have received mine own with usury. [28]Take therefore the talent from him, and give *it* unto him which hath ten talents. [29]For unto every one that hath shall be given, and he shall have abundance: but from him that hath not shall be taken away even that which he hath. [30]And cast ye the unprofitable servant into outer darkness: there shall be weeping and gnashing of teeth.

There is a wonderful paradox here that encourages close critical reading. The lord of the story gives the same commendation to the person who doubled two and the one who doubled five. Notice that verses 21 and 23 are identical. Then in verse 28 the person who hid the single talent away loses his talent altogether, as it is taken from him and given to the person who doubled five talents. Now if both doubled their talents and were given the same blessing/commendation, why did the single talent go to the doubler of five and not the doubler of two? Furthermore, if doubling two million is more difficult than doubling five million, why didn't the reward for extra effort go to the man who apparently worked the hardest?

The discussion continues as students compare a fable, Aesop's "The Miser," with the parable and notice that the conclusion or moral of the story is clear in the fable. (Aesop's Fables is online at http://www.pacificnet.net/~johnr/aesop. This site even includes lesson plans for those who wish to teach the fables.)

> A MISER sold all that he had and bought a lump of gold, which he buried in a hole in the ground by the side of an old wall and went to look at daily. One of his workmen observed his frequent visits to the spot and decided to watch his movements. He soon discovered the secret of the hidden treasure, and digging down, came to the lump of gold, and stole it. The Miser, on his next visit, found the hole empty and began to tear his hair and to make loud lamentations. A neighbor, seeing him overcome with grief and learning the cause, said, "Pray do not grieve so; but go and take a stone, and place it in the hole, and fancy that the gold is still lying there. It will do you quite the same service; for when the gold was there, you had it not, as you did not make the slightest use of it." Wealth unused might as well not exist.

The point is made that parables are difficult. That is what makes them good. They speak to our imagination and allow us to bring our own experience to the story. But allegorical imaginations can get carried away, perhaps too far. To demonstrate this idea I have students read another familiar parable, the parable of the Good Samaritan in Luke 10:29–37:

> [29]But he, willing to justify himself, said unto Jesus, And who is my neighbour? [30]And Jesus answering said, A certain *man* went down from Jerusalem to Jericho, and fell among thieves, which stripped him of his raiment, and wounded *him*, and departed, leaving *him* half dead. [31]And by chance there came down a certain priest that way: and when he saw him, he passed by on the other side. [32]And likewise a Levite, when he was at the place, came and looked *on him*, and passed by on the other side. [33] But a certain Samaritan, as he journeyed, came where he was: and when he saw him, he had compassion *on him*, [34]And went to *him*, and bound up his wounds, pouring in oil and wine, and set him on his own beast, and brought

> him to an inn, and took care of him. [35]And on the morrow when he departed, he took out two pence, and gave *them* to the host, and said unto him, Take care of him; and whatsoever thou spendest more, when I come again, I will repay thee. [36]Which now of these three, thinkest thou, was neighbour unto him that fell among the thieves? [37]And he said, He that shewed mercy on him. Then said Jesus unto him, Go, and do thou likewise.

Symbolically, two religious people (a Levite and a priest) passed by, but only the third passerby, a Samaritan, offered service and was a neighbor. A *kohen* (Jewish priest) is not supposed to have contact with the dead. Students enjoy trying to put this parable in a modern context. We discuss Good Samaritan laws as examples of how the parable has become a metaphor for our times. We then look at an old allegorical reading that most students think takes us too far:

> St. Augustine provided the classic example of ancient allegorizing with his interpretation of the parable of the good Samaritan (Luke 10:30–37): the wounded man stands for Adam; Jerusalem, the heavenly city from which he has fallen; the thieves, the devil who deprives Adam of his immortality; the priest and Levite, the Old Testament Law which could save no one; the Samaritan who binds the man's wounds, Christ who forgives sin; the inn, the church; and the innkeeper, the apostle Paul. (Blomberg 31)

Blomberg gives his reference for Augustine's work as *Quaest. Evang.* II, 19.

Ryken, in *How to Read the Bible as Literature*, suggests a way to approach a parable that seems to work (151). He suggests a four step process:

1. Analysis of the Literal Story
2. Interpreting Symbolic Details
3. Determining the Theme(s)
4. Application

Ryken's approach is helpful, but parables are also an opportunity to teach form criticism. They seem to have an identifiable form:

1. There is a problem.
2. A story is introduced ("And he spake a parable"; "it is like").
3. The parable is repeated.

4. There is often a sentence or two about how to apply the lesson of the parable.

5. A quotation from the Bible sometimes follows ("it is written that").

For many classes, the discussion is enough. We read and discuss. Sometimes, however, students enjoy writing a parable, and I ask them to follow the traditional form.

Chapter 12

TEACHING A GRAND THEME:
THE UNIVERSAL PROBLEM OF SUFFERING

The lesson starts with a vocabulary word. *Theodicy* is the vindication or justification of God. It is an attempt to justify the ways of God to humans, who see suffering and sadness and wonder why a loving and all powerful God can allow such misery. It is *the* question for theists and atheists alike. It is a normative question in literature and philosophy classes.

We read the story of Job, a perfect/blameless man who is afflicted without cause. He has his family taken from him, loses his home and fortune, is afflicted with boils, and is berated by comforters. His story is the closest we get to a biblical novel that reads like a drama.

It is a difficult read, and often a modern-language translation is necessary. My personal favorite translations of *The Book of Job* are by Mitchell and Scheindlin. Both include excellent notes (see Works Cited).

We could read such a story about how the good suffer in the literature of many cultures. In India it would be the story of Hariscandra. In Babylonia, there was a text saying "I Will Praise the Lord of Wisdom." In this story there is a monologue in which there are complaints about an unjust God (Marduk) who allows his followers to suffer. In ancient Egypt "The Tale of the Eloquent Peasant" is a dialogue between the suffering individual and his own soul. I often select companion readings that take a different look at the problem of suffering. "A Job of the Plains," a short story by William Humphrey, has worked over the years. It is not only a modern setting of the Job story, the trial is entirely different. The wealth itself is the trial.

There are other examples in Ackerman and Warshaw's *The Bible as/in Literature*, a text with biblical narratives and companion readings on biblical themes. These include the following:

- "A Masque of Reason," a dramatic poem by Robert Frost
- "The Prologue in Heaven," a passage from the novel *The Undying Fire* by H. G. Wells
- "Job," a poem by Elizabeth Sewell
- A scene from *J.B.*, a play by Archibald Macleish
- "New Hampshire, February," a poem by Richard Eberhart

Job emerges frequently in the literature we teach. Chaucer has the Clerk and Wife of Bath make reference to Job, and Milton uses Job in *Paradise Regained* and in *Samson Agonistes*. *Othello* is still required reading in some high schools, and the oblique reference to Job's comforter suggests that Othello's lot is harder than Job's (4.2.48–57). We also find one of Job's comforters in *Moby Dick*. Bildad is half-owner of Captain Ahab's ship. As part owner he aims to convert the sailors in order to have a prosperous voyage.

But we will read about the problem of suffering from the Bible, a sacred text to Christians and Jews and a philosophical text to philosophers, who, like Kant, find failure after failure in attempts to explain theodicy (Despland 283). We read about the innocent suffering where even the name Job is an enigma. The root in Hebrew is *enmity* or *hostility*. In Arabic the root is *return* or *repent*, as in "the penitent one." Students can see the paradox of a man named either Repentant or Hostile.

Job is a masterpiece that addresses the most fundamental philosophical question: Why do bad things happen to good people? Not only is the story good but "the very presuppositions by which we read, our expectations of what literature can do, are predetermined by the decisive early model of the Bible. . . . It is probably more than a coincidence that the very pinnacle of ancient Hebrew poetry was reached in Job, the biblical text that is most daring and innovative in its imagination of God, man, and creation." This is according to Robert Alter in *The World of Biblical Literature*. (54)

Over the years I have taught Job many times with no strong objections from students. I have collected supporting materials, such as copies of the etchings of Robert Blake and a dramatization of Job recorded by the BBC in England. In the recording, Paul Scofield is Job and Robert Harris is God.

Students love the story of Job. I think they like it because they agree with Alter: "It wants to draw me out of myself using the medium of narrative to transform my sense of the world, urgently alert me to spiritual realities and moral imperatives I might have misconceived, or not conceived at all" (9). Students enjoy the story if they are willing to go beyond preconceived ideas and recognize that "the one thing modern readers should not do, even if they have secularist scruples in regard to this dimension of biblical literature, is condescend to it as 'primitive'"(21).

Every time I teach in a public college from the Bible, I like to ask students what they think the worldview would be of those early Americans who used the Bible as a primary book to learn how to read. What about the worldview of the early translators that gave us the Bible in English? Besides the fact that these early readers were reading sometimes difficult material, what were they learning about the world as they read? I am particularly interested in how students explain the goodness of God in the context of terrible suffering in the world and how they think others answer questions about suffering when they read the Book of Job.

Job is part of a genre we call wisdom literature. I ask students to name examples, as I do when teaching Proverbs, and after a little prodding they recognize that we are talking about the self-help department of a bookstore, where we find titles like the following:

God's Little Instruction Book

Chicken Soup for the Soul

Seven Habits of Highly Effective People

How to Win Friends and Influence People

Think and Grow Rich

All I Needed to Know I Learned in Kindergarten

When Bad Things Happen to Good People (a commentary on the Story of Job that is a multimillion-copy best-seller)

Students will need to know that they aren't reading a conventional story. Even though it may not look like it in older Bible translations, it is almost all poetry. Only the first two chapters and verses 7–17 in the last chapter are prose. Except for the prose passages, the book is a conversation where characters give long speeches. The conversation isn't like a dialogue, with questions, answers, interruptions, and clarifications. The conversation is more like a debate, in which one person gets a few minutes to make a case and then another gets a few minutes to make a case and then each has a brief rebuttal. In many places it feels like a courtroom drama, the prosecutor gives a speech about the defendant's guilt and the defense attorney offers a rebuttal.

It is a difficult read in any translation, but students are successful with some introduction and help.

Job in Our Mind and Job in the Story

My dad used to compliment those who suffer without complaint by saying that "they had the patience of Job." When I finally read the third chapter of Job I wondered where he got this idea. Even the heading of chapter 3 in the KJV admits that Job is not necessarily patient: "Job curses the day of his birth. He speaks of the quietness and rest of death. His complaint of life."

Where did my dad get his idea? I think it is from the story of Job that is in our cultural consciousness. It comes from the fact that "the patience of Job" is a metaphor for those who suffer in silence, even though Job of the Bible doesn't. Perhaps it is from the only New Testament reference to Job in James 5:11, which says, "we count them happy which endure. Ye have heard of the patience of Job, and have seen the end of the Lord; that the Lord is very pitiful, and of tender mercy." This passage may be evidence that the collective consciousness had already changed the Job story of the Hebrew Bible when the passage in James was written, that the Hebrew Bible text is "corrupt" or that my reading of Job's lament is just plain wrong.

In any case the idea of a patient Job gives us pause when we read Job's lament in chapter 3. It gives students pause to discover that the biblical text sometimes disagrees with what seems to be our collective opinion about the stories. The problem is at least an argument that Job is a difficult text and that we all bring our own preconceived ideas to it. That is part of what makes it good.

Students bring their own template to the study of Job. The challenge is to allow them to read through this template and at the same time consider other readings. Pointing out that Job may be both patient and impatient can help students to consider other views. A good way of pointing this out is to have students read chapter 3, then ask them, "Is Job patient?"

The Structure of the Story

Chapters 1 and 2 constitute the prologue. It is written in prose. It sets up the story by recounting a discussion between God and Satan in which it is decided that Job should be tested. There is much to discuss in this section, including the idea that the testing is taking place even though Job is "perfect and upright, and one that feared God, and eschewed evil" (Job 1:1). Many translations use "blameless" rather than "perfect," and this makes a good discussion point. A person driving a licensed and inspected car according to the law could hit a child. The person may not be perfect because of causing an injury, yet be blameless in life and in the accident.

Chapter 3 is Job's Lament. Students will want to know that "lament" is sometimes " complaint," but the two words are not always synonyms. This is a nice point of discussion. Close reading of verse 25 offers the hint of a reason for Job's troubles for some readers. "For the thing which I greatly feared is come upon me, and that which I was afraid of is come unto me." Are Job's troubles a self-fulfilling prophecy? Do we bring troubles on ourselves by worrying that we will have troubles? "I haven't had a cold in months; I'm afraid I'm due for one." "Things are going so well with my friend; I hope we don't have an argument. I've never had an accident, knock on wood."

Chapters 4–31 are a dialogue between Job and three comforters/ friends: Eliphaz, Bildad, and Zophar. Each friend makes a speech to Job, and Job replies. This debate consists of three cycles of arguments, but the third cycle presents problems because of a corrupted text that many have tried to reconstruct. It is also interrupted with a meditation on wisdom (chapter 28). "It is the only poetry in the book that is not attributed to any particular speaker" (Scheindlin 36–38). It is a good stand alone read and also a chapter that prepares the reader for the divine speeches at the end of the story.

Because each comforter seems to present the same idea in each speech, but each one becomes more emphatic, one strategy is to have students read all the arguments of one comforter and then all of Job's responses to those speeches. Teachers who want to try this approach can use the following:

Eliphaz's Three Speeches	Job's Responses
chapters 4–5	chapters 6–7
chapter 15	chapters 16–17
chapter 22	chapters 23–24

Bildad's Three Speeches	**Job's Responses**
chapter 8	chapters 9–10
chapter 18	chapter 19
chapters 25:1–6, 26:5–14	chapters 26:1–4, 27:1–12

Zophar's Three Speeches	**Job's Responses**
chapter 11	chapters 12–14
chapter 20	chapter 21
chapters 24:18–24 (?), 27:13–23 (?)	chapters 29–31

Another way to have students read is to use an edited version like the one used by Ackerman and Warshaw (269–283). This text uses the following passages from the Revised English Bible: Job 1:1–3:4, 20–23; 4:1–9; 5:17–18; 6:1, 14–15, 21, 24; 7:9–12, 16–18, 20–21; 8:1–3, 8–10, 20–21; 9:1–2, 19–24, 30–33; 11:1–8; 12:1–3; 13:4–9, 12; 14:1–2, 12b, 14–22; 19:23–27; 27:1–6; 29:2, 7–10, 15–16; 31:1–2, 5–6, 9,13 , 16–17, 19–20, 22, 29, 33, 35–37; 38:1–7, 34–38; 39:19–22, 25–28; 40:2–8, 10, 12–14; 41:1–5, 31–34; 42:1–17.

Chapters 32–37 are the Elihu speeches. At the end of chapter 31, Job wishes that "the Almighty would answer me" (35). This foreshadows a future speech from God in a whirlwind, but prior to the whirlwind Elihu has a say. Elihu apologizes for being young and then berates both Job and the comforters. He blames Job for his own problems and says that the comforters should have persuaded Job that he deserved the trials.

Chapters 38:1–42:6 are called the theophany or speeches of God from the whirlwind. They are the centerpiece of the story, for it is the only explanation of Job's troubles that are from God. All other explanations are from Job, his comforters, or Elihu. Job doesn't seem to get his questions answered directly. In fact, he is asked a list of questions, none of which he even tries to answer. Could it be that there is no answer for Job? Even if there are no answers, does he receive comfort from God?

Chapter 42:7–17 is the epilogue. In many ways it is a postscript that offers the equivalent of "The moral of the story is . . ." Many scholars think this tag was added much later because there appears to be no answer to Job's problem in the story itself. It is a good point of discussion for students. Do they think the epilogue is an addition to try and explain the story? How effectively does the epilogue serve this purpose? Would the story be better without it?

The Purpose of Job's Suffering

The central question of the story is the purpose of Job's suffering. Is it really just to decide a bet between God and Satan, or is the suffering some test of Job's character? If it is a test, did Job pass?

There are many good commentaries that address this question. One can be found at http://cspar181.uah.edu/RbS/JOB/job.html There are many other good websites for the Job narrative, but it is important to tell students to search for "Book of Job" rather than "Job." When they search the latter they will find numerous employment opportunities and resume services.

One of the most popular commentaries on Job is in Harold S. Kushner's best seller, *When Bad Things Happen to Good People*. Chapter 2, "The Story of a Man Named Job," is quite accessible for high school students, and I've found that most students who discover this book read it all and recommend it to others.

I use a paradox that Kushner proposes in his book as a place to start the discussion. It is a multiple choice dilemma. On the board are Kushner's three propositions (37):

1. God is all-powerful and causes everything that happens in the world. Nothing happens without His willing it.

2. God is just and fair, and stands for people getting what they deserve, so that the good prosper and the wicked are punished.

3. Job is a good person.

The idea is that all three of these statements are true as long as Job receives blessings. Can they all be true when Job suffers? Kushner's commentary suggests that the author of the story rejects one of these statements, the comforters reject another and Job rejects a third. The comforters obviously reject C. They think that Job has done something to deserve his punishment. Job maintains his innocence and rejects B. He just doesn't think it is fair. The author, according to Kushner, rejects A.

The discussion about which, if any, statement we must reject is lively. Some students have suggested that they can reconcile the three statements even in the light of Job's suffering if they change "causes" in A to "allows." I leave it open. As a teacher I may teach *about* religion but not teach religion. However, I may teach values, and I will make a suggestion about this later in the chapter.

When I explore the purposes of Job's sufferings I generally use, with some modification, the standard explanations that are found in

The Interpreters' Dictionary of the Bible (Buttrick 922).

1. Perhaps this is a test. This is usually the first suggestion students make. I ask them to consider: Why does Job need testing when he is "perfect/blameless"? What is the test? Does Job pass the test? Are replacement children (even beautiful daughters named Dove, Cinnamon, and Eye Shadow) as good as the first ones? Can children be replaced?

2. I explain that in the cultural context of the Job story is an idea called *exact retribution*. Every bad deed is punished and every good deed rewarded. Perhaps the story refutes this idea. God may not be a cosmic vending machine that never malfunctions. It may be that every good deed put in the machine doesn't get a blessing and every bad deed isn't punished. Job was a good (perfect or blameless) person, and he still had trials.

3. Perhaps the punishments and rewards come after this life. That is the suggestion that students usually make after discussing option number two. If this is a possibility, it is time for a close reading of Job 19:25–27. Does it really say what we want it to say? Is there some ambiguity? Does it clarify the passage to read multiple translations?

    [25]For I know *that* my redeemer liveth, and *that* he shall stand at the latter *day* upon the earth: [26]And *though* after my skin *worms* destroy this *body*, yet in my flesh shall I see God: [27]Whom I shall see for myself, and mine eyes shall behold, and not another; *though* my reins be consumed within me.

Students will notice that this last verse doesn't make it into some translations.

4. Perhaps the purpose of Job's suffering is to put humans in their proper place in relation to God. Job is asked a litany of questions that he can't answer. The list that comes from the voice in the whirlwind whirls in each of us. Is Job being told "there is no answer for you Your answer is that there is no answer"? Maybe we all give our own meaning to suffering because we can't find a satisfactory standard explanation. One only has to look at the variety of meanings given to a school tragedy to understand that we all bring our own meaning to a horrific event. Some will say it is God's will. Others will blame the media. Others say the law is at fault. Some say it is a test, and others say there is no reason for it.

5. Perhaps the purpose is to show that disinterested piety is possible because suffering serves some larger purpose. Students like the idea that some people just do what they know to be right regardless of the consequences. Whether threatened with skin worms or rewarded with wealth, some, like Job, do what something inside them tells them they should do. Is Job good because he expects a reward? Is he any less good when he suffers? Does the suffering change him in some fundamental way?

Values Education

It is at this point that the story can be used to teach a value that is beyond any religious dogma. Job is a man of integrity. In spite of unspeakable suffering; in spite of the deaths of his children; in spite of the lack of support from his wife; in spite of lost wealth, comforters who don't comfort, and a God who doesn't explain his suffering, Job sticks to his story. "I didn't do anything to deserve this." He is a man of integrity: "³And the LORD said unto Satan, Hast thou considered my servant Job, that *there is* none like him in the earth, a perfect and an upright man, one that feareth God, and escheweth evil? and still he holdeth fast his integrity, although thou movedst me against him, to destroy him without cause" (Job 2:3).

Job starts out with an honest response. He doesn't know what the reader knows, that Satan moves against him without cause. He doesn't know this when he honestly admits that he feared this could happen: "For the thing which I greatly feared is come upon me, and that which I was afraid of is come unto me" (Job 3:25).

Job gets more credit for honesty after his affliction, in chapter 2:

> ⁷So went Satan forth from the presence of the LORD, and smote Job with sore boils from the sole of his foot unto his crown. ⁸And he took him a potsherd to scrape himself withal; and he sat down among the ashes. ⁹Then said his wife unto him, Dost thou still retain thine integrity? curse God, and die. ¹⁰But he said unto her, Thou speakest as one of the foolish women speaketh. What? shall we receive good at the hand of God, and shall we not receive evil?
> In all this did not Job sin with his lips.

Another reading might be, "Job says what he thinks, and he believes that what he said was not a sin." He asks rhetorical questions that make the point in chapter 6:

[26] Do ye imagine to reprove words, and the speeches of one that is desperate, *which are* as wind? [27] Yea, ye overwhelm the fatherless, and ye dig *a pit* for your friend. [28] Now therefore be content, look upon me; for *it is* evident unto you if I lie. [29] Return, I pray you, let it not be iniquity; yea, return again, my righteousness *is* in it. [30] Is there iniquity in my tongue? Cannot my taste discern perverse things?

In chapter 27 Job again affirms his integrity. He is honest. He says what he knows.

[1]Moreover Job continued his parable, and said, [2]*As* God liveth, *who* hath taken away my judgment; and the Almighty, *who* hath vexed my soul; [3]All the while my breath *is* in me, and the spirit of God *is* in my nostrils; [4]My lips shall not speak wickedness, nor my tongue utter deceit. [5]God forbid that I should justify you: till I die I will not remove mine integrity from me. [6]My righteousness I hold fast, and will not let it go: my heart shall not reproach *me* so long as I live.

Wow! In the face of tremendous pressure from his friends and suffering he doesn't understand, he still sticks to his story, and he plans to stick to the story until he dies. "If I have walked with vanity, or if my foot hath hasted to deceit; [6]Let me be weighed in an even balance, that God may know mine integrity" (Job 31:5–7).

In 42:7 we learn that Job was right and his comforters were wrong. Job was truthful and the comforters were not. "And it was *so*, that after the LORD had spoken these words unto Job, the LORD said to Eliphaz the Temanite, My wrath is kindled against thee, and against thy two friends: for ye have not spoken of me *the thing that is* right, as my servant Job *hath*"

Job spoke the things that are right. This is a story of someone who says the truth as he knows it despite affliction, peer pressure, punishment or reward.

Deconstructing the Story

There is tension in this story. There is so much tension that the story itself undermines the ideas promoted in the story. The complete version of this argument is found in an article by David Clines, "Deconstructing the Book of Job" (65–80).

In the purposes listed above, the second option was that the story refutes the idea of exact retribution. It refutes the idea that every good deed is rewarded and every bad deed punished. The idea that every bad deed is punished is refuted by the fact that Job did nothing wrong to deserve his punishment. "Thou movedst me against him, to destroy him without cause" (Job 2:3). However, at the end of the story, Job is given a replacement family and new wealth. "Also the Lord gave Job twice as much as he had before" (Job 42:10). If this is a reward for his righteousness, a blessing for his integrity, it deconstructs the idea that not all good deeds are rewarded, for here he has been rewarded for being good.

Over the years it has seldom worked for me to try to explain deconstruction to high school students or undergraduates. This is the closest I've come to an example that most students seem to understand. It is reason enough to teach Job as literature.

Chapter 13

TEACHING DUAL NARRATIVES:
DEBORAH THE PROPHETESS

Only 111 of the 1,426 people given names in the Hebrew Bible are women. The Bible "describes a succession of societies over a period of roughly 1,200 years whose public life was dominated by men. And because the Bible's focus is predominantly on public rather than private life, it talks almost only about men" (Murphy 42).

Of the 111 women, the Talmud (Megillah) mentions seven female prophets[15] from the Bible, Sarah, Miriam, Deborah, Hannah, Abigail, Huldah, and Esther. Deborah is a member of a very small minority. When she is mentioned in Judges 5:7, it is the first time we hear her called "mother in Israel" in the Bible, and she seems to be the only judge who actually "judges" as we think of the word today. This judgment results in a glorious victory for Israel.

Her judgment elevates her as a woman and a prophet. When Barak asks for her judgment, he also asks for her to go to battle with him. "If you will go with me, I will go: but if you will not go with me, I will not go" (Judges 4:8). Deborah replies to the request. "I will surely go with you; nevertheless, the road on which you are going will not lead to your glory, for the LORD will sell Sisera into the hand of a woman" (Judges 4:9). Deborah says that the victory will be at the hand of a woman.

The time is after the forty years in the wilderness, when Israel is settled in the land of Canaan. The judges seem to descend in character as we proceed through the stories of Othniel, then left-handed Ehud (whom we met in chapter 4), then Shamgar the son of an idolator. The fourth judge is Deborah, who saves Israel in a war with Canaan and composes a poem or song about it, sung by her and Barak, the general of her army. Her name means "bee" or "hornet," depending on the translator. This alone gives us two contrasting views of her. Her husband is Lappidoth, "torches," and we don't learn much about him. Deborah's military general is Barak, "lightning" or "lightning flash." Deborah's song celebrates Jael, whose name means "mountain goat" and the "headache" Jael gives Sisera, the Canaanite general (when she drives a tent peg through his skull as he sleeps).

The note in the NRSV agrees with most source criticism scholars: "The Song of Deborah may be the oldest part of the Hebrew Bible." It could date from 1155 B.C.E. (Religious scholars and secular scholars do not differ greatly on this date, because the 12th century B.C.E. is when the story happened. What they differ on is whether the earlier part of the Bible—the Hexateuch—was already written or not.)

If we were studying English literature, we would teach "Beowolf" as an important artifact, if not an interesting poem. We would teach it because it may be the oldest epic poem in English. If not "Beowolf" we could teach "Cædmon's Hymn," the earliest poem recorded in English. In an American literature class we might cut through the sermons and letters and go back to Native American trickster tales or stories of the beginning of the world like those recorded in the fifth edition of *The Norton Anthology of American Literature*. If we look for the oldest English American poetry, we may settle on the works of Anne Bradstreet (c. 1612–1672). If we study Hebrew poetry, we begin with Judges 5, the Song of Deborah and Barak. We study it as the oldest poem, a rare poem in the mouth of a female prophet who judges Israel.

There is another reason to teach it. It is one of many parallel accounts that can be used to teach close reading. Just as there are two Creation and Flood stories, two David narratives, and three synoptic Gospels with various versions of the parables, there are two stories of Deborah, in Judges 4 and 5. The two chapters are cited side by side and students are asked to compare and contrast. The citation is from the NRSV. This is a departure from my favorite KJV and there are reasons for this departure. First, the old text is corrupted and this newer translation tries to clarify some of the long-standing problems. Second, this translation shows chapter 5 as a poem, something the KJV doesn't do. It also uses quotation marks, which are helpful. They raise the question of who is speaking. When I ask students to compare Judges 4 and Judges 5, I want them to notice that chapter 5 is a poem. I want them to notice what makes it a poem.

NRSV Judges 4

¹The Israelites again did what was evil in the sight of the Lord, after Ehud died.

²So the Lord sold them into the hand of King Jabin of Canaan, who reigned in Hazor; the commander of his army was Sisera, who lived in Harosheth-ha-goiim.

³Then the Israelites cried out to the Lord for help; for he had nine hundred chariots of iron, and had oppressed the Israelites cruelly twenty years.

⁴At that time Deborah, a prophetess, wife of Lappidoth, was judging Israel.

⁵She used to sit under the palm of Deborah between Ramah and Bethel in the hill country of Ephraim; and the Israelites came up to her for judgment.

⁶She sent and summoned Barak son of Abinoam from Kedesh in Naphtali, and said to him, "The Lord, the God of Israel, commands you, 'Go, take position at Mount Tabor, bringing ten thousand from the tribe of Naphtali and the tribe of Zebulun.

⁷I will draw out Sisera, the general of Jabin's army, to meet you by the Wadi Kishon with his chariots and his troops; and I will give him into your hand.' "

⁸Barak said to her, "If you will go with me, I will go; but if you will not go with me, I will not go."

⁹And she said, "I will surely go with you; nevertheless, the road on which you are going will not lead to your glory, for the Lord will sell Sisera into the hand of a woman." Then Deborah got up and went with Barak to Kedesh.

¹⁰Barak summoned Zebulun and Naphtali to Kedesh; and ten thousand warriors went up behind him; and Deborah went up with him.

¹¹Now Heber the Kenite had separated from the other Kenites, that is, the descendants of Hobab the father-in-law of Moses, and had encamped as far away as Elon-bezaanannim, which is near Kedesh.

¹² When Sisera was told that Barak son of Abinoam had gone up to Mount Tabor,

¹³ Sisera called out all his chariots, nine hundred chariots of iron, and all the troops who were with him, from Harosheth-ha-goiim to the Wadi Kishon.

¹⁴Then Deborah said to Barak, "Up! For this is the day on which the LORD has given Sisera into your hand. The LORD is indeed going out before you." So Barak went down from Mount Tabor with ten thousand warriors following him.

¹⁵And the LORD threw Sisera and all his chariots and all his army into a panic before Barak; Sisera got down from his chariot and fled away on foot,

¹⁶ while Barak pursued the chariots and the army to Harosheth-ha-goiim. All the army of Sisera fell by the sword; no one was left.

¹⁷Now Sisera had fled away on foot to the tent of Jael wife of Heber the Kenite; for there was peace between King Jabin of Hazor and the clan of Heber the Kenite.

¹⁸Jael came out to meet Sisera, and said to him, "Turn aside, my lord, turn aside to me; have no fear." So he turned aside to her into the tent, and she covered him with a rug.

¹⁹Then he said to her, "Please give me a little water to drink; for I am thirsty." So she opened a skin of milk and gave him a drink and covered him.

²⁰He said to her, "Stand at the entrance of the tent, and if anybody comes and asks you, 'Is anyone here?' say, 'No.' "

²¹But Jael wife of Heber took a tent peg, and took a hammer in her hand, and went softly to him and drove the peg into his temple, until it went down into the ground—he was lying fast asleep from weariness—and he died.

²²Then, as Barak came in pursuit of Sisera, Jael went out to meet him, and said to him, "Come, and I will show you the man whom you are seeking." So he went into her tent; and there was Sisera lying dead, with the tent peg in his temple.

²³So on that day God subdued King Jabin of Canaan before the Israelites.

²⁴Then the hand of the Israelites bore harder and harder on King Jabin of Canaan, until they destroyed King Jabin of Canaan.

NRS Judges 5:1

¹ Then Deborah and Barak son of Abinoam sang on that day, saying:

² "When locks are long in Israel,
   when the people offer themselves willingly—
      bless the LORD!

³ "Hear, O kings;
  give ear, O princes;
    to the LORD I will sing,
    I will make melody to the LORD, the God of Israel.
⁴ "LORD, when you went out from Seir,
    when you marched from the region of Edom,
      the earth trembled,
      and the heavens poured,
      the clouds indeed poured water.
⁵ The mountains quaked before the LORD,
      the One of Sinai,
    before the LORD,
      the God of Israel.
⁶ "In the days of Shamgar son of Anath,
    in the days of Jael,
      caravans ceased and
      travelers kept to the byways.
⁷ The peasantry prospered in Israel,
        they grew fat on plunder,
    because you arose, Deborah,
    arose as a mother in Israel.
⁸ When new gods were chosen,
        then war was in the gates.
    Was shield or spear to be seen
        among forty thousand in Israel?
⁹ My heart goes out to the commanders of Israel
        who offered themselves willingly among the people.
    Bless the LORD.
¹⁰ "Tell of it, you who ride on white donkeys,
        you who sit on rich carpets
        and you who walk by the way.
¹¹ To the sound of musicians at the watering places,
        there they repeat the triumphs of the LORD,
        the triumphs of his peasantry in Israel.
    "Then down to the gates marched the people of the LORD.
¹² "Awake, awake, Deborah!
    Awake, awake, utter a song!

Arise, Barak, lead away your captives,
    O son of Abinoam.
13 Then down marched the remnant of the noble;
    the people of the LORD marched down for him against the mighty.
14 From Ephraim they set out into the valley,
        following you, Benjamin, with your kin;
    from Machir marched down the commanders,
        and from Zebulun those who bear the marshal's staff;
15 the chiefs of Issachar came with Deborah,
        and Issachar faithful to Barak;
        into the valley they rushed out at his heels.
    Among the clans of Reuben there were great searchings of heart.
16 Why did you tarry among the sheepfolds,
        to hear the piping for the flocks?
    Among the clans of Reuben
        there were great searchings of heart.
17 Gilead stayed beyond the Jordan;
        and Dan, why did he abide with the ships?
    Asher sat still at the coast of the sea,
        settling down by his landings.
18 Zebulun is a people that scorned death;
        Naphtali too, on the heights of the field.
19 "The kings came, they fought;
        then fought the kings of Canaan,
        at Taanach, by the waters of Megiddo;
        they got no spoils of silver.
20 The stars fought from heaven,
        from their courses they fought against Sisera.
21 The torrent Kishon swept them away,
        the onrushing torrent, the torrent Kishon.
        March on, my soul, with might!
22 "Then loud beat the horses' hoofs
        with the galloping, galloping of his steeds.
23 "Curse Meroz, says the angel of the LORD,
        curse bitterly its inhabitants,
    because they did not come to the help of the LORD,
        to the help of the LORD against the mighty.

²⁴ "Most blessed of women be Jael,
>   the wife of Heber the Kenite,
>   of tent-dwelling women most blessed.
²⁵ He asked water and she gave him milk,
>   she brought him curds in a lordly bowl.
²⁶ She put her hand to the tent peg
>   and her right hand to the workmen's mallet;
>   she struck Sisera a blow,
>   she crushed his head,
>   she shattered and pierced his temple.
²⁷ He sank, he fell,
>   he lay still at her feet;
>   at her feet he sank, he fell;
>   where he sank, there he fell dead.
²⁸ "Out of the window she peered, the mother of Sisera gazed
>   through the lattice:
>   'Why is his chariot so long in coming?
>   Why tarry the hoofbeats of his chariots?'
²⁹ Her wisest ladies make answer,
>   indeed, she answers the question herself:
³⁰ 'Are they not finding and dividing the spoil?—
>   A girl or two for every man;
>   spoil of dyed stuffs for Sisera,
>   spoil of dyed stuffs embroidered,
>   two pieces of dyed work embroidered for my neck as spoil?'
³¹"So perish all your enemies, O Lord!
>   But may your friends be like the sun as it rises in its might."
And the land had rest forty years.

Besides the fact that chapter 4 is a narrative and chapter 5 a poem, students may notice other differences. The following citation from "Deborah" in the *Britannica CD Encyclopaedia* describes some of the distinctions of the two chapters and illustrates what a good teaching resource an encyclopedia can be.

> The two narratives of her exploit, the prose account in Judg. 4 (evi-
> dently written after Judg. 5) and the martial poem comprising [sic]
> Judg. 5 (a lyric outburst showing a high standard of poetic skill in

ancient Israel), differ in some important details. The most obvious discrepancy is in the identity of the chief foe of the Israelites. Judg. 4 makes the chief enemy Jabin, king of Hazor (present Tell el-Qedah, about three miles southwest of Hula Basin), though a prominent part is played by his commander in chief, Sisera of Harosheth-ha-goiim (possibly Tell el-'Amr, approximately 12 miles [19 kilometres] northwest of Megiddo). In the poem Jabin does not appear, and Sisera is an independent king of Canaan. Other important contradictions include the action sites (Mount Tabor in Judg. 4 is not found in Judg. 5, for example); which Israelite tribes joined Deborah and her chief commander, the Naphtalite Barak (only Zebulun and Naphtali in Judg. 4, additional tribes in Judg. 5); and the manner of Sisera's death (in Judg. 4 he is murdered in his sleep, in Judg. 5 he is struck down from behind while drinking a bowl of milk).

Even though the Britannica is good with plot, geography, and historical context, it doesn't look at the poetic qualities. There is another good encyclopedic source that can help with the Hebrew Bible, The *Encyclopaedia Judaica*. The following is from the CD-ROM version:

> The poetic form of the Song of Deborah is characterized by parallelism and the repetition of a word, or a combination of words, in various lines of most of the verses. Also characteristic is the frequency of the tricolon, that is, the three line verse (e.g., 5:2, 3b). According to tradition, the Song of Deborah is written in a form called "blank over script and script over blank," that is, a line of three hemistiches followed by a line of two longer hemistiches, and so on (similar to the form of the Song of Moses, Ex. 15). There is, however, no established tradition on the division of the words into hemistiches in the Song of Deborah. Great similarity exists between this song and Psalm 68, which appears to have been composed under the former's influence. Tradition has assigned the Song of Deborah to the *haftarah* of the weekly portion of *Be-Shallah*, whose central section is Moses' Song by the Sea (Ex. 15), which, in turn, bears a direct relationship in spirit, style, and content to the Song of Deborah.

There is also good information about Deborah in the arts in the *Encyclopaedia Judaica*. It notes Deborah's prominence in oratorios such as the *Deborah* of Handel. It notes the art, music, and illuminated manuscripts of Deborah, including the Rembrandt pen-drawing of Jael and the Gobelin tapestry in the Vienna Museum.

The Song of Deborah is a good place to remind students of the parallelism of biblical poetry and an excellent place to study irony. Just after the death of Sisera in chapter 5, the scene shifts to his mother, who is peering out the window to wonder why her son is so slow in returning. The reader knows her son is dead, but listens as his mother and "her wisest ladies" assure themselves in parallel lines that he is all right.

Students also like the scene in verse 24, where Sisera asks for water and Jael offers an ever greater hospitality by offering some refreshing milk and curds in a lordly bowl. And then the deed is done. After milk and cookies comes the tent peg to the temple and then the parallel lines in verse 27:

> He sank, he fell,
> > he lay still at her feet;
> at her feet he sank, he fell;
> > Where he sank, there he fell dead.

Because the song puts words in the mouth of Deborah and Barak, I suggest to students that we are listing to antiphonal music. It is like listening to a choral piece in which there is a choir at each end of the auditorium. The choir sings back and forth to each other, sometimes separately, sometimes together.

To teach close reading I ask students to try and identify which lines can be attributed to Deborah and which to Barak. One approach is to find parts that Deborah could not have sung and that Barak could not have sung. For example, Deborah could not call on herself to awake, as in Judges 5:12, and neither could Barak exhort himself in the same verse. Barak could sing that Deborah arose "a mother in Israel" (5:7), but some translations read "I, Deborah, arose a mother in Israel," which would be hard to put in Barak's mouth. Verse 30, gloating over the rape of Israelite women ("a girl or two for every man") is a quote of the "wisest ladies" of Sisera"s mother.

The song is taught as a historical artifact, a first Hebrew poem, one that celebrates a female biblical prophet and a feisty woman handy with tent pegs.

Note

15 The term *prophetess* is still used in most English Bible translations to describe a female prophet. This text uses the gender neutral term prophet for men and women who prophesy.

Chapter 14

TEACHING FAMOUS LAST WORDS: WRITING EPITAPHS

T he old man said that he had the epitaph ready for his grave marker: "I told you I was sick."

Not all last words are an epitaph on a life. Some are whimsical and fun to write. We will start with the last words that have been submitted in class over the years and then look at the last words of David—the epitaph of a legendary king, shepherd, warrior, poet, prophet, musician, adulterer, and murderer. David's last words are especially interesting because they conclude a double narrative, a binocular look at his life that offers poetic depth perception.

First, the last words written by students:

I'm sure the power is off.

You won't have to unplug it. I'll have it fixed in a minute.

I wonder what this button does?

Cut that wire first.

What happens if I touch these two wires together?

You can stay at my place.

Of course I've done this before.

I can do it with my eyes closed.

It isn't loaded.

This won't hurt.

It's fireproof.

It's foolproof.

He's a perfectly safe driver.

Don't worry, they'll find us.

I saw this on television.

What duck?

I'm not superstitious.

This is the last time.

We made it this far OK.

Good dog.

I'll be honest. You do look a bit fat in that dress.

I'll kick his butt.

I have another couple gallons when it says empty.

The stuff is harmless; it's herbal.

I'll beat the light.

I got it fresh last week.

I can identify safe mushrooms.

This doesn't taste right.

We won't need a reservation.

I'll do the talking here.

It will be fun.

I know the way.

We won't need a map.

Does something smell like gas?

One student submitted a more extended list of last words that she found on the Internet. I haven't checked these out for historical accuracy and haven't found sources, but the site address she gave me is http://www.corsinet.com/braincandy/index.html. Many of the epitaphs on the "Brain Candy" site above sound familiar, and many sound too good to be true. That is the nature of the last words of the famous. It's hard to track them down, the last words and the dead people. The words have a quality of folklore about them, as if they were a punctuation mark on a life supplied by those who remember the life as much as the words.

The words are often part of a lifelong attribution based on a reputation. For example, the title of Yogi Berra's book *I Really Didn't Say*

Everything I Said is an admission that many of his intentional and unintentional malapropisms aren't his. He says that many of the things he is supposed to have said, he doesn't remember saying. My hunch is that some jokes or lines are funnier if attributed to the Yankee philosopher and so somehow the lines just get attributed to him. They sound like something he'd say:

> I never answer anonymous letters.
>
> A nickel isn't worth a dime anymore.
>
> You can see a lot by looking.
>
> The past just isn't what it used to be.

Last words take on the flavor of the life. For example, when Nathan Hale was shot by the British as a spy in 1776, he said, "It is the duty of every good officer to obey any orders given him by his commander-in-chief." What has been attributed to him over the centuries is, "I only regret that I have but one life to lose for my country." What did he actually say? I suppose we could collect the evidence and try to decide, but in the end there is no way of knowing exactly what was said. The news media was not present when it happened. In the end, we have to rely on some witnesses to these last words, who may have faulty memories or even ulterior motives for selective memory.

Even though unreliable, last words punctuate a life. They sum it all up in a usually brief and memorable statement. They may be lofty or whimsical. The website that includes an extended list (http://www.corsinet.com/braincandy/index.html) of famous and not so famous last words, includes: "Father, into thy hands I commend my spirit," words spoken by Jesus in Luke 23:46.

The examples can put students in a frame of mind to look at some lofty last words that define one of the best-developed heroes of the Bible: King David. To understand David's last words, they should be put in the context of the first time we meet him—twice, in 1 Samuel 16 and 17. Just as David offers two sets of last words, the narrative starts with two beginnings. Two chapters in Robert Alter's *The Art of Biblical Narrative* are especially good teacher resources for this comparison. Chapter 6, "Characterization and the Art of Reticence," is an extended look at character development and David, who is "the most complex and elaborately presented of biblical characters" (115). The last seven pages of chapter 7, "Composite Artistry," focus on 1 Samuel 16 and 17, the introduction to David as "the most elaborate biblical instance" (147) of composite narrative.

KJV 1 Samuel 16

¹And the L ORD said unto Samuel, How long wilt thou mourn for Saul, seeing I have rejected him from reigning over Israel? fill thine horn with oil, and go, I will send thee to Jesse the Bethlehemite: for I have provided me a king among his sons. ²And Samuel said, How can I go? if Saul hear *it*, he will kill me. And the L ORD said, Take an heifer with thee, and say, I am come to sacrifice to the L ORD. ³And call Jesse to the sacrifice, and I will shew thee what thou shalt do: and thou shalt anoint unto me *him* whom I name unto thee. ⁴And Samuel did that which the L ORD spake, and came to Bethlehem. And the elders of the town trembled at his coming, and said, Comest thou peaceably? ⁵And he said, Peaceably: I am come to sacrifice unto the L ORD: sanctify yourselves, and come with me to the sacrifice. And he sanctified Jesse and his sons, and called them to the sacrifice.

⁶And it came to pass, when they were come, that he looked on Eliab, and said, Surely the L ORD's anointed *is* before him. ⁷But the L ORD said unto Samuel, Look not on his countenance, or on the height of his stature; because I have refused him: for *the* L ORD *seeth* not as man seeth; for man looketh on the outward appearance, but the L ORD looketh on the heart. ⁸Then Jesse called Abinadab, and made him pass before Samuel. And he said, Neither hath the L ORD chosen this. ⁹Then Jesse made Shammah to pass by. And he said, Neither hath the L ORD chosen this. ¹⁰Again, Jesse made seven of his sons to pass before Samuel. And Samuel said unto Jesse, The L ORD hath not chosen these. ¹¹And Samuel said unto Jesse, Are here all *thy* children? And he said, There remaineth yet the youngest, and, behold, he keepeth the sheep. And Samuel said unto Jesse, Send and fetch him: for we will not sit down till he come hither. ¹²And he sent, and brought him in. Now he *was* ruddy, *and* withal of a beautiful countenance, and goodly to look to. And the L ORD said, Arise, anoint him: for this *is* he. ¹³Then Samuel took the horn of oil, and anointed him in the midst of his brethren: and the Spirit of the L ORD came upon David from that day forward. So Samuel rose up, and went to Ramah.

¹⁴But the Spirit of the L ORD departed from Saul, and an evil spirit from the L ORD troubled him. ¹⁵ And Saul's servants said unto him, Behold now, an evil spirit from God troubleth thee. ¹⁶Let our lord now command thy servants, *which are* before thee, to seek out a man, *who is* a cunning player on an harp: and it shall come to pass, when the evil spirit from God is upon thee, that he shall play with his hand, and thou shalt be well. ¹⁷And Saul said unto his servants, Provide me now a man that can play well, and bring *him* to me. ¹⁸Then answered

one of the servants, and said, Behold, I have seen a son of Jesse the Bethlehemite, *that is* cunning in playing, and a mighty valiant man, and a man of war, and prudent in matters, and a comely person, and the LORD *is* with him.

[19]Wherefore Saul sent messengers unto Jesse, and said, Send me David thy son, which *is* with the sheep. [20]And Jesse took an ass *laden* with bread, and a bottle of wine, and a kid, and sent *them* by David his son unto Saul. [21]And David came to Saul, and stood before him: and he loved him greatly; and he became his armourbearer. [22]And Saul sent to Jesse, saying, Let David, I pray thee, stand before me; for he hath found favour in my sight. [23]And it came to pass, when the *evil* spirit from God was upon Saul, that David took an harp, and played with his hand: so Saul was refreshed, and was well, and the evil spirit departed from him.

KJV 1 Samuel 17

[1]Now the Philistines gathered together their armies to battle, and were gathered together at Shochoh, which *belongeth* to Judah, and pitched between Shochoh and Azekah, in Ephesdammim. [2]And Saul and the men of Israel were gathered together, and pitched by the valley of Elah, and set the battle in array against the Philistines. [3]And the Philistines stood on a mountain on the one side, and Israel stood on a mountain on the other side: and *there was* a valley between them.

[4]And there went out a champion out of the camp of the Philistines, named Goliath, of Gath, whose height *was* six cubits and a span. [5]And *he had* an helmet of brass upon his head, and he *was* armed with a coat of mail; and the weight of the coat *was* five thousand shekels of brass. [6]And *he had* greaves of brass upon his legs, and a target of brass between his shoulders. [7]And the staff of his spear *was* like a weaver's beam; and his spear's head *weighed* six hundred shekels of iron: and one bearing a shield went before him. [8]And he stood and cried unto the armies of Israel, and said unto them, Why are ye come out to set *your* battle in array? *am* not I a Philistine, and ye servants to Saul? choose you a man for you, and let him come down to me. [9]If he be able to fight with me, and to kill me, then will we be your servants: but if I prevail against him, and kill him, then shall ye be our servants, and serve us. [10]And the Philistine said, I defy the armies of Israel this day; give me a man, that we may fight together. [11]When Saul and all Israel heard those words of the Philistine, they were dismayed, and greatly afraid.

¹²Now David *was* the son of that Ephrathite of Bethlehemjudah, whose name *was* Jesse; and he had eight sons: and the man went among men *for* an old man in the days of Saul. ¹³And the three eldest sons of Jesse went *and* followed Saul to the battle: and the names of his three sons that went to the battle *were* Eliab the firstborn, and next unto him Abinadab, and the third Shammah. ¹⁴And David *was* the youngest: and the three eldest followed Saul. ¹⁵But David went and returned from Saul to feed his father's sheep at Bethlehem. ¹⁶And the Philistine drew near morning and evening, and presented himself forty days. ¹⁷And Jesse said unto David his son, Take now for thy brethren an ephah of this parched *corn*, and these ten loaves, and run to the camp to thy brethren; ¹⁸And carry these ten cheeses unto the captain of *their* thousand, and look how thy brethren fare, and take their pledge. ¹⁹Now Saul, and they, and all the men of Israel, *were* in the valley of Elah, fighting with the Philistines.

²⁰And David rose up early in the morning, and left the sheep with a keeper, and took, and went, as Jesse had commanded him; and he came to the trench, as the host was going forth to the fight, and shouted for the battle. ²¹For Israel and the Philistines had put the battle in array, army against army. ²²And David left his carriage in the hand of the keeper of the carriage, and ran into the army, and came and saluted his brethren. ²³And as he talked with them, behold, there came up the champion, the Philistine of Gath, Goliath by name, out of the armies of the Philistines, and spake according to the same words: and David heard *them*. ²⁴And all the men of Israel, when they saw the man, fled from him, and were sore afraid. ²⁵And the men of Israel said, Have ye seen this man that is come up? surely to defy Israel is he come up: and it shall be, *that* the man who killeth him, the king will enrich him with great riches, and will give him his daughter, and make his father's house free in Israel. ²⁶And David spake to the men that stood by him, saying, What shall be done to the man that killeth this Philistine, and taketh away the reproach from Israel? for who *is* this uncircumcised Philistine, that he should defy the armies of the living God? ²⁷And the people answered him after this manner, saying, So shall it be done to the man that killeth him.

²⁸And Eliab his eldest brother heard when he spake unto the men; and Eliab's anger was kindled against David, and he said, Why camest thou down hither? and with whom hast thou left those few sheep in the wilderness? I know thy pride, and the naughtiness of thine heart; for thou art come down that thou mightest see the battle. ²⁹And David said, What have I now done? *Is there* not a cause?

³⁰And he turned from him toward another, and spake after the same manner: and the people answered him again after the former manner. ³¹And when the words were heard which David spake, they rehearsed *them* before Saul: and he sent for him.

³²And David said to Saul, Let no man's heart fail because of him; thy servant will go and fight with this Philistine. ³³And Saul said to David, Thou art not able to go against this Philistine to fight with him: for thou *art but* a youth, and he a man of war from his youth. ³⁴And David said unto Saul, Thy servant kept his father's sheep, and there came a lion, and a bear, and took a lamb out of the flock: ³⁵ And I went out after him, and smote him, and delivered *it* out of his mouth: and when he arose against me, I caught *him* by his beard, and smote him, and slew him. ³⁶Thy servant slew both the lion and the bear: and this uncircumcised Philistine shall be as one of them, seeing he hath defied the armies of the living God. ³⁷David said moreover, The LORD that delivered me out of the paw of the lion, and out of the paw of the bear, he will deliver me out of the hand of this Philistine. And Saul said unto David, Go, and the LORD be with thee.

³⁸And Saul armed David with his armour, and he put an helmet of brass upon his head; also he armed him with a coat of mail. ³⁹And David girded his sword upon his armour, and he assayed to go; for he had not proved *it*. And David said unto Saul, I cannot go with these; for I have not proved *them*. And David put them off him. ⁴⁰And he took his staff in his hand, and chose him five smooth stones out of the brook, and put them in a shepherd's bag which he had, even in a scrip; and his sling *was* in his hand: and he drew near to the Philistine. ⁴¹And the Philistine came on and drew near unto David; and the man that bare the shield *went* before him. ⁴²And when the Philistine looked about, and saw David, he disdained him: for he was *but* a youth, and ruddy, and of a fair countenance. ⁴³And the Philistine said unto David, *Am* I a dog, that thou comest to me with staves? And the Philistine cursed David by his gods. ⁴⁴And the Philistine said to David, Come to me, and I will give thy flesh unto the fowls of the air, and to the beasts of the field. ⁴⁵ Then said David to the Philistine, Thou comest to me with a sword, and with a spear, and with a shield: but I come to thee in the name of the LORD of hosts, the God of the armies of Israel, whom thou hast defied. ⁴⁶This day will the LORD deliver thee into mine hand; and I will smite thee, and take thine head from thee; and I will give the carcases of the host of the Philistines this day unto the fowls of the air, and to the wild beasts of the earth; that all the earth may know that there is a God in Israel. ⁴⁷And all this assembly shall

know that the LORD saveth not with sword and spear: for the battle *is* the LORD's, and he will give you into our hands. ⁴⁸And it came to pass, when the Philistine arose, and came and drew nigh to meet David, that David hasted, and ran toward the army to meet the Philistine. ⁴⁹And David put his hand in his bag, and took thence a stone, and slang *it*, and smote the Philistine in his forehead, that the stone sunk into his forehead; and he fell upon his face to the earth. ⁵⁰So David prevailed over the Philistine with a sling and with a stone, and smote the Philistine, and slew him; but *there was* no sword in the hand of David. ⁵¹Therefore David ran, and stood upon the Philistine, and took his sword, and drew it out of the sheath thereof, and slew him, and cut off his head therewith. And when the Philistines saw their champion was dead, they fled. ⁵²And the men of Israel and of Judah arose, and shouted, and pursued the Philistines, until thou come to the valley, and to the gates of Ekron. And the wounded of the Philistines fell down by the way to Shaaraim, even unto Gath, and unto Ekron. ⁵³And the children of Israel returned from chasing after the Philistines, and they spoiled their tents. ⁵⁴And David took the head of the Philistine, and brought it to Jerusalem; but he put his armour in his tent.

⁵⁵And when Saul saw David go forth against the Philistine, he said unto Abner, the captain of the host, Abner, whose son *is* this youth? And Abner said, *As* thy soul liveth, O king, I cannot tell.

⁵⁶And the king said, Enquire thou whose son the stripling *is*.

⁵⁷And as David returned from the slaughter of the Philistine, Abner took him, and brought him before Saul with the head of the Philistine in his hand.

⁵⁸And Saul said to him, Whose son *art* thou, *thou* young man? And David answered, I *am* the son of thy servant Jesse the Bethlehemite.

Students are used to the exercise I give them now. I first ask them to find evidence in each of the narratives that an author may not have been familiar with the other story. Is there evidence that both stories were written by the same author? The students are then asked for more specifics that require close reading: How is David different when you compare 1 Samuel 16 and 1 Samuel 17? Knowing this will help us to better understand David's last words. Here are Robert Alter's words:

> In the first account, the prophet Samuel is sent to Bethlehem to anoint one of the sons of Jesse as successor to Saul, whose violation of divine injunction has just disqualified him for the kingship that was conferred on him. Samuel, after mistaking the eldest of

the brothers as the divinely elected one, is directed by God to anoint David, the youngest (a pattern of displacing the firstborn familiar from Genesis). Following the anointment, David is called to Saul's court to soothe the king's mad fits by playing the lyre, and he assumes the official position of armor-bearer to Saul. In the second account, David is still back on the farm while his older brothers (here three in number rather than seven) are serving in Saul's army against the Philistines. These is no mention here of any previous ceremony of anointing, no allusion to David's musical abilities or to a position as royal armor-bearer (indeed, a good deal is made of his total unfamiliarity with armor). In this version David, having arrived on the battlefield with provisions for his brothers, makes his debut by slaying the Philistine champion, Goliath, and he is so unfamiliar a face to both Saul and Abner, Saul's commander-in-chief, that, at the end of the chapter, they both confess they have no idea who he is or what family he comes from, and he has to identify himself to Saul.

Logically, of course, Saul would have had to meet David for the first time either as music therapist in his court or a giant-killer on the battlefield, but he could not have done both. Both stories are necessary, however, for the writer's binocular vision of David. (ABN 147–148)

The second introduction to David is almost three times as long as the first, and in the second we hear David's words. In the first he is shy and silent. In the second version he not only finds his voice but wins the debate and the battle with Goliath. And speaking of voices, in the second version God does not speak. David is the spokesman.

According to Alter, "The whole event [first story] is an exercise in seeing right, not only for Jesse and his sons and the implied audience of the story, but also for Samuel, who was earlier designated seer" (149). In the second, "the motif of the unknown young man who astonishes his elders and slays the dread giant is common to many folkloric traditions, but here is woven persuasively into the texture of historical fiction, given the concreteness of vividly verisimilar dialogue" (150).

Alter seems to agree with other close readers, like Kenneth R. R. Gros Louis, that we are reading the private and the public story of David. "These two views correspond in part, but only in part, to the public and private David, the David Saul envies, then hates as his rival, and the one whom he loves as his comforter. David will be the brilliant warrior-king and (as Shemei of the house of Saul one day will call him) the 'man of blood,' and for this identity the Goliath story is the fitting introduction. But he is also to figure as the eloquent elegist, the composer of psalms, the sensitive and passionate man who loves Jonathan and weeps for his dead sons; and this side of him is properly introduced in the story of his debut as a court musician with the gift of driving out evil spirits through his song" (Alter, ABN 152).

Not only are there two introductions to David in 1 Samuel, there are a multitude of imaginings of David in art. I note a few examples here in case some teachers wish to teach more than epitaphs and last words. For example, Goliath of Gath looks as though death is inevitable. He is on his back with his head cocked back to expose a large neck that is an easy target for the sword of a gentle shepherd boy poet who straddles the near dead giant's shoulders. David looks reluctant. Stunning the giant with a stone thrown from a sling was easier than face to steel combat. David doesn't seem to swing the sword with the vengeance of a champion gladiator.

This David of the Vyner window, designed by Sir Edward Burne-Jones and executed by William Morris in 1874–1875, is in Christchurch, Oxford. David is reborn in this art as a reluctant shepherd drafted to champion the Israelites against the Philistine.

Another David straddles the shoulders of a felled Goliath on the ceiling of the Sistine Chapel. This David is more a warrior and less a shepherd. Although his raised arm and sword is in a cocked position for a mortal blow as in the Vyner window, Michelangelo's David is ready to strike a still-struggling Goliath with vengeance. This Goliath is face down but pushing the earth and twisting as if straining to turn to see the face of his conqueror. David holds Goliath's hair in his fist as he prepares the mortal blow.

These two imaginings of David were born of the same narrative, a narrative of more chapters in the Bible than are devoted to any other monarch. Perhaps this is because David, the second king of Israel, ruled for forty years, longer than any other king of Israel. The biblical narrative imagines a monarch destined to be reborn in the imaginations of artists and writers as David himself was a writer, musician, and "Renaissance man." The Davids of the artists, poets, musicians, and writers who have imagined their own Davids all find some attachment to the biblical narrative of the books of Samuel and 1 Kings 1–2. These sources are paralleled, with significant omissions and some additions, in 1 Chronicles 11–29. These references are the place to start a study of the art of characterization in biblical literature.

The study of the characterization of David is an opportunity to integrate ideas from the humanities disciplines using ideas from a common source. The variety of imaginings of David by artists and writers exists in part because there are at least two histories of David. One history consists of what really happened. The other history is the *record* of what happened and is flavored with the imaginations of the people who compiled it. The first history we will never know, but the second is left for us each to discover from biblical literature and the work it has inspired.

Some teachers may wish to look at the victory of David over Goliath in sculpture. This was a popular subject with the great sculptors of the Renaissance. The most exciting examples are the sculptures of David by Donatello (1430–1432, Florence, Bargello), Andrea del Verrocchio (1476, Florence, Bargello), and Michelangelo (1503, Florence, Accademia). There is a baroque version of the subject sculpted by Bernini (1623) that I often include as we compare the imaginings of four sculptors.

Before looking at David's last words, public and private, I like to give students the context of two more dramatic events in the life of David. The events help to continue the idea of the dual narratives looking at private and public behavior. The first is David's very public dance before the ark and the second is his public affair with Bathsheba. The second event he obviously wished were more private. Both events have a private subtext. I admit that the choice of these two events is a bit arbitrary. There are so many good narratives from which teachers can choose:

- The friendship of David and Jonathan (1 Samuel 18, 19, 20, 23)
- David spares Saul's life (1 Samuel 24, 26)
- The Rebellion of Absalom (2 Samuel 13:1–20; 14:25; 15:2–6; 18:9)
- If I choose to teach an extended unit on David I assign 1 Samuel 16–30; 2 Samuel 1–6, 11–18, 19:1–8, 23:1–5; 1 Kings 2.

Another good resource to assign is the history of David in *Wanderings: Chaim Potok's History of the Jews* (142–154). This is a short and poetic reading that helps students to make sense of the fragmentary reading of Samuel and Kings. Potok writes his history with the skill of a novelist. His history reads like a good story.

Before the last words we watch David dance in 2 Samuel 6:

¹²And it was told king David, saying, The LORD hath blessed the house of Obededom, and all that *pertaineth* unto him, because of the ark of God. So David went and brought up the ark of God from the house of Obededom into the city of David with gladness. ¹³And it was *so*, that when they that bare the ark of the LORD had gone six paces, he sacrificed oxen and fatlings. ¹⁴And David danced before the LORD with all *his* might; and David *was* girded with a linen ephod. ¹⁵So David and all the house of Israel brought up the ark of the LORD with shouting, and with the sound of the trumpet. ¹⁶And as the ark of the LORD came into the city of David, Michal Saul's daughter looked through a window, and saw king David leaping and dancing before the LORD; and she despised him in her heart. ¹⁷And they brought in the ark of the LORD, and set it in his place, in the midst of the tabernacle that David had pitched for it: and David offered burnt offerings and peace offerings before the LORD. ¹⁸And as soon as David had made an end of offering burnt offerings and peace offerings, he blessed the people in the name of the LORD of hosts. ¹⁹And he dealt among all the people, *even* among the whole multitude of Israel, as well to the women as men, to every one a cake of bread, and a good piece *of flesh*, and a flagon *of wine*. So all the people departed every one to his house.

²⁰Then David returned to bless his household. And Michal the daughter of Saul came out to meet David, and said, How glorious was the king of Israel to day, who uncovered himself to day in the eyes of the handmaids of his servants, as one of the vain fellows shamelessly uncovereth himself! ²¹And David said unto Michal, *It was* before the LORD, which chose me before thy father, and before all his house, to appoint me ruler over the people of the LORD, over Israel: therefore will I play before the LORD. ²²And I will yet be more vile than thus, and will be base in mine own sight: and of the maidservants which thou hast spoken of, of them shall I be had in honour. ²³Therefore Michal the daughter of Saul had no child unto the day of her death.

The questions for students are as follows:

1. What do we learn about David's character from this story?
2. What do we learn about the private David?
3. What do we learn about the public David?
4. What tone of voice is Michal using when she says "How glorious was the King . . ."
5. What is David's tone when he says "it was before the Lord?"

The next narrative that gives David's last words context is the Bathsheba story of 2 Samuel 11 and 12:

¹And it came to pass, after the year was expired, at the time when kings go forth *to battle*, that David sent Joab, and his servants with

him, and all Israel; and they destroyed the children of Ammon, and besieged Rabbah. But David tarried still at Jerusalem. ²And it came to pass in an eveningtide, that David arose from off his bed, and walked upon the roof of the king's house: and from the roof he saw a woman washing herself; and the woman *was* very beautiful to look upon. ³And David sent and enquired after the woman. And *one* said, *Is* not this Bathsheba, the daughter of Eliam, the wife of Uriah the Hittite? ⁴And David sent messengers, and took her; and she came in unto him, and he lay with her; for she was purified from her uncleanness: and she returned unto her house. ⁵And the woman conceived, and sent and told David, and said, I *am* with child.

⁶And David sent to Joab, *saying*, Send me Uriah the Hittite. And Joab sent Uriah to David. ⁷And when Uriah was come unto him, David demanded *of him* how Joab did, and how the people did, and how the war prospered. ⁸And David said to Uriah, Go down to thy house, and wash thy feet. And Uriah departed out of the king's house, and there followed him a mess *of meat* from the king. ⁹But Uriah slept at the door of the king's house with all the servants of his lord, and went not down to his house. ¹⁰And when they had told David, saying, Uriah went not down unto his house, David said unto Uriah, Camest thou not from *thy* journey? why *then* didst thou not go down unto thine house? ¹¹And Uriah said unto David, The ark, and Israel, and Judah, abide in tents; and my lord Joab, and the servants of my lord, are encamped in the open fields; shall I then go into mine house, to eat and to drink, and to lie with my wife? *as* thou livest, and *as* thy soul liveth, I will not do this thing. ¹²And David said to Uriah, Tarry here to day also, and to morrow I will let thee depart. So Uriah abode in Jerusalem that day, and the morrow. ¹³And when David had called him, he did eat and drink before him; and he made him drunk: and at even he went out to lie on his bed with the servants of his lord, but went not down to his house.

¹⁴And it came to pass in the morning, that David wrote a letter to Joab, and sent *it* by the hand of Uriah. ¹⁵And he wrote in the letter, saying, Set ye Uriah in the forefront of the hottest battle, and retire ye from him, that he may be smitten, and die. ¹⁶And it came to pass, when Joab observed the city, that he assigned Uriah unto a place where he knew that valiant men *were*. ¹⁷And the men of the city went out, and fought with Joab: and there fell *some* of the people of the servants of David; and Uriah the Hittite died also. ¹⁸Then Joab sent and told David all the things concerning the war; ¹⁹And charged the messenger, saying, When thou hast made an end of telling the matters of the war unto the king, ²⁰And if so be that the king's wrath arise, and he say unto thee, Wherefore approached ye so nigh unto the city when ye did fight? knew ye not that they would shoot from the wall? ²¹Who smote Abimelech the son of Jerubbesheth? did not a woman cast a piece of a millstone upon

him from the wall, that he died in Thebez? why went ye nigh the wall? then say thou, Thy servant Uriah the Hittite is dead also. ²²So the messenger went, and came and shewed David all that Joab had sent him for. ²³And the messenger said unto David, Surely the men prevailed against us, and came out unto us into the field, and we were upon them even unto the entering of the gate. ²⁴And the shooters shot from off the wall upon thy servants; and *some* of the king's servants be dead, and thy servant Uriah the Hittite is dead also. ²⁵Then David said unto the messenger, Thus shalt thou say unto Joab, Let not this thing displease thee, for the sword devoureth one as well as another: make thy battle more strong against the city, and overthrow it: and encourage thou him. ²⁶And when the wife of Uriah heard that Uriah her husband was dead, she mourned for her husband. ²⁷And when the mourning was past, David sent and fetched her to his house, and she became his wife, and bare him a son. But the thing that David had done displeased the LORD.

¹And the LORD sent Nathan unto David. And he came unto him, and said unto him, There were two men in one city; the one rich, and the other poor. ²The rich *man* had exceeding many flocks and herds: ³But the poor *man* had nothing, save one little ewe lamb, which he had bought and nourished up: and it grew up together with him, and with his children; it did eat of his own meat, and drank of his own cup, and lay in his bosom, and was unto him as a daughter. ⁴And there came a traveller unto the rich man, and he spared to take of his own flock and of his own herd, to dress for the wayfaring man that was come unto him; but took the poor man's lamb, and dressed it for the man that was come to him. ⁵And David's anger was greatly kindled against the man; and he said to Nathan, *As* the LORD liveth, the man that hath done this *thing* shall surely die: ⁶And he shall restore the lamb fourfold, because he did this thing, and because he had no pity. ⁷And Nathan said to David, Thou *art* the man. Thus saith the LORD God of Israel, I anointed thee king over Israel, and I delivered thee out of the hand of Saul; ⁸And I gave thee thy master's house, and thy master's wives into thy bosom, and gave thee the house of Israel and of Judah; and if *that had been* too little, I would moreover have given unto thee such and such things. ⁹Wherefore hast thou despised the commandment of the LORD, to do evil in his sight? thou hast killed Uriah the Hittite with the sword, and hast taken his wife *to be* thy wife, and hast slain him with the sword of the children of Ammon. ¹⁰Now therefore the sword shall never depart from thine house; because thou hast despised me, and hast taken the wife of Uriah the Hittite to be thy wife. ¹¹Thus saith the LORD, Behold, I will raise up evil against thee out of thine own house, and I will take thy wives before thine eyes, and give *them* unto thy neighbour, and he shall lie with thy wives in the sight of this sun. ¹²For thou didst *it* secretly: but I will do this thing before all Israel, and before the sun. ¹³And David said unto Nathan, I have sinned against the LORD. And Nathan said unto David,

The LORD also hath put away thy sin; thou shalt not die. [14]Howbeit, because by this deed thou hast given great occasion to the enemies of the LORD to blaspheme, the child also *that is* born unto thee shall surely die.

[15]And Nathan departed unto his house. And the LORD struck the child that Uriah's wife bare unto David, and it was very sick. [16]David therefore besought God for the child; and David fasted, and went in, and lay all night upon the earth. [17]And the elders of his house arose, *and went* to him, to raise him up from the earth: but he would not, neither did he eat bread with them. [18]And it came to pass on the seventh day, that the child died. And the servants of David feared to tell him that the child was dead: for they said, Behold, while the child was yet alive, we spake unto him, and he would not hearken unto our voice: how will he then vex himself, if we tell him that the child is dead? [19]But when David saw that his servants whispered, David perceived that the child was dead: therefore David said unto his servants, Is the child dead? And they said, He is dead. [20]Then David arose from the earth, and washed, and anointed *himself*, and changed his apparel, and came into the house of the LORD, and worshipped: then he came to his own house; and when he required, they set bread before him, and he did eat. [21]Then said his servants unto him, What thing *is* this that thou hast done? thou didst fast and weep for the child, *while it was* alive; but when the child was dead, thou didst rise and eat bread. [22]And he said, While the child was yet alive, I fasted and wept: for I said, Who can tell *whether* God will be gracious to me, that the child may live? [23]But now he is dead, wherefore should I fast? can I bring him back again? I shall go to him, but he shall not return to me. [24]And David comforted Bathsheba his wife, and went in unto her, and lay with her: and she bare a son, and he called his name Solomon: and the LORD loved him. [25]And he sent by the hand of Nathan the prophet; and he called his name Jedidiah, because of the LORD.

Now some of the same questions apply as before:

1. What does the narrative show about the private David?

2. What does the narrative show about the public David?

3. Another question that seems to promote good discussion is, Why can't the poet, the sweet psalmist of Israel, recognize the meaning in Nathan's good parable?

The reason for the public-private questions is that the last words of David are both public and private. The public words are even given a musical setting. The one-beat double forte of a bass B played in three octaves, and then a brief glissando to a unison D of a full choir, heralds the bombastic pronouncement of David: "He that ruleth over men must be just . . . ruling in the fear of God." The passage that follows in Randall Thompson's choral work, however, makes the first blast seem like an apology for a life of hypocrisy. It is a soft, flowing, poetic interpretation worthy of the poet laureate David, the sweet psalmist of Israel. "And he shall be as the light of the morning, when the sun riseth, even a morning without clouds; as the tender grass springing out of the earth by clear shining after rain."

There is a good recording of the Thompson anthem by the Mormon Tabernacle Choir. It is track 2 on side 2 of "The Lord is My Shepherd" released by Columbia Masterworks (MT 6019).

The public last words of David (2 Samuel 23: 1–5) are as follows:

> ¹Now these *be* the last words of David. David the son of Jesse said, and the man *who was* raised up on high, the anointed of the God of Jacob, and the sweet psalmist of Israel, said, ²The Spirit of the LORD spake by me, and his word *was* in my tongue. ³The God of Israel said, the Rock of Israel spake to me, He that ruleth over men *must be* just, ruling in the fear of God. ⁴And *he shall be* as the light of the morning, *when* the sun riseth, *even* a morning without clouds; *as* the tender grass *springing* out of the earth by clear shining after rain. ⁵Although my house *be* not so with God; yet he hath made with me an everlasting covenant, ordered in all *things*, and sure: for *this is* all my salvation, and all *my* desire, although he make *it* not to grow.

The private last words (1 Kings 2: 1–10) are to David's son Solomon:

> ¹Now the days of David drew nigh that he should die; and he charged Solomon his son, saying, ²I go the way of all the earth: be thou strong therefore, and shew thyself a man; ³And keep the charge of the LORD thy God, to walk in his ways, to keep his statutes, and his commandments, and his judgments, and his testimonies, as it is written in the law of Moses, that thou mayest prosper in all that thou doest, and whithersoever thou turnest thyself: ⁴That the LORD may continue his word which he spake concerning me, saying, If thy children take heed to their way, to walk before me in truth with all their heart and with all their soul, there shall not fail thee (said he) a man on the throne of Israel. ⁵Moreover thou knowest also what Joab the son of Zeruiah did to me, *and* what he did to the two captains of the hosts of Israel, unto Abner the son of Ner, and unto Amasa the son of Jether, whom he slew, and shed the blood of war in peace, and put the blood of war upon his girdle that *was* about his loins, and in his shoes that *were* on his feet. ⁶Do therefore according to thy wisdom, and let not his hoar head go down to the grave in peace. ⁷But shew kindness unto the sons of Barzillai the Gileadite, and let them be of those that eat at thy table: for so they came to me when I fled because of Absalom thy brother. ⁸And, behold, *thou hast* with thee Shimei the son of Gera, a Benjamite of Bahurim, which cursed me with a grievous curse in the day when

> I went to Mahanaim: but he came down to meet me at Jordan, and
> I sware to him by the LORD, saying, I will not put thee to death with
> the sword. ⁹Now therefore hold him not guiltless: for thou *art* a
> wise man, and knowest what thou oughtest to do unto him; but
> his hoar head bring thou down to the grave with blood. ¹⁰So David
> slept with his fathers, and was buried in the city of David.

Thus we have a paradox to discuss. On the one hand, a king must
be just and fear God. On the other hand he orders the murder of two
people while on his death bed.

I add some context to the discussion so that students know a bit
about these two victims, since Solomon does as he is told by his father. Joab is one of David's closest commanders. He took care of the
Bathsheba-Uriah problem by putting Uriah in the front lines so he
would be killed. He is also a close relative to David, the son of David's
sister Zeruiah. Some suggest that Joab was the military power behind David's throne.

But Joab crossed David at least three times and was part of the
cabal that tried to put Solomon's older brother, Adonijah, on the throne
after David's death. The three unsanctioned murders committed by
Joab include the murders of two commanders in the army—Abner,
the son of Ner (2 Samuel 3:26–30) and Amasa, the son of Jether (2
Samuel 20:4–13). Most serious of all, Joab had Absolom killed when
David had ordered otherwise (2 Samuel 18:1–15). Absolom was
David's rebellious son.

Shimei belong to the household of Saul, who lost the kingship to
David. Once Shimei cursed David and threw stones and dust at him
(2 Samuel 16:5–13). Shimei later asked for forgiveness when he met
David on his return to Jerusalem after Absalom's revolt (2 Samuel
19:16–23). David made an oath and granted Shimei clemency but
apparently had second thoughts about this on his deathbed.

1. Can the two sets of last words be reconciled?
2. Is the death order just a political expediency that must occur if
   Solomon is to maintain the kingdom?
3. Is David's motive revenge?
4. Who is David, really? At the end, what does he stand for? Is
   David different in public than in private?

After musing over the last words, I generally take one of two
approaches. I let students write the last words of someone. The idea
is to put words in the mouth of someone else, words that seem to
capture the essence of a life. They usually choose historical figures

or modern icons of music and film. I have on occasion asked students to write their own last words. It is only fair to mention that writing one's own last words as an assignment hasn't always met with a positive response. Sometimes I've learned things I really don't want to know. Nevertheless, that a life should have an epitaph that punctuates its quality and dreams and ambitions is a concept students like to discuss.

Chapter 15

RECOGNIZING SATIRE: IS JONAH A FISH STORY OR WHAT?

There is more than one way to read a story, especially a fish story. Reading it as satire may be the most difficult for students, but it seems to help them if they recognize that the story can be read as history, parable, short story, prophecy, allegory, and satire. For Steven C. Walker, Jonah is the best joke in the Bible. Walker's "Jonah as Joke: A Glance at God's Sense of Humor," is included in this chapter.

One would think that students would be good at recognizing satire. Their daily discourse is laced with sarcasm, a first cousin of satire, and humor is the staff of life for some students. They say one thing and mean another. The compliment is often the ultimate insult. However, satire is more subtle than sarcasm and that is part of the reason we read Jonah and read it as humor. It is a short story, only four chapters. (The citation is from the KJV except that I have put the poetic second chapter in verse.)

The Book of Jonah

Chapter 1

¹NOW the word of the LORD came unto Jonah the son of Amittai, saying, ²Arise, go to Nineveh, that great city, and cry against it; for their wickedness is come up before me. ³But Jonah rose up to flee unto Tarshish from the presence of the LORD, and went down to Joppa;

and he found a ship going to Tarshish: so he paid the fare thereof, and went down into it, to go with them unto Tarshish from the presence of the LORD.

⁴But the LORD sent out a great wind into the sea, and there was a mighty tempest in the sea, so that the ship was like to be broken. ⁵Then the mariners were afraid, and cried every man unto his god, and cast forth the wares that [were] in the ship into the sea, to lighten [it] of them. But Jonah was gone down into the sides of the ship; and he lay, and was fast asleep. ⁶So the shipmaster came to him, and said unto him, What meanest thou, O sleeper? arise, call upon thy God, if so be that God will think upon us, that we perish not. ⁷And they said every one to his fellow, Come, and let us cast lots, that we may know for whose cause this evil [is] upon us. So they cast lots, and the lot fell upon Jonah. ⁸Then said they unto him, Tell us, we pray thee, for whose cause this evil [is] upon us; What [is] thine occupation? and whence comest thou? what [is] thy country? and of what people [art] thou? ⁹And he said unto them, I [am] an Hebrew; and I fear the LORD, the God of heaven, which hath made the sea and the dry [land]. ¹⁰Then were the men exceedingly afraid, and said unto him, Why hast thou done this? For the men knew that he fled from the presence of the LORD, because he had told them.

¹¹Then said they unto him, What shall we do unto thee, that the sea may be calm unto us? for the sea wrought, and was tempestuous. ¹²And he said unto them, Take me up, and cast me forth into the sea; so shall the sea be calm unto you: for I know that for my sake this great tempest [is] upon you. ¹³Nevertheless the men rowed hard to bring [it] to the land; but they could not: for the sea wrought, and was tempestuous against them. ¹⁴Wherefore they cried unto the LORD, and said, We beseech thee, O LORD, we beseech thee, let us not perish for this man's life, and lay not upon us innocent blood: for thou, O LORD, hast done as it pleased thee. ¹⁵So they took up Jonah, and cast him forth into the sea: and the sea ceased from her raging. ¹⁶Then the men feared the LORD exceedingly, and offered a sacrifice unto the LORD, and made vows. ¹⁷Now the LORD had prepared a great fish to swallow up Jonah. And Jonah was in the belly of the fish three days and three nights.

Chapter 2

¹THEN Jonah prayed unto the LORD his God out of the fish's belly, ²And said,

I cried by reason of mine affliction unto the LORD,
    and he heard me;
out of the belly of hell cried I,
    [and] thou heardest my voice.
³For thou hadst cast me into the deep,
    in the midst of the seas;
and the floods compassed me about:
    all thy billows and thy waves passed over me.
⁴Then I said, I am cast out of thy sight;
    yet I will look again toward thy holy temple.
⁵The waters compassed me about, [even] to the soul:
    the depth closed me round about,
    the weeds were wrapped about my head.
⁶I went down to the bottoms of the mountains;
    the earth with her bars [was] about me for ever:
    yet hast thou brought up my life from corruption, O
LORD my God.
⁷When my soul fainted within me
    I remembered the LORD:
    and my prayer came in unto thee,
        into thine holy temple.
⁸They that observe lying vanities
    forsake their own mercy.
⁹But I will sacrifice unto thee
    with the voice of thanksgiving;
I will pay [that] that I have vowed.
    Salvation [is] of the LORD.
¹⁰And the LORD spake unto the fish, and it vomited out Jonah upon the dry [land].

Chapter 3

¹AND the word of the LORD came unto Jonah the second time, saying, ²Arise, go unto Nineveh, that great city, and preach unto it the preaching that I bid thee. ³So Jonah arose, and went unto Nineveh, according to the word of the LORD. Now Nineveh was an exceeding great city of three days' journey. ⁴And Jonah began to enter into the

city a day's journey, and he cried, and said, Yet forty days, and Nineveh shall be overthrown.

⁵So the people of Nineveh believed God, and proclaimed a fast, and put on sackcloth, from the greatest of them even to the least of them. ⁶For word came unto the king of Nineveh, and he arose from his throne, and he laid his robe from him, and covered [him] with sackcloth, and sat in ashes. ⁷And he caused [it] to be proclaimed and published through Nineveh by the decree of the king and his nobles, saying, Let neither man nor beast, herd nor flock, taste any thing: let them not feed, nor drink water: ⁸But let man and beast be covered with sackcloth, and cry mightily unto God: yea, let them turn every one from his evil way, and from the violence that [is] in their hands. ⁹Who can tell [if] God will turn and repent, and turn away from his fierce anger, that we perish not? ¹⁰And God saw their works, that they turned from their evil way; and God repented of the evil, that he had said that he would do unto them; and he did [it] not.

Chapter 4

¹BUT it displeased Jonah exceedingly, and he was very angry. ²And he prayed unto the LORD, and said, I pray thee, O LORD, [was] not this my saying, when I was yet in my country? Therefore I fled before unto Tarshish: for I knew that thou [art] a gracious God, and merciful, slow to anger, and of great kindness, and repentest thee of the evil. ³Therefore now, O LORD, take, I beseech thee, my life from me; for [it is] better for me to die than to live. ⁴Then said the LORD, Doest thou well to be angry?

⁵So Jonah went out of the city, and sat on the east side of the city, and there made him a booth, and sat under it in the shadow, till he might see what would become of the city. ⁶And the LORD God prepared a gourd, and made [it] to come up over Jonah, that it might be a shadow over his head, to deliver him from his grief. So Jonah was exceeding glad of the gourd. ⁷But God prepared a worm when the morning rose the next day, and it smote the gourd that it withered. ⁸And it came to pass, when the sun did arise, that God prepared a vehement east wind; and the sun beat upon the head of Jonah, that he fainted, and wished in himself to die, and said, [It is] better for me to die than to live. ⁹And God said to Jonah, Doest thou well to be angry for the gourd? And he said, I do well to be angry, [even] unto

death. [10]Then said the LORD, Thou hast had pity on the gourd, for the which thou hast not laboured, neither madest it grow; which came up in a night, and perished in a night: [11]And should not I spare Nineveh, that great city, wherein are more than sixscore thousand persons that cannot discern between their right hand and their left hand; and [also] much cattle?

Parallelism

In the section on poetry, students discovered parallelism. Jonah is structured in such a way that it is symmetrically parallel. This has been pointed out by various commentators over the years. One of the best extended rhetorical criticisms of the Jonah story is by Phyllis Trible, *Rhetorical Criticism: Context, Method, and the Book of Jonah*. The book is recommended for teachers who wish to teach the structure of Jonah.

Trible's analysis is much more detailed and better argued than what I teach at the introductory level. It is found on pages 111 and 112 and in an extended appendix in her book.

The following is the parallel version I teach:

Chapter 1	Chapter 3
Verse 2: There is a call (arise and go).	Verse 2: There is a second call (arise and go).
Verse 3: Jonah arises but goes to Tarshish (identified as Spain by Malbim).	Verse 3: Jonah arises and goes to Nineveh (the capital of Assyria on the eastern bank of the Tigris).
Verse 4: God *acts* and causes a storm	Verse 4: Jonah *acts* and prophesies destruction.
Verse 5: Sailors call to their god.	Verse 5: Ninevites believe Jonah, fast, and put on sackcloth.
Verses 7–14: Sailors seek the will of God and pray that they won't perish.	Verses 6–8: King wears sackcloth and seeks God's will. He orders the people to pray that they don't perish.
Verse 15: The storm stops.	God spares the city.

cont.

Chapter 2	Chapter 4
Jonah is saved.	Jonah is angry.
Jonah prays.	Jonah prays.
God acts.	God acts.

Story or Parable

It is good to point out the symmetry to make the point that maybe this is a carefully crafted story, perhaps not a history or an allegory. Most of the symmetry is synonymous. Since a few of the parallels are not synonymous, I suggest that these are the ones to which an imaginative author is suggesting we pay close attention.

It may be that an author had an entertainment/teaching motive rather than recording history or writing a lesson, or it may be that the story is a lesson. At any rate there seems to be some poetic form and some other poetic qualities. Jonah means "dove." The teacher may wish to ask students to identify dovelike qualities in Jonah as, suggested in Buttrick:

- Does he moan and lament when in distress? (Nahum 2:7; Isaiah 38:14, 59:11)
- Perhaps he seeks secure refuge in the mountains. (Ezekiel 7:16; Psalms 55: 6–8)
- Is he easily put to flight—flighty as a dove?
- Is he like a dove of peace?
- Is he like the Holy Spirit, which descends in the form of a dove? (Matthew 3:15)
- Is he like the dove released from the ark by Noah? (Genesis 8:8–12)

There are symbols in the story. Ninevah represents evil that repents. Jonah may be symbolic of the mission of a prophet. The sailors are gentiles, with all that that implies. And besides the great fish that rescues the reluctant prophet, there are other critters and symbolic objects that are actually characters in the story. There is a treelike plant, complete with a worm, that offers temporary protection. And there is an east wind that makes conditions on the side of the mountain difficult for Jonah. The story is written is such a way as to invite the reader to anthropomorphize these things and make them actors in the tale.

The most important question if Jonah is a parable is "What does it mean?" Perhaps it is a lesson in forgiveness and mercy or a lesson that one can't run from God. Even prophets can't hide. The usual parabolic reading suggests that we should be like Jonah in some way. What way?

History

It could be that we've been too hasty. Perhaps this is a history. Perhaps this is a factual account in spite of Ira Gershwin's "Porgy and Bess":

> It ain't necessarily so: it ain't necessarily so.
> De t'ings dat yo' li'ble to read in de Bible,
> It ain't necessarily so.

> Oh, Jonah, he lived in de whale; oh, Jonah, he lived in de whale.
> Fo he made his home in dat fish's abdomen.
> O Jonah, he lived in de whale.

There is evidence. At least, there is safety in numbers, and Jonah is mentioned in other Bible passages. Jesus mentions him in Matthew 12:39–41 and he is given a father, Amittai in 2 Kings 14:25. He isn't the first or last prophet to undertake a journey to unfaithful people. Elijah and Elisha undertake similar missions to the unfaithful, and there are similar rescue motifs in Daniel's divine rescue from the lion's den and the rescue of the three men from the fiery furnace.

Of course there are also problems considering this as a historical narrative. First is the idea that someone can live for three days in the belly of a great fish. There are more miracles that could be suspect: the conversion of an entire city after a one sentence sermon, a plant that grows up in the night, animals that wear sackcloth and ashes. On the other hand, there are events more miraculous than this in the Bible that are read as historical by many readers.

Also a bit confusing is the fact that Jonah's psalm from the belly of the great fish is a song of thanksgiving. He is offering thanks for his deliverance and hasn't been delivered yet. Not only is the thanks offered before the deliverance, it is in a crafty poetic chiasmus, according to Trible's analysis (163–173).

Allegory

The word *allegory* comes from two Greek works: *allos* meaning "other" and *agoreuein* meaning "to speak." An allegory is a story whose characters, things, and happenings have another meaning. Allegories are written to explain ideas about good and evil, or about moral or religious principles. What makes a piece of writing an allegory is that the characters actually *become* what they stand for (Padgett 7).

Jonah means "dove." This is a traditional symbol of Israel and may be taken as a hint that the story can be read allegorically. Jonah becomes Israel. This is a view taken in The *Interpreter's Dictionary of the Bible*:

We may see in Jonah's flight to Tarshish Israel's avoidance of its mission before the Exile, turning its back upon God, embarking upon the sea of world politics in the ship of diplomatic intrigue. The storm which broke upon it and upon the Gentile world (the sailors), when the center of power moved from Assyria to Babylon, was followed, for Israel, by exile in Babylon (the whale; cf. Jeremiah 51:34). Delivered from this chastening experience, Israel, having turned to God in captivity like Jonah, has the task of proclaiming its faith to its pagan neighbors. (Buttrick 967)

Satire

Satire is the exposure of human vice or folly through rebuke or ridicule. It can appear in any form or genre, including expository prose, narrative, poetry or visionary writing. It can be either a minor part of a work or the main point. It might consist of an entire book (e.g., Amos [or Jonah]), or it can be as small as an individual proverb. One of the conventions of satire is the freedom to exaggerate, overstate or oversimplify to make a satiric point. Overall, satire is a subversive form that questions the status quo, unsettles people's thought patterns and aims to bake people uncomfortable. (Buttrick 762)

The following commentary does unsettle, overstate, and is subversive to many modern readers who view it as anti-Semitic.

the book is a satire–the exposure of human vice through ridicule. In fact, the book is a handbook on how *not* to be a prophet. The object of satiric attack is the kind of nationalistic zeal that tried to make God the exclusive property of Israel, refusing to accept the universality of God's grace (i.e., its transcendence of national bounds). The satiric norm—the standard by which Jonah's ethnocentrism is judged—is God's character and the breadth of his grace. In this story Jonah is a great nationalist, but God is a great internationalist. The satiric tone is light and mocking as Jonah is held up to scorn by being rendered ridiculous–a pouting prophet foolish enough to undertake an anti-quest to run away from God. (Buttrick 458)

Students better understand the less strident satire if they see the gentle humor. Following is the work of Steven C. Walker of Brigham Young University. It is very funny the way he tells it and it is usually good advice to let funny people have the last word.

Jonah as Joke: A Glance at God's Sense of Humor

When it comes to biblical humor, we miss the point. In fact, we mostly miss the humor. The Bible is the last place most modern readers would find a laugh. But the main reason we fail to find it there is that the Bible is the last place we'd look. Given how persistently humor smiles and chuckles and sometimes laughs right out loud in virtually every book of the Bible, it's astonishing how consistently we manage to overlook it. It's also unfortunate. Humor informs biblical texts. To miss the humor of the Bible is to miss not only much of its fun, but much of its meaning.

We are so bent on revering this literary text instead of enjoying it that we may have developed a cultural blind spot toward biblical humor. The problem is one of perspective; we view the Bible through sanctimonious glasses. Consider what a difference it would make, for example, if in place of Gregory Peck in our Cecil B. DeMille version of *David and Bathsheba* we cast Jerry Lewis.

Yet the Jerry Lewis version may better illuminate the biblical context. When in 1 Samuel 16:7 God directs the disappointed prophet to "Look not on [David's] countenance . . . for man looketh on the outward appearance, but the Lord looketh on the heart," Lewis's buck teeth, crossed eyes, and dopey grin drive home the point better than Gregory Peck's perfect features. And certainly Lewis would be more appropriate as the teenage David trying on the armor of that mighty Saul who "from his shoulders and upward . . . was higher than any of the people" (1 Samuel 9:2)—the Jerry Lewis David is easier to imagine with that oversize mail dragging on the ground, helmet down over his eyes, overweight spear clutched desperately in both hands.

Anyone who has seen Richard Pryor in *Holy Moses* or heard Bill Cosby's rendition of Noah will recognize that there can be as much insight as laughter in humorous readings of the Bible. Biblical humor is as much concerned with informing us as delighting us. That capacity of humor to illuminate biblical meaning is easiest to see in the funniest biblical character—not David, nor Cosby's Noah nor Pryor's Moses, not (to mention but a few of the prime nominees) Peter nor Eve nor Samson nor Balaam nor Sarah nor Herod nor even Gideon. The funniest biblical character is Jonah.

And the Book of Jonah is the funniest book of the Bible. Its structure is deliberately comic. On Michael Tueth's list of the five key comic elements in scripture, *Jonah* scores high in every category. The book features "the downfall of the serious"—it's harder to get much more serious than Jonah, with his endless groanings of "it is better for me to die than to live" (4:3, 4:8, 4:9). *Jonah* features the comic "element of surprise" in the prophet's flight, in the storm, in the whale, in the Ninevite conversion, in the withering gourd. *Jonah* "emphasizes the value of innocence and childlikeness" in its concern for those morally untutored Ninevites who "cannot discern between their right hand and their left hand" (4:11). The story "reverses previously held assumptions and values"; the whole point of the book is that God's love extends beyond the limits Hebrew prophets had imagined until *Jonah*. And, to complete its perfect alignment with Tueth's catalogue of the comic, *Jonah* "thrives" on "physical danger": "Harold Lloyd hanging from the clock, Abbot and Costello meeting Frankenstein, or even the fat man slipping on the banana peel" (Tueth 2) have nothing on Jonah going overboard or disappearing into the whale's gullet or venturing singlehanded into mighty Nineveh.

But it isn't only that *Jonah* fits abstract literary categories of the comic; the book is genuinely funny in its own right. Every scene in this story invites a smile—the picture of the recalcitrant prophet, for example, fresh from the belly of the whale, reeking of whale vomit, trailing seaweed and barnacles and old fishheads, bleached of all his color by gastric juices, his robe shrunk up to his knees and elbows by that interior humidity, disheveled and disgruntled, trudging into Nineveh muttering his message of doom in a language the Ninevites can't even understand.

Scenes that laughable dominate the book. The first chapter alone proposes enough ridiculous situations for a Marx Brothers' movie. God calls Jonah to the Ninevite "Mission" at a time when there were no foreign missions. God says to go east; Jonah goes due west, as far as he can. God pulls out all stops to threaten Jonah with a "mighty tempest in the sea, so that the ship was like to be broken" (1:4); Jonah remains "fast asleep" (1:5). The heathen shipmaster urges God's prophet to "call upon thy God" (1:6). God demands that Jonah be thrown into a watery grave, then rescues him. For the means of that gracious rescue, God devises the decidedly ungracious "belly of the fish" (1:17).

From its initial parody of the prophetic call to its concluding picture of those "much cattle" (4:11) penitently attired in sackcloth and ashes, *Jonah* is a funny book. And the funniness matters. As its pervasiveness suggests, the humor in *Jonah* is not incidental, not superficial decoration. The humor is not only fun, but functional. There is moral to the *Jonah* joke.

To a Hebrew of the fifth century B.C.E., the very premise of the story is absurd. *Jonah* is a midrashic tale, in the usual form of "imagine if." But in *Jonah's* case the "imagine if" is unimaginable. The story's narrative situation is impossible for Jonah's Hebrew audience; the tale is for the Israelite of the time an invitation to think about the unthinkable. God in those days just did not go around inviting heathen nations to repent. Even if He had, the hopeless heathens never would have repented. As Leslie Allen suggests, "The audience is asked to ponder a theological riddle: what would have happened if no less a den of foreign devils than Nineveh had repented?" (82).

The opening scene of the book sets the tone of that playing with biblical convention. The first thing we see in Jonah is a parody of the prophetic call. Prophetic convention dictated a certain shy reluctance in responding to the Lord's call; hesitance hallmarks responses to the call by such model prophets as Isaiah (6:5) and Jeremiah (1:6) and even Moses, who says demurely to the burning bush: "I am not eloquent . . . I am slow of speech, and of a slow tongue" (Exodus 4:10). But Jonah carries that traditional reluctance to extremes that suggest parody. When the Lord calls Jonah, he refuses to answer at all. "Jonah's silence has the parodic impact of silence after the question 'Do you take this woman to be your lawfully wedded wife?'" (Miles 172).

Another indication that the humor of the Book of Jonah is deliberate is that it is climactic; it gets funnier as it goes along. The closing statement of *Jonah* is not so much a statement as a punchline, its whimsicality underlined by its form as a question. And that concluding question is quietly hilarious: "And should not I," God wonders out loud to Jonah in that closing verse, "spare Nineveh, that great city, wherein are more than sixscore thousand persons that cannot discern between their right hand and their left hand; and also much cattle?"

That great exit line seems to me funny in at least five ways. The quantification is an insult to Jonah's accountant mentality, an early Hebrew equivalent of, "You want justice, I'll give you justice times 120,000—"the quality of mercy is not strained," let alone the quantity. The reference to Jonah's relative sophistication, the implication that the prophet of the Lord ought to know better than "persons that cannot discern between their right hand and their left hand," hints that, morally speaking, "Jonah may not know his gourd from a hole in the ground." (Whitney 1). The reversal of Jonah's earlier "I told you so"—his insistent "was not this my saying, when I was yet in my country" (4:2)—turns the tables on Jonah with a "he who laughs last laughs best" twist.

The most obvious source of humor in that closing line is the animal reference. That anticlimactic apparent afterthought, "and also much cattle," is wonderfully prepared for by earlier jokes hinging upon creatures ranging from great whales to tiny worms. God as Trickster is not missing a trick. God's compassionate awareness extends to all creatures—not so much as a sparrow shall "fall on the ground without your Father" (Matthew 10:29). That "also much cattle" jibe suggests something very close to: "Jonah, I'd save the city despite— or even to spite—your petulance for the sake of its camels or even its cats, let alone its people. Especially," the text smiles between its understated lines, "when those camels are so penitently dressed in sackcloth and ashes." Kelly McIlrath suspects that the humor of the bestial imagery runs still deeper, that "the worm referred to in 4:4 may be a simile for Jonah himself," that "Jonah is the worm that the Lord brought to Ninevah to perform the smiting" (1).

The funniest thing about that divine last word at the conclusion of *Jonah* is the direct moral that it gives to the story, like David Letterman heightening the intensity of a joke by patiently explaining the punchline to Paul Shafer. There is strong implication here of gentle divine ribbing: "The reason you have too little compassion, Jonah, is that you have no sense of humor." There is also strong implication that that is what God would have us have—both the sense of humor and the compassion to which this book so warmly relates it. That anticlimactic closure focuses us back upon the second verse of this final chapter, where Jonah in his condemnation of God ironically vivifies the moral of the story: "I knew that thou art a gracious God, and merciful, slow to anger, and of great kindness, and repentest thee of the evil" (4:2).

That is the greatest joke of all in *Jonah*. What for Jonah is condemnation is for us—and for God—commendation. Jonah reprimands God for His unreliability. The omniscient and omnipotent Ruler of the Universe responds to Jonah's impertinent attempt to put Him in His divine place by gently allowing Jonah to put himself in his very human place with a smiling question about being humane: "Doest thou well to be angry?" (4:4). Jonah tells God how to be God; God shows Jonah how to be human. God invites Jonah out of his narrow theological certainties into life, into that risky and uncertain human life where things get unpredictable and as a result potentially funny.

The message of the book of *Jonah* is delivered with a divine smile that directly contrasts with Jonah's sullen message of doom to the Ninevites. That message is: live. The God of *Jonah*, much to His prophet's chagrin, transcends expectations. He urges us to expect the unexpected. Jonah reads that moral as "damned if you don't and damned if you do"; we are likelier to read it as God does: "blessed if you do, and blessed if you don't." Life with the God of *Jonah* is not far from C. S. Lewis's view of heaven—"better than we could ever imagine, and full of wonderful surprises" (17). Those surprises are chancy business, like casting lots on a deck pitching in storm so wild the dice don't have to be thrown. That undependability is an understandable threat to Jonah. But to us it is also a promise, a promise of fuller life, of God "come that ye might have life, and that ye might have it more abundantly" (John 10:10).

The laughter of the Book of Jonah urges us in the direction of that abundance, in the direction of those wonderful surprises. The laughter urges us to find a way to laugh at ourselves, to laugh off our restrictive expectations, to laugh away our confining certitudes about our just deserts. The humor informs us that things may not be as bound by our expectations as we'd expect, that the "first [could] be last; and the last . . . be first" (Matthew 19:30). "Among David's ancestors there may be a Ruth the Moabite, among the righteous a Job the Edomite; among the penitents a city of Nineveh" (Lacocque 94). "History would be more intelligible if God's word were the last word, final and unambiguous like a dogma or an unconditional decree . . . Yet, beyond justice and anger lies the mystery of compassion" (98)—and that compassion reveals itself in laughter.

The God of Jonah may be closer to us than we thought, closer even than we wanted. The point of His intersection with us is marked by laughter. Being "vomited out" by a great fish (2:10) is for Jonah trauma tinged with insult—"here's another fine mess you've gotten me into." For God the vomiting out is, like all of His acts in the book, an act of compassion. For the whale it's a relief—Jonah may have been "the worst case of indigestion he ever had" (Miller 1). For us, standing precariously between divine love and human selfishness, that incongruous juxtaposition of sublime possibilities and ridiculous actualities lies very close to laughter.

Robert Alter thinks the following:

> "The monotheistic revolution of biblical Israel . . . left little margin
> for neat and confident views about God . . . it repeatedly had to
> make sense of the intersection of incompatibles—the relative and
> the absolute, human imperfection and divine perfection, the brawl-
> ing chaos of historical experience and God's promise to fulfill a
> design in history. The biblical outlook is informed, I think, by a
> sense of stubborn contradiction, of a profound and ineradicable
> untidiness in the nature of things." (154)

Jonah is an invitation to that ineradicably untidy biblical outlook. Like every other book of the Bible—where we even more thoroughly manage to overlook the humor—*Jonah* is an invitation to life. I think that invitation depends upon laughter because life does, and because that God who invented life loves the laughter.

Chapter 16

Artists Imagine Bible Characters: Joseph as a Developing Character

There is so much that can be done with Joseph. He is in our culture, an archetypal foreigner in the court who helps and even saves a nation. In this respect he is like Esther and Daniel. As a foreigner, he may be like Henry Kissinger or Zbigniew Brzezinski or Madeleine Albright. His narrative is the longest of the Genesis narratives, and his story isn't just fragments and snippets here and there. It is, with the exception of Genesis 38, continuous. And even Genesis 38 is interjected to contrast Judah's sexual behavior—soliciting a "prostitute"—with Joseph's resisting the advances of his master's wife.

Joseph is probably more developed than any character in the Bible, even more than Job or Jesus. His story is like a biographical novel. He starts as the favorite son with dreams of greatness. His father's favoritism and his dreaming angers his brothers, who throw him into a pit, where he is removed by slavetraders and sold in Egypt. He is resilient. He wins the favor of foreign leaders and despite the difficulties he encounters, becomes right hand man to Pharaoh. The difficulties along the way include sibling rivalry, slavery, sexual harassment and imprisonment.

The *Encyclopaedia Judaica* makes the point that the Bible narrative of Joseph seems to be secular rather than religious:

> Most striking and, in fact, unique, is the secularistic complexion of
> the narrative. There are no miraculous or supernatural elements;
> no divine revelations are experienced by Joseph, who also had no

associations with altars or cultic sites. On the other hand, the discourse is permeated with the consciousness of God at work, and if there is no direct intervention by Him in human affairs, no doubt is left that the unfolding of events is the directed act of Providence.

We know the popular musical and the symbolic technicolor coat. There is so much that can be done with the Joseph narrative that I've tried over the years to focus on what he does best: (1) Joseph is a developing character, and (2) Joseph has a foil or two that makes him look even better.

The Developed Character

It is an old article of faith among literature teachers that "good readers are less interested in actions done by characters than in characters doing actions":

> Reading for character is more difficult than reading for plot, for character is much more complex, variable, and ambiguous. Anyone can repeat what a person has done in a story, but considerable skill may be needed to describe what a person *is*. (Perrine 65)

The goal in teaching the Joseph narrative is to discover what Joseph is by what he does. This is a challenge because Joseph is a developing character. He is different in the end than at the beginning. He goes from spoiled child to world leader. He is believably different because the change is clearly within his possibilities. He is motivated and there is sufficient time for the change (Perrine 69).

The story is in Genesis 37–45, except for chapter 38. I usually assign the entire narrative and then focus a lesson on the final scene, when Joseph, after testing his brothers, forgives them for their abuse of him. This final scene in Genesis 45 is printed here, but it really requires the context of the earlier events:

> ¹Then Joseph could not refrain himself before all them that stood by him; and he cried, Cause every man to go out from me. And there stood no man with him, while Joseph made himself known unto his brethren. ²And he wept aloud: and the Egyptians and the house of Pharaoh heard. ³And Joseph said unto his brethren, I *am* Joseph; doth my father yet live? And his brethren could not answer him; for they were troubled at his presence. ⁴And Joseph said unto his brethren, Come near to me, I pray you. And they came near. And he said, I *am* Joseph your brother, whom ye sold into

Egypt. [5]Now therefore be not grieved, nor angry with yourselves, that ye sold me hither: for God did send me before you to preserve life. [6]For these two years *hath* the famine *been* in the land: and yet *there are* five years, in the which *there shall* neither *be* earing nor harvest. [7]And God sent me before you to preserve you a posterity in the earth, and to save your lives by a great deliverance. [8]So now *it was* not you *that* sent me hither, but God: and he hath made me a father to Pharaoh, and lord of all his house, and a ruler throughout all the land of Egypt. [9]Haste ye, and go up to my father, and say unto him, Thus saith thy son Joseph, God hath made me lord of all Egypt: come down unto me, tarry not: [10]And thou shalt dwell in the land of Goshen, and thou shalt be near unto me, thou, and thy children, and thy children's children, and thy flocks, and thy herds, and all that thou hast: [11]And there will I nourish thee; for yet *there are* five years of famine; lest thou, and thy household, and all that thou hast, come to poverty. [12]And, behold, your eyes see, and the eyes of my brother Benjamin, that *it is* my mouth that speaketh unto you. [13]And ye shall tell my father of all my glory in Egypt, and of all that ye have seen; and ye shall haste and bring down my father hither. [14]And he fell upon his brother Benjamin's neck, and wept; and Benjamin wept upon his neck. [15]Moreover he kissed all his brethren, and wept upon them: and after that his brethren talked with him.

As an aside, Joseph is considered a prominent prophet in Islam. It is instructive for students to understand another view of him by reading sura (chapter) 12 of the Qur'an. The Moslem text isn't reprinted here, but a summary of the Islamic text from the CD-Rom version of the *Encyclopaedia Judaica* is helpful. The plot differences are interesting since the narratives are well developed in both sources:

Yusuf was one of Muhammad's most beloved characters; he consecrated a whole *sura* (the 12th) to him ("the Sura of Joseph"), which contains "the most beautiful tale," in 111 continuous verses. The tale begins with Jacob's warning to his son not to tell his dream of the sun, the moon, and the stars to his brothers because it might arouse their jealousy. Indeed, Joseph became the object of his brothers' hatred and they availed themselves of the first opportunity to throw him into the pit. Muhammad . . . embellishes . . . when he tells of Joseph's enticement by the wife of his master (Qitfir = Potiphar), whom Muhammad knows only by the name of al-Aziz ("the Mighty"; verses 30, 51). Joseph was saved from her designs because Allah was with him. His shirt, which was torn from behind, was definite proof that the woman had not protected herself from the intentions of Joseph, but that she had attacked and attempted to seize hold of him when he had fled from her presence. The Egyptian women mocked the stupid woman, and when the latter invited them to a feast, she presented each of them with a knife, together with the refreshments. She then ordered Joseph to appear before the guests, and when they looked upon him, they were so enraptured by his beauty that they cut their fingers with the knives. The tale then returns to its biblical course. Before Joseph was appointed head of the king's granaries, the woman came to Pharaoh and confessed that Joseph was one of the *al-\adiqin*, "the righteous" (verse 51), and that she had sought to entice him (similarly, the chief butler refers to him (Joseph) as *al-\iddiq*, "the righteous one"; verse 46). According to Speyer, this was due to the influence of a Syrian legend, so that Joseph would not desire vengeance against her and her husband, who had imprisoned him. Before the brothers went to Egypt for the second time, their father advised them not to enter together, through one gate (verse 67). The latter detail is taken from the Jewish *aggadah* (Gen[esis] R[abbah] 91:2).

After students have read the forgiveness scene from the Bible, they ask questions before watching three video versions of the same scene and a just-for-fun screening, a remix from the *Amazing Technicolor Dreamcoat*:

1. Why did Joseph test the brothers for so long before offering his forgiveness? He could have told them who he was the moment they first met in Egypt, but he required a return trip to Egypt so that his younger brother, Benjamin, could be present. He also tested the brothers by putting gold and a cup in their grain sacks. Why?

2. Why would Joseph forgive them at all? After all, they threw him into a pit, plotted to sell him into slavery, and told their father he was dead.

3. Based on what we see Joseph doing in this scene, what or who is he?

4. How is Joseph different in the end of the story from when he

was the little brother with dreams of greatness that so annoyed his brothers?

The first video interpretation of the scene is quite literal. It uses a narrator and the text of the KJV. *Joseph and His Brothers* is part of the New Media Bible filmed by a cooperative group from various Christian denominations called the Genesis Project. I haven't seen the collection in video stores but it is available from many churches, including Deseretbook.com.

The second reconciliation scene is from an older film version. *Joseph and His Brethren* is available in video stores. It was directed by Irving Rapper in 1962 and released on video in 1989. Geoffrey Horen, Robert Morley, and Belinda Lee are the main actors. This version is interesting because of changes in the text. Joseph's father, Jacob, is present in the reconciliation scene. Students can discuss how this effects the story. Most important, I want to know if this changes who Joseph is. The focus is on Joseph as a developing character and this scene is the climax of his development.

The third video is so available that it falls into shopping carts in discount stores. It is the Turner Broadcasting version titled *Joseph*. It is directed by Roger Young and stars Ben Kingsley, Paul Mercurio, Martin Landau and Lesley Ann Warren. This is the most emotional of the three versions. In it Joseph embraces each of the brothers in turn in the reconciliation scene. The music, setting, and drawn-out plot set the viewer up for the scene. Students sense that the emotion is a bit contrived in the movie, yet most seem to think that this version most closely presents the Bible text.

Since students usually rate this version as closest to the text, we ask: Based on what we see him doing in text and film, who is Joseph? Who is he in the different versions?

Just for fun and for at least one serious question, I like to show *Joseph Mega-Remix.* from the Premiere Collection Encore: Andrew Lloyd Webber, PolyGram Video, New York, 1992. The remix doesn't show the reconciliation scene, but one wonders if any scene could be taken seriously after the dancing in the aisles. The point, aside from sheer entertainment, is the same point made earlier in a citation from *Encyclopaedia Judaica*: "Most striking and, in fact, unique, is the secularistic complexion of the narrative. There are no miraculous or supernatural elements; no divine revelations are experienced by Joseph, who also had no associations with altars or cultic sites."

Thus Andrew Lloyd Webber has created a secular musical. It offers no religious message, but it is biblical. The same questions, however, are relevant: Who is Joseph in the musical? How is he like or unlike the biblical Joseph? Is he a developing character?

Joseph and His Foils

It isn't exactly fair. A foil should be from the same narrative. The Bible is a collection of narratives, even a collection of books, but we are used to thinking of it as one book. Maybe this illusion is justified long enough to teach about the literary foil.

Anyone who has shopped for jewelry knows what a foil is. Jewels are displayed in such a way as to make them look good. They used to be placed on a "foil" so that what is good about them would look even better. Nowadays the carefully lighted cases lined with velvet are foils for the jewels, which somehow look less when they are carried out into the honest light of day.

Literary foils do the same thing. One character accents another. A minor character can make a good but somewhat flawed protagonist look better, and Samson certainly makes Joseph look good. With Samson's help, we look past the spoiled-youngest-child Joseph and past the slow-to-forgive Joseph and admire the honest teller of dreams and forgiving world leader. The comparison has been made by many, but I'm indebted to E. Glenn Oscarson for many of these ideas.

Both men have a great start, as Joseph is "most loved" of his father and Samson is a Nazirite from his birth, consecrated to God. Both are destined to be saviors of their people. Joseph is to save his family from the famine, and Samson is to save his people from the Philistines. Further comparisons include the following:

- Joseph acknowledges the inspiration of God in his dreams, but Samson's contacts with God are through his parents.
- Joseph rejects the advances of Potiphar's wife, but sexual desire clearly motivates Samson.
- The life of Joseph is "serious and lofty," but "the life of Samson, in spite of its spectacular ending, is really rather funny." (Davis).
- On the way, Joseph translates dreams. Samson tosses off barnyard sayings and lame riddles.
- Joseph avoids Mrs. Potiphar, but Samson seeks foreign women.
- God blesses Joseph for his faithfulness, but Samson is left to fend for himself, until he brings the house down in the end.
- Joseph is brutally honest with his brothers, Pharaoh, and oth-

ers who ask for help. Samson doesn't know what truth is.

- Joseph has an attitude of service. Samson is into self-service.
- Revenge is not part of Joseph's character, but Samson represents the spirit of revenge. When his wife and father-in-law were burnt, he reacted and killed.

The most important point of comparison is that Joseph is a developing character and Samson is not. Joseph matures from one who tattles on his brothers to one who forgives the most personal wrongdoings of his brothers. In the end he saves his family. Samson is predictably the same from beginning to end. As one student put it, "he never grows up."

Chapter 17

TEACHING THE BIBLE AS MYTH: MYTH IS WHY WE BELIEVE

I generally don't sense that students in my undergraduate Bible as literature class are really challenged until about five minutes after I take roll call on the first day of class. The challenge comes as I mention in passing that the course will consider the issue of myth and the narratives of the Bible. I say we will study biblical "myth" and they hear "untrue." I say that we swim in a surging sea of experience that requires the buoyant support of mythic symbols, and they check to see what other courses fill the Humanities and Arts general education requirement.

I respect these students and their often literal Bible reading. Surveys show that many of us are very literal Bible readers. In a 1998 survey, 34% of people in the United States who were given the following three choices selected the first:

- The Bible is the actual word of God and is to be taken literally, word for word.

- The Bible is the inspired word of God, but not everything should be taken literally word for word.

- The Bible is an ancient book of fables, legends, history, and moral precepts recorded by man. (Seaberry and Anderson)

Teachers usually read literally with students and wrestle with difficult passages. Teachers can help students by showing that one way of wrestling is to read the Bible as myth. This biblical myth explains why we believe.

I have affection for the students who struggle, and I don't want to be a professorial iconoclast who breaks their fragile images, which are still wanting the refined fire of study and experience. Although good scholarship requires that those who study willingly ask any question about any text, being a teacher also requires that the teacher only break an image that can be replaced with something better, and I am often in no position to replace what I could easily tear down. Besides, inflicting damage on fragile images would also be self-destructive.

A homiletic, if not literary, reading of Matthew 12:43–45 and Luke 11:24–26 may make my point. When an evil spirit is driven out of a person and there is nothing to replace it, seven other spirits more wicked than the first enter and dwell there. An idea can be driven out of a student by professorial force or by new ideas encountered in new texts, but if it is not replaced by something with the help of a teacher, seven ideas worse than the first may take its place. The point is that I'm trying to be helpful when suggesting that we read the Bible as myth.

Driving out the idea that reading myth is the same as reading fiction is not helpful unless replaced with a better idea. Showing how we read and live myth is a more modest goal. Perhaps a more modest goal than driving out bad ideas is to help students recognize new ways of looking for answers by closely reading the text. As they look, they may come to understand that mythic knowledge is a matter of recognition. In a sense we already know, but we often do not realize it without the help of myth. Then we say "That's it. That explains it for me."

When I say *myth* on this first day of class, I am talking about something beyond verifiable truth. *Myth* is what I use to explain what I believe. *Historicity* is not as important. "Why is there sin in the world?" For many of us the answer is in Genesis. It isn't in Genesis as a theological discourse on sin and it isn't there in a perfectly accurate historical transcription of events in 4004 B.C.E.. The answers are there because Genesis is mythic literature that speaks to us as only myths can. For many of our students the answer to the sin question could be in some other myth.

It is at this point that I can see behind the students' eyes. "Do I really need this class? This is Brigham Young University, isn't it?" Only a few are brave enough to confront me; that's a shame. I enjoy the visits of those few students who want to look me in the eye and ask. Some will seek refuge in the religion courses, where good people will patiently answer questions and will often call me to discover what I really said. In my previous experience at Snow College, I suppose some people wondered about church and state issues in a Bible as literature course taught at a state college. That was before they decided that the first five minutes proved that the Church is not involved in the issue of literature at secular colleges and that theology is not usually part of the discussion in secular Bible courses. The course is strictly a literature course at schools with no religious ties. That is sad in some ways.

In English 350 at Brigham Young University, there is freedom even to discuss "the m word" in the context of biblical literature, and there is the same freedom in public schools, where it is legal to teach any mythic narratives for their educational value. Reading the Bible as myth is not frightening to those who understand what myth means and who study in a value supportive environment. It doesn't take a parochial school to support student values.

The most terrible consequence of my use of "the m word" is for the student who mentally capitulates and thinks that it's "another class where I just have to put down what the teacher wants and hold my own belief or knowledge inside. Saying what I think will only penalize me in the class and open what I believe to ridicule and challenge by someone who could obviously clobber my true ideas with the weight of a grade and a Ph.D. in secular humanism." The answer to this student is that capitulation, not the myth, is the lie.

I try to say *myth* with some reverence. It is the *summon bonum*, the highest good. How else could I explain the most personal and sacred of beliefs? How else could I defend what I feel? Science and history, with reliance on the sandy foundation of the verifiable isn't enough. I need myth.

I need it as those who wrote the sacred texts, including the Bible, needed it to explain what they believe. I need it as did the people who positioned these texts in the middle of the myth that came before and the myth with legend that comes after.

Students must understand that my definition of myth is not my own invention. It has scholarly support. The first sentence of *Sacred Narrative* puts it this way: "A myth is a sacred narrative explaining how the world and humanity came to be in their present form" (Dundes 1). Notice that we don't need hard evidence to believe how the world and man came to be. I sometimes think that we confuse the purpose of mythic truth and scientific truth. The scientists try to discover *how* the world was created, and those who rely on myth seem more interested in *why*. What is the purpose of the world?

Genesis is the logical place to start with in myth, but it is so laden with emotion for many students that it is a serious land mine. It is the place from which people explain why they believe that Creation took seven days, why there is sin in the world, why there are so many languages, why capital punishment is either proscribed or prescribed, and even why women are inferior to men. We would do well to notice that these are *why* questions not *how* questions. Science seems to be best equipped to explain how things happen, and myth seem best to explore the truths of *why*.

I generally start somewhere other than Genesis when I teach, but I like to point out in passing that there are other places in the Bible than the first book to read about Creation, and the stories don't all agree. A good teacher resource for this is *Hebrew Myths: The Book of Genesis* by Robert Graves and Raphael Patai, which lists in chapter 2 five other creation myths of the Bible.

Modern writers try to distinguish between myth, legend, and folktale. Perhaps a look at this distinction will defuse the pejorative attitude we sometimes have toward myth. These definitions are from the same text cited above in an essay by William Bascom:

> Folktales are prose narratives which are regarded as fiction. (8)

> Myths are prose narratives which, in the society in which they are told, are considered to be truthful accounts of what happened in the remote past. (9)

> Legends are prose narratives which, like myths, are regarded as true by the narrator and his audience, but they are set in a period considered less remote, when the world was much as it is today. (9)

Let me give an example that I think teachers could use in a unit on mythology. I'll take my example away from the emotion of Genesis, creation, fall, and sin. Elijah will be my example. We'll go with Elijah to Mt. Carmel to discover the myth he confronted on the mountain and then follow him into our world to see what his myth explains for us. Surely Elijah, in a short and stormy career, establishes a myth for our day as he responds to the myth of his day. A prophet seems to come from nowhere, demands a drought in the name of Yahweh, is fed by ravens, raises the dead, calls down fire from heaven, and ascends to a heavenly realm in a chariot of fire, leaving his successor with his mantle. This is the stuff of myth that explains what we believe. It does what Elie Wiesel says that myth should do in the parable preface of *The Gates of the Forest*:

When the great Rabbi Israel Baal Shem-Tov saw misfortune threatening the Jews it was his custom to go into a certain part of the forest to meditate. There he would light a fire, say a special prayer, and the miracle would be accomplished and the misfortune averted.

Later, when his disciple, the celebrated Magid of Mezritch, had occasion, for the same reason, to intercede with heaven, he would go to the same place in the forest and say: "Master of the Universe, listen! I do not know how to light the fire, but I am still able to say the prayer." And again the miracle would be accomplished.

Still later, Rabbi Moshe-Leib of Sasov, in order to save his people once more, would go into the forest and say: "I do not know how to light the fire, I do not know the prayer, but I know the place and this must be sufficient." It was sufficient and the miracle was accomplished.

Then it fell to Rabbi Israel of Rizhyn to overcome misfortune. Sitting in his armchair, his head in his hands, he spoke to God: "I am unable to light the fire and I do not know the prayer; I cannot even find the place in the forest. All I can do is to tell the story, and this must be sufficient." And it was sufficient. (preface)

Maybe all of us who have forgotten how to call down the fire of Elijah to destroy false gods can read the story together, and that will be sufficient.

At this point it is probably a good idea to read the actual text, 1 Kings 17–19 and teachers may want to read it now in order to understand the remainder of this chapter.

The Mythology Before Elijah

To dig under the text for the mythic foundation is difficult. The sources are few and are not unbiased. The first source is the Hebrew Bible. The Christian Old Testament, in which people die for serving Baal. Baal and his worshipers are treated with disdain.

A second source is Sanchuniathon's *Phoenician History*. It would be an especially good source if we actually had it. In the work of Eusebius of Caesarea (c. 315 C.E.) called *Preparation for the Gospel*, we find fragments of the *Phoenician History*, written by the sage named Sanchuniathon who is reputed to have lived in Beirut before the Trojan War. It was translated by Philo of Byblos in about 100 C.E. and then it found its way to the writings of Eusebius. It is available in Greek or French. The fragments of Sanchuniathon's *Phoenician His-*

tory, as well as that which Eusebius and Philo of Byblos and others write about the history, have been collected and published by Carolus Mullerus in *Fragmenta Historicorum Graecorus*.

The discovery of the Ras Shamra tablets of ancient Ugarit were extremely important. Ancient Ugarit is an archeological site on the Mediterranean coast of Syria. The city Ugarit was the capital of a kingdom of the same name that flourished around 1400 B.C.E. The writings, discovered around 1929, reveal cultural, religious, and mythical traditions from the 14th through the 13th centuries B.C.E. The only problem is that Ugarit is a bit to the north of biblical Canaan. Ugarit even revealed a new but related language to Hebrew. It's close, and the texts are wonderful myths that can be supported by what we know of biblical mythology. However, to say that the Ugaritic texts are tales of the biblical Canaanite gods is helpful, but not quite accurate. One advantage of Ugarit not being Canaan is that it removes some of the problem faced by the public school teacher. At this point students are learning about the myths of Ugarit rather than the myths of the Bible.

With these cautions, it will help to look at the texts of Ugarit because the story here is at least continuous. *Canaanite Myths and Legends* by G.R. Driver is a good analysis and interpretation of the texts, and it also contains both a transliteration and a translation of the myths. Driver seems to have established the definitive translation of the Ras Shamra texts.

From this source (not the Bible) comes the following summary of the mythology to be confronted by Elijah at Mount Carmel. The central conflict of the poem is a struggle between Baal and Yam-Nahar, who is god of the seas and rivers, including the subterranean waters that are the source of lakes and rivers. Baal himself is god of lightning and thunder and rain. Athtar, a third god, has charge of springs and wells. All three, then, are responsible for water and, through this, the fertility of the earth.

The throne of El, the kindly white-haired old god who reigns in heaven, is vacant. The struggle for the throne involves an attack on Yam by Baal, who is victorious and obtains the right to build a palace or temple. There is some difficulty with the temple project because Baal wants no windows, and windows are required because through them rain is poured down to earth. This little detail may echo in another biblical place. "Bring ye all the tithes into the storehouse, that there may be meat in mine house, and prove me now herewith, saith the LORD of hosts, if I will not open you the windows of heaven, and pour you out a blessing, that there shall not be room enough to receive it" (Malachi 3:11). Don't jump to conclusions: the echo may be in the mind of the reader. The point, however, is that the tithes and sacrifice of the people open the windows of heaven in the Baal myth.

Baal then proceeds to found an empire by conquering a number of cities. An obstacle to this is Mot, the god of death. Since Mot will be responsible for all the deaths caused by drought when Baal is for any reason unwilling or unable to provide rain, Baal decides that Mot must be destroyed. While Baal is in the world below in search of Mot, rain ceases and life on earth fails. Baal himself is reported to be dead, and El therefore nominates Athtar, the old rival of Baal, to the vacant throne. Athtar just can't measure up. He is too small for the throne, unmarried, and a minor; and, in other words, artificial irrigation alone is insufficient for the earth.

Baal is revived and restored with the help of his sister and future consort Anat. Mot is defeated. He takes his sister Anat as wife and has offspring, including a bull. Because Baal is back in his heaven, rain falls on the earth. In the land of Canaan there is a seven-year cycle during which this myth is reenacted, and during the struggles there is no rain. Baal requires some sacrifice to assist in his struggles that will put him back in his aspect of rain god.

Robert Alter in *The Art of Biblical Narrative* offers another good reminder of why we need to be careful looking in for biblical mythology at Ugarit:

> Among other things, the Ugaritic texts report in epic detail a battle between the regnant land god, Baal, and the sea god, Yamm. Suddenly, a whole spate of dimly apprehended allusions in Psalms and Job came into focus: an antecedent epic tradition had been assimilated into the recurrent imagery of God's breeding the fury of the elemental sea or shackling a primordial sea monster. Thus, when Job cries out (Job 7:12), *ha-yam 'ami 'im tanin*, [am I a sea, or a whale, that thou settest a watch over me?] he is not asking rhetorically whether he is the sea (*yam*), but, with a pointed sardonic allusion to the Canaanite myth, he is saying: "Am I Yamm, am I the Sea Beast, that you should set a guard over me?" (13)

Just imagine what havoc would be wreaked in the name of scholarship if in search of a dissertation topic an enterprising graduate student changed all "the seas" in the Bible to the poper name of the Canaanite God Yam ("sea" in Hebrew is *yam*). The Red or Reed sea— it's looking for a mythology where there is none. Perhaps we could also listen to Alter's caution as we look for mythology behind Elijah's confrontation with the priests of Baal on Mt. Carmel. After all, Elijah does specify that the altar of the LORD be soaked with sea water. Does the water represent Yam who is destroyed in the conflagration on Mt. Carmel?

Besides the caution of Alter, there is the caution of good judgment, which can get clouded by names that look and sound alike. *Asherah* in the Bible is a tree. The pagan altars had at least one tree near by, if not an entire grove. *Ashtoreth* was a Phoenician goddess. Ashtaroth, its plural, is the name of a group of goddesses worshiped with Baal in Canaan and by Israel in the time of the Judges.

Baal is in these ancient Ugaritic texts and in the Hebrew Bible, principally as a god of agriculture, a god who controls storms and fertility, and who with his power over both the seasonal and the seven-year cycles of the earth, was thought to control life and death. His symbol is the bull. His epithet is "he who rides on clouds." His antagonist on Mt. Carmel is also powerful. "His excellency is over Israel, and his strength is in the clouds" (Psalm 68:34). Baal rides the clouds; Yahweh's strength is in the clouds. This sounds like the stuff of which confrontations are made.

There were 450 priests of Baal on Mt. Carmel and 400 priests of Asherah, "she who walks in the sea," prophets of the groves. In Ugaritic tradition she is the wife of El, who is represented by Melchizedek, the high priest at Salem (Genesis 14:18), priest of the "most high God," *El = Elyon* in Hebrew.

In the Bible Asherath is Baal's mother and consort. She is the groves and has a significant role in the Baal cult, since Ahab erected an altar for Baal with an Asherah (1 Kings 16:32, 33): "And Ahab did more to provoke the LORD God of Israel to anger than all the kings of Israel that were before him". It is easy to get confused between the consort Asherath and the image Asherah, which is not approved by the LORD.

Why is there conflict between the prophets of Baal and the prophets of the LORD? Kenneth R. R. Gros Louis points out in *Literary Interpretations of Biblical Narratives* that through Elijah and Elisha, we understand exactly what God controls:

> He controls fire, the symbol of civilization; he controls rain and
> storm, which nourish the land; he controls agriculture, suggested
> by the multiplication of Elisha's twenty loaves and Elijah's jar of
> flour and flask of oil; he controls fertility, seen both in the ending
> of the drought and in the son that Elisha promises to a barren
> woman; he controls life and death—he can heal Naaman and res-

> urrect the two young men from the dead; he controls the heavens, where he takes his prophet's body, the body not found by Elijah's followers (183).

Behind the confrontation of Elijah and the priests of Baal on Mt. Carmel is both history and myth. Yahweh was "a jealous God" (El-Cana) and had told the people, "Thou shalt have no other gods before me" (Exodus 20:3). This one of the Ten Commandments is a reminder, after a confrontation between YHVH and the gods and goddesses of Egypt which culminated in God promising to "pass through the land of Egypt this night, and . . . smite all the firstborn in the land of Egypt, both man and beast; and against all the gods of Egypt I will execute judgment; I am the LORD" (Exodus 12:12).

Even Moses' father-in-law, Jethro, the old priest of Midian, understands. "And Jethro said, Blessed be the LORD, who hath delivered you out of the hand of the Egyptians, and out of the hand of Pharaoh, who hath delivered the people from under the hand of the Egyptians. Now I know that the LORD is greater than all gods: for in the thing wherein they dealt proudly he was above them" (Exodus 18:10–11).

Even as Jethro understands, however, we sense some possible trouble with foreign gods in a new land. As the Israelites flee the land of Egypt, they encounter a new idolatrous world to take the place of the idolatrous world of Egypt. They are redirected around Baal-Zephon, a city named for Baal's highest summit (*zephon* is Hebrew for "north"). (Exodus 14:2).

Perhaps the Israelite lapse into the worship of the golden calf also foreshadows Elijah's confrontation on Mt. Carmel. After all, it was a calf and Baal is represented by a bull. When Aaron fashioned the calf and announced "These be thy gods, O Israel, which brought thee up out of the land of Egypt" (Exodus 32:4), he was not then halting between two opinions. He was offering a confrontation to the God who had brought them out of the land of Egypt. When the people "rose up early on the morrow, and offered burnt offerings, and brought peace offerings; and the people sat down to eat and to drink, and rose up to play" (Exodus 32:6), did they "play" before the idol of Aaron in such a way as to forecast an adoption of the sexual fertility practices of Baal? On the other hand, does the command to remember the Exodus have some hint of toleration for the practices of other gods? Even the command of the holidays would seem to hint that some Canaanite customs are salvageable. "And thou shalt observe the feast of weeks, of the firstfruits of wheat harvest, and the feast of ingathering at the year's end . . . The first of the first fruits of thy land thou shalt bring unto the house of the LORD thy God" (Exodus 34:22–26). These are the Jewish festivals of Shavuot and Sukkot, respectively.

The confrontation on Carmel was not the first confrontation with a Baal. These gods of the Canaanites quickly filled the void left by the gods of the Egyptians. In the wilderness, the Israelite men were easily seduced by the priestesses of Baal-Peor (Numbers 25):

> [1]And Israel abode in Shittim, and the people began to commit whoredom with the daughters of Moab. [2]And they called the people unto the sacrifices of their gods: and the people did eat, and bowed down to their gods. [3]And Israel joined himself unto Baal-Peor: and the anger of the LORD was kindled against Israel. [4]And the LORD said unto Moses, Take all the heads of the people, and hang them up before the LORD against the sun, that the fierce anger of the LORD may be turned away from Israel. [5]And Moses said unto the judges of Israel, Slay ye every one his men that were joined unto Baal-Peor.

Joshua (22:17–19) remembered the grim lesson of Baal-Peor and uses it to focus on another problem that we see in the confrontation of Elijah, where there are two altars side by side:

> Is the iniquity of Peor too little for us, from which we are not cleansed until this day, although there was a plague in the congregation of the LORD, but that ye must turn away this day from following the LORD? And it will be, seeing ye rebel today against the LORD, that tomorrow he will be wroth with the whole congregation of Israel. Notwithstanding, if the land of your possession be unclean, then pass ye over unto the land of the possession of the LORD, wherein the LORD's tabernacle dwelleth, and take possession among us: but rebel not against the LORD, nor rebel against us in building you an altar beside the altar of the LORD our God.

Joshua must have been wrong. The lesson of Baal-Peor must have dimmed quickly for the Israelites to erect an altar to Baal beside the altar of the LORD on Mt. Carmel. By the time Elijah confronts the prophets of Baal, the altar of the LORD has been torn down.

In recounting the history of the nation of Israel, Joshua warns against the problem through the ages of following other gods. "Thus saith the LORD God of Israel, Your fathers dwelt on the other side of the flood in old time, even Terah, the father of Abraham, and the father of Nachor: and they served other gods" (Joshua 24:2).

Joshua would do well to remember Rachel, the favored wife of Jacob, trying to preserve the household gods of her past as she left with her husband to found the nation. The vow of Jacob, "With whomsoever thou findest thy gods, let him not live" (Genesis 31:32) and her death in childbirth should be a reminder that there can be no other gods.

In the end Joshua reminds the people that they are between the gods of two cultures and thus there are two dangers, going back and going forward. It is as if the Israelites should halt between two opinions. "Now therefore fear the LORD, and serve him in sincerity and in truth: and put away the gods which your fathers served on the other side of the flood, and in Egypt; and serve ye the LORD. And if it seem evil unto you to serve the LORD, choose you this day whom ye will serve: whether the gods which your fathers served that were on the other side of the flood, or the gods of the Amorites, in whose land ye dwell: but as for me and my house, we will serve the LORD" (Joshua 24:14–15).

The best view of historical context may be the text itself. Although not necessarily the best history, it provides the best historical context because it is the context. Ahab, the king, is superficially tied to the God of Israel but has a pagan wife, Jezebel, who worships Baal. Jezebel attempts to introduce her Phoenician cult worship into Israel. She is not content with private worship but chooses to impose her religion from Tyre by building high places, inviting her prophets to eat at her table, and killing her opponents. The true prophets who have survived are hidden in caves with the help of Obadiah, who is governor of Ahab's house.

The context shows more than a battle for territory, despite 1 Kings 18:30, which notes that the altar of the LORD was broken down. The erection of an altar was a conventional way of staking a claim to disputed territory. This, however, was a contest between the political establishment of Ahab and Jezebel with their foreign gods and the God who brought Israel out of the land of Egypt and deeded the chosen people a promised land by divine covenant.

And what is this place, Mt. Carmel? I wonder that every time I turn west off Highway 89 in southern Utah to visit Zion National Park, where the view, after a strenuous hike to Angel's Landing and to the Patriarchs, evokes feelings of the sacred. I wonder because I turn at Mt. Carmel junction. Mt. Carmel is on the way to Zion for me.

In Israel I would find Haifa on the northeastern slope of Ha-Carmel, which is 1,791 feet above sea level. A guide may tell me that a northwest village, a vineyard or an orchard, was mentioned as a holy mountain in records of 16th century B.C.E. Is this part of the history or the myth? Both are true.

Mt. Carmel in Haifa was sacred to Christians as early as the sixth century. There are convenient caves for hermits, caves like that of Elijah. The Carmelite monastic order was founded there in the Middle Ages. The first rules or laws of the order are from 1206–1214. They live near the traditional site of Elijah's miracle.

It was quite recently, in 1952, that Michael Avi-Yonah, an Israeli archaeologist, made an important discovery as he visited the museum of the Monastery of Elijah. His finding was a stone foot inscribed in Greek: "To Heliopoleitan Zeus Carmel from Gaius Julius Eutychas, citizen of Caesarea." The inscription suggests a date around 200 C.E. according to D. R. Ap-Thomas.

It seems like a nondescript inscription. It's like a signature and no personal message on a Hallmark greeting card. Its simplicity belies its importance, for the word *Carmelos* is used as a divine name. The confrontation on Mt. Carmel may have been with a local Baal and not Jezebel's Tyrian Baal, an echo of the destruction of a sanctuary of the local Baal on Mt. Carmel by YHVH zealots.

If we assume that the showdown on Mt. Carmel is with the Baal that Jezebel imported, there is another question to be asked. There were two gods worshiped at this period in Tyre, Jezebel's hometown. There was Baal-Melkart and Baal-Shamem. The question may really be academic since all Phoenician and Canaanite mountain gods were sky gods, but asking the question mixes true history and true myth.

To look for history or myth uncovers other inconsistencies. In 1 Kings 18:22 and 19:10 Elijah claims that he alone is left of God's prophets, but in 18:13 Obadiah tells him that he himself preserved the lives of 100. In addition, is it probable that Ahab allowed Jezebel to slay the prophets of God at the time suggested, since in 22:6 Ahab still has a band of God's prophets on call?

Elijah, who stopped up the heavens and stated what he knows is God's will, confronts the priests of Baal. The reader, if not Elijah, knows that lack of rain is not a new punishment for serving other gods. "Take heed to yourselves, that your heart be not deceived, and ye turn aside, and serve other gods, and worship them: And then the LORD's wrath be kindled against you, and he shut up the heaven, that there be no rain, and that the land yield not her fruit; and lest ye perish quickly from off the good land which the LORD giveth you" (Deuteronomy 11:16–17).

It is not, then, a new idea to blame God for the weather. The *New York Times*, on July 24, 1993, reported a poll that tried to fix blame for the rain and the flooding of the Mississippi River on the Midwest. Twenty-one percent said that it was a punishment by God for sin. The poll didn't say what sin—or, for that matter, what God.

Elijah has had time to consider, three years since the rain stopped. He has been fed by ravens during the drought. Ravens, birds of omen who can imitate human voices. Perhaps even *'arebium*, ravens or *'arabium*, arabs. Now myth raps at chamber door,/ the allusion strained, evermore./ Like hot air term papers poor,/ tis the wind and nothing more.

Before the confrontation we are examining, let us look at a confrontation after Elijah's, in 2 Kings 10:

> [18]And Jehu gathered all the people together, and said unto them, Ahab served Baal a little: but Jehu shall serve him much. [19]Now therefore call unto me all the prophets of Baal, all his servants, and all his priests; let none be wanting; for I have a great sacrifice to do to Baal; whosoever shall be wanting, he shall not live. But Jehu did it in subtilty, to the intent that he might destroy the worshippers of Baal. [20]And Jehu said, Proclaim a solemn assembly for Baal. And they proclaimed it. [21]And Jehu sent through all Israel: and all the worshippers of Baal came, so that there was not a man left that came not. And they came into the house of Baal; and the house of Baal was full from one end to another. [22]And he said unto him that was over the vestry, Bring forth vestments for all the worshippers of Baal. And he brought them forth vestments. [23]And Jehu went, and Hehonadab the son of Rechab, into the house of Baal, and said unto the worshippers of Baal, Search, and look that there be here with you none of the servants of the LORD, but the worshippers of Baal only. [24]And when they went in to offer sacrifices and burnt offerings, Jehu appointed forescore men without, and said, If any of the men whom I have brought into your hands escape, he that letteth him go, his life shall be for the life of him. [25]And it came to pass, as soon as he had made an end of offering the burnt offering, that Jehu said to the guard and to the captains, Go in, and slay them; let none come forth. And they smote them with the edge of the sword; and the guard and the captains cast them out, and went to the city of the house of Baal. [26]And they brought forth the im-

ages out of the house of Baal, and burned them. [27]And they brake down the image of Baal, and brake down the house of Baal, and made it a draught house unto this day. [28]Thus Jehu destroyed Baal out of Israel.

Our look back before the confrontation could also include Moses in the cleft of rock (Exodus 33:22) like Elijah in his cave, the fire of Moses' vision (Exodus 3:2), or the pillar of fire that leads the way by night (Exodus 13:21), but this look back could be in the mind of the reader. It may be pushing the text to say that it takes us back there. Elijah does, however, push me back to the first offerings of Aaron. "And there came a fire out from before the LORD, and consumed upon the altar the burnt offering and the fat; which when all the people saw, they shouted, and fell on their faces" (Leviticus 9:24). Perhaps the Chronicler was also pushed by some text or tradition when saying of David's offering, "And David built there an altar unto the LORD, and offered burnt offerings and peace offerings, and called upon the LORD; and he answered him from heaven by fire upon the altar of burnt offering" (1 Chronicles 21:26). The recorder of Solomon's sacrifice may have been pushed by text or tradition. "Now when Solomon had made an end of praying, the fire came down from heaven, and consumed the burnt offering and the sacrifices; and the glory of the LORD filled the house" (2 Chronicles 7:1). What pushes the reader and the scribe from text to text is not text itself; it is the myth behind the text.

In our look back to Mt. Carmel, we can consider the parallels of Sinai (or Horeb). The work of Frank Moore Cross is especially helpful. You can read his complete essay in *Canaanite Myth and Hebrew Epic: Essays in the History of Religion of Israel*. It was published by Harvard University Press in 1973 and cited here by permission.

Cross finds the account of Elijah a sequel to Moses. He notes that even the translation of Elijah is reminiscent of Moses death. Further, Elisha is a minister of Elijah much as Joshua was to Moses. In both cases the minister suceeds the prophet. (193)

But the most important comparisons for Cross are in the experiences of Elijah and Moses on the mountain where Moses builds an and includes twelve stones (Exodus 24:4) like Joshua (Joshua 4:3) and Elijah (1Kings 17:31). Cross notes that the words of Elijah echo each other as Elijah asks "how long will you straddle either side: If Yahweh be God follow him, and if Baal, follow him" and Moses saying "Whoever is on the side of Yahweh, [rally] to me." After these Words Elijah commanded that the prophets of Baal be killed and Moses led the Levites in killing those who worshipped the bull. (193)

Cross finds further parallels between Moses and Elijah in the episode at Sinai in 1Kings 19 even more striking. He especially notes the comparison between Elijah's experience and Moses' second visit to the mountain: At all events, Elijah's sojourn in Sinai is parallel . . . In fear, rage, and despair, Elijah fled, and under divine guidance and care was led to Sinai. The account of the sojourn in the mount in 1Kings 19:9-14 shows direct dependence on the archaic lore of Exodus 33:17-23; 34:6-8. Elijah "came thence to the cave," that is, the "hole in the rock" where Moses had been hidden. Not only did Elijah return to the holy mountain; he returned to the very site of Yahweh's supreme revelation to Moses, the theophany in which Yahweh passed by Moses in the cave, reciting his own names in Moses' hearing, and, granting Moses his request, permitted him, a mortal, a glimpse of the back of his "Glory." From the point of view of the traditionist who composed the pericope in Exodus 33:12-23, Yahweh's "passing" and Moses' glimpse of his back represented the ultimate approach of the godhead to Israel, the definitive revelation. The narrative in 1Kings 18 and 19 has prepared us for a repetition of this theophany, the most audacious parallelism between Moses and Elijah. (193)

Although there is some textual corruption, Cross notes that . . . "the basic intention of the account seems to be clear. The narrative leads up to an expected theophany in pattern of the traditional theophany at Sinai: The Epic description of the original theophany at Sinai Portrays Yahweh as communicating freely with Moses in the manner in which he (later) imparts his word to the prophets, alongside the theophanic form in which he speaks from the cloud or storm, or from his "Glory." Yahweh does pass by Elijah in the cave on Sinai. There is repetition as required. The god of Moses approaches his great prophet Elijah. Again Sinai is wracked by storm wind, by quaking and by fire—the three hallmarks of the theophany of the storm god. At this point the repetition abruptly ends, and the expectations of the hearer (or reader) of the tale are shattered by a surprise ending. Three times the narrator repeats,

"Yahweh was not in the fire." Yahweh passed in a "thin whisper of sound," that is to say, imperceptibly, in silence. Perhaps we should translate in each case, "Yahweh was no longer in the storm." In any case, Yahweh was not immanent in the storm. The thunderous voice of Baal has become the imperceptible whisper. And Elijah does not see the hidden god. (194)

I sense that this may be more than public school teachers want to know or teach about the mythology of Elijah. It is here for a few reasons:

1. It demonstrates that the study of mythology is complex. It is more than just saying that the Bible or any sacred text is myth.
2. Students are interested in the Cannanite myth stories even when they don't connect the stories to biblical narrative.
3. The free association that goes on in mythic reading is obvious as the chapter winds from Bible to Midrash to Elie Wiesel to Mormon belief to Ugarit to Jewish folklore and to personal belief.
4. The Cannanite myth helps understand the biblical narrative. This myth is just under the surface in the biblical narrative of Elijah. as noted in the next section.

Confrontation between Elijah and the Priests of Baal

Now that we have looked back with Frank Moore Cross, let's look at the narrative of the contest of Mt. Carmel. I am impressed with the symmetry. Elijah speaks twice to the children of Israel and twice to the prophets of Baal. Elijah comes near to all the people and, after the failed attempt by Baal's prophets, invites the people to come near. There are the two bulls and the two choices. "If the LORD be God, follow him: but if Baal, then follow him" (1 Kings 18:21).

The reader has been set up. The symmetry ends as the preparations begin. The frantic attempts of the prophets of Baal serve to make the preparations of Elijah seem even more confident. The taunting by Elijah of Baal's prophets serves the purpose of pure enjoyment along with contributing to the confidence of Elijah's preparation. When he suggests that they cry aloud, the prophets already are doing so. When he suggests that their god may be sleeping, they are already trying to awake him. When he suggests that their god may be pursuing, he may be suggesting that Baal is only human and attending to some bodily function. When Elijah suggests that he is on a journey, he may well be.

After the pyrotechnics and a bloody slaughter, the sacrifice, wood, rocks, water, and dust have been consumed. Here is where the Cannanite myth comes to the surface. Did God symbolically consume the Canaanite pantheon? Perhaps not, since the prophets of the groves still live, but surely Baal, Yam, and Mot could be part of the carnage of the wood, rocks, water, and dust. Elijah continues a more private supplication in a crouching position out on a promontory.

It is just like this prophet who comes and goes so rapidly to leave behind unresolved problems. Why weren't the 400 prophets of the groves killed along with the 450 prophets of Baal? Why did Elijah tell us three times that he was the only prophet left when Obadiah had hid 100 prophets of the LORD? Why was God in the fire that rained from heaven on Mt. Carmel and not in the fire at the cave of Horeb? Is any of this narrative an exaggeration? This is the stuff of which class discussions are made.

The Myth after the Confrontation

This narrative is the stuff of myth and legend. The events spawn more events and legend perpetuates itself. Ask me what I believe, and I could explain in terms of the myths and legends of Elijah. This seems to be what later writers and commentators do. Aggadic literature tries to give Elijah a bit of history. One source puts him in the tribe of Gad, descended from Leah. Another source makes him a Benjaminite or a Levite.

In the Midrash, Jewish commentary on the Hebrew Bible written between 400 and 1200 C.E., the rabbis offers commentary on a person we meet only once: Hiel the Bethelite in the last verse of 1 Kings 34, just before Elijah stops the rain in chapter 17. According to the Midrash, he hid himself on Mt. Carmel at the great trial between Elijah and the prophets of Baal in order to kindle the wood surreptitiously and make the people believe that it had been done by Baal. He was punished by being bitten by a snake. (See chapter 7 for more about serpents and snakes.) The Midrash is serious literature to Jews. It is an explanation of the sacred. It is also the way that myth is built and believed.

In midrashic commentary on Abraham, we find a note about the importance of remembering Abraham that also contributes to the literature of Elijah.

You will thus find that Elijah offered up many supplications on Mount Carmel for the fire to descend, as it says *Hear me, O Lord, hear me* (I Kings 18:37), but the Lord did not hearken unto him. As soon, however, as he mentioned the dead, and said: *O Lord, the God of Abraham, of Isaac, and of Israel*, he was immediately answered; for what does it say? *Then the fire of the Lord fell*.

The forbidden place of the sacrifice was a midrashic issue.

God said that no man must come and criticize Elijah, who hailed from Gilead, for sacrificing on the forbidden high place, building an altar on Mount Carmel and offering a sacrifice thereon while the Temple was in existence, although the Torah forbade it: as it says, *Take heed to thyself that thou offer not thy burnt-offerings in every place...but in the place which the Lord shall choose* (Deut 12:13). 'It was I,' said the Holy One, blessed be He, 'who told him to do so'; as may be inferred from the text, *I have done all these things at Thy word* (I Kings 18:36).

Perhaps we could be permitted one more read in the Midrash. Its commentary adds a story within the story and can demonstrate the stunted growth of myth that didn't persist.

Learn a lesson from the bullock of Elijah. When Elijah said to the worshippers of Baal: *Choose you one bullock for yourselves, and dress it first; for ye are many* (I Kings 18:25), for four hundred and fifty prophets of Baal and the four hundred prophets of the Asherah gathered round but could not move the bullock's feet from the ground. For observe what is written in that connection: *Let them therefore give us two bullocks; and let them choose one bullock for themselves, and cut it in pieces, and lay it on the wood, and put no fire under; and I will dress the other bullock, and lay it over the wood, and put no fire under* (ibid.23). What did Elijah do? He said to them: "Select two bullocks, equal in all respects, coming from the same mother and reared on the same pasture, then cast lots for them, one to be for the Lord and one for Baal, and choose for yourselves one bullock." Elijah's bullock followed him immediately, while as regards the bullock assigned for Baal, though all the prophets of Baal and the prophets of the Asherah gathered round it, they could not move its foot. At last Elijah began to speak to it and said to it: "Go with them!" The bullock replied by saying to him in the presence of all the people: "My fellow cow, and I have both come from the same womb, from the same cow, and have grown up on the same pasture, that he has fallen to the lot of the Omnipresent and the name of the Holy One, blessed be He, is sanctified by him, while I have fallen to the lot of Baal and shall have to provoke my Creator!" Said Elijah to it: "Bullock, bullock, fear not! Go with them and let them not find any excuse for their failure. Indeed, even as the name of the Holy One, blessed be He, shall be sanctified by means of the bullock that is with me, so will it be sanctified by means of you!" The bullock answered him: "Seeing that you give me such advice, I swear that I will not budge from this spot until you hand me over into their hand!" *As it says, And they took the bullock which he gave them* (ibid.26). Who gave it them? Elijah. And you can infer this from the fact that Elijah said to them, *"Let them therefore give us two bullocks,'* and then again he told them, *'Choose you one bullock, and dress it first."* While finally it is written, *"And they took the bullock which he gave them."* For the above reasons it is written, *"Who teacheth us by means of the beasts of the earth."* By the expression, *"And maketh us wise by means of the fowls of heaven,"* the Holy One, blessed be He, implies: Learn a lesson from the ravens who fed Elijah; for it says *"And I have commanded the ravens to feed thee there"* (I Kings 17:4). And from where did they bring him *bread and flesh in the morning, and bread and flesh in the evening* (ibid. 5)? From Jehoshaphat's table. The ravens would not enter the house of that wicked man Ahab to take anything from his table for the righteous man, because there was idolatry in his house! This explains the text, *"Maketh us wise by means of the fowls of heaven."* The Holy One, blessed be He, said: "Learn a lesson from the bullock of Elijah and from the ravens, and do not turn to the idols to gaze upon them." Whence were they to infer that this was so? From what they read in the context, THEN YE SHALL DRIVE OUT ALL THE INHABITANTS OF THE LAND FROM BEFORE YOU.

Elijah's departure from the world is dramatic. "And it came to pass, as they still went on, and talked, that, behold, there appeared a chariot of fire, and horses of fire, and parted them both asunder; and Elijah went up by a whirlwind into heaven" (2 Kings 2:11). This dramatic exit, along with Malachi's prophecy "Behold, I will send you Elijah the prophet before the coming of the great and dreadful day of the LORD" (Malachi 4:5), pushed the Elijah story into the Apocrypha, the New Testament, Jewish tradition and liturgy, Christianity, and even current Mormon belief.

A passage in the historical book of 1 Maccabees (2:58) refers to Elijah's ascent into heaven, but the most extensive reference in the Apocrypha is in Ecclesiasticus, also called the Wisdom of Sirach, or Ben Sirach after its 180 B.C.E. author, Jesus the son of Sirach. This book found its way into the worship of the early Christian Church but not into the Synagogue.

> [1] Then stood up Elias the prophet as fire, and his word burned like a lamp. [2] He brought a sore famine upon them, and by his zeal he diminished their number. [3] By the word of the Lord he shut up the heaven, and also three times brought down fire. [4] O Elias, how wast thou honoured in thy wondrous deeds! and who may glory like unto thee! [5] Who didst raise up a dead man from death, and his soul from the place of the dead, by the word of the most High: [6] Who broughtest kings to destruction, and honourable men from their bed: [7] Who heardest the rebuke of the Lord in Sinai, and in Horeb the judgment of vengeance: [8] Who anointedst kings to take revenge, and prophets to succeed after him: [9] Who wast taken up in a whirlwind of fire, and in a chariot of fiery horses: [10] Who wast ordained for reproofs in their times, to pacify the wrath of the Lord's judgment, before it brake forth into fury, and to turn the heart of the father unto the son, and to restore the tribes of Jacob. [11] Blessed are they that saw thee, and slept in love; for we shall surely live.

This is an important question about the creation of myth that we see in evidence in the new ideas of this passage: Where in the story of Elijah in 1 Kings would a future writer get the idea that Elijah would restore the tribes of Jacob or Israel, and what does this mean? Maybe there is more to Elijah repairing the altar of the LORD with stones representing the twelve tribes than we first recognized. Where would a reader come to the idea that those who saw Elijah were honored with his love? This is evidence of myth making. The writer is trying not to hide truth but reveal it.

Elijah appears in the New Testament as suddenly as he did in the Hebrew Bible. As a certain priest named Zacharias executed the priest's office, an angel made the announcement about him and his aged wife, Elizabeth. Despite their ages they would have a baby, John. "And he shall go before him in the spirit and power of Elias [Elijah], to turn the hearts of the fathers to the children, and the disobedient to the wisdom of the just; to make ready a people prepared for the Lord" (Luke 1:17). It is interesting to ask why this announcement departs from Malachi's formula. Luke turns the "disobedient to the wisdom of the just" rather than the "hearts of the children to the fathers." Are these both the same idea? Maybe the angel's announcement is homiletic and another example of how myth is made. Do angels edit texts?

John must have looked somewhat like Elijah with his raiment of camel's hair and a leather girdle. It is the clothing worn by Elijah (2 Kings 1:8). When John is asked if he is Elijah, he answered "no" (John 1:19–23). There is evidence, however, that Jesus himself put John in the role of Elijah. Matthew 17:12–13 is a good example. "But I say unto you, that Elias is come already, and they knew him not, but have done unto him whatsoever they listed. Likewise shall also the Son of Man suffer of them. Then the disciples understood that he spake unto them of John the Baptist." There are also references where Jesus himself was thought to be Elias (Mark 6:14–15).

The most dramatic reference to Elijah in the New Testament is the transfiguration of Jesus in the presence of three disciples on a mountain (Matthew 17:16; Mark 9:2–8; Luke 9:28–36). On the mountain, first Moses and then Elijah talk with Jesus. As they are coming down, the disciples ask whether and when the earthly appearance of Elijah is to be expected, and they receive the answer mentioned in the passages cited above: he has already appeared.

An interesting twist in the story of Elijah's confrontation with the prophets of Baal finds its way into the Epistle of Paul to the Romans. Apparently Elijah did not understand the whole truth when he told God "I am left alone, and they seek my life. But what saith the answer of God unto him? I have reserved to myself seven thousand men, who have not bowed the knee to the image of Baal" (Romans 11:4). This myth making by Paul illustrates the changes that occur in how events are perceived.

From here Elijah finds his way into Christian liturgy and tradition. In early Christian liturgy, the description of Elijah's ascent was read from the Bible on Ascension Day. At the consecration of water, Elijah's sacrifice and prayer on Mt. Carmel for rain was recited. The Syrian Church introduced as Elijah's Fast a forty-day period of fasting. beginning on the Sunday after Pentecost and lasting till July 20, which was celebrated as the Day of Elijah the Holy. References to Elijah abound in early Christianity. Even while reading these sources I recall wondering as I walked as a youth past the Greek Orthodox Church in Salt Lake City why it was called the Church of the Prophet Elias.

What is clear is that quite a few churches are named for Elijah. A monastery exists on present day Mt. Carmel. His life reads like *Leg-*

ends of the Saints—or is it the other way around? Does *Legends of the Saints* read like Elijah? The saint is fed miraculously by birds or by angels. He controls the weather, multiplies food, raises the dead to life, and performs feats of endurance. But for the strength of one myth over another the marathon would not be the 26 miles 385 yards to Athens, but the 17 miles to Jezreel in Elijah's running foot steps.

What does the footnote mean in the Oxford Study edition of the NEB at Revelation 11:3? It says that in some traditions, two witnesses that prophesy clothed in sackcloth are probably Elijah and Moses.

It may be a point to just mention in passing that Elijah is acknowledged in the Qur'an.

> We also sent forth Elias, who said to his people: "Have you no fear of Allah? Would you invoke Baal and forsake the Most Gracious Creator: Allah is your Lord and the Lord of your forefathers." But they denied him, and thus incurred Our punishment, except Allah's true servants. We bestowed on him the praise of later generation: "Peace on Elias!" Thus We reward the righteous. He was one of Our believing servants" (Sura 37: 123–133).

The former student who gave me a story from Jewish tradition when we were reading the Book of Ruth in a literature class told me that the Talmud says that "he who finds the woman who corresponds to him is kissed by Elijah." I found a reference for her talmudic citation (*Kiddushin* 70a) but not for her story. She said that the story came from her rabbi.

> A very wealthy man with an observant family celebrated the seder every year. "For many years I have opened the door for Elijah every seder night waiting for him to come, but he never does. What is the reason?" His wise rabbi answered: "In your neighborhood there lives a very poor family with many children. You should call on the man and propose that you and your family celebrate the next Passover in his house, and for this purpose provide him and his whole family with everything necessary for the eight days of Passover. If you do this, then on the seder night Elijah will surely come." The pious man did as the rabbi told him, but after Passover he came to the rabbi and said that he had again waited in vain to see Elijah. The rabbi answered: "I know very well that Elijah came on the seder night to the house of your poor neighbor, but you could not see him." The rabbi held a mirror before the face of the man and said: "Look, this was Elijah's face that night."

It is a wonderful tale, but is it the same Elijah who called fire from the heavens and put 450 prophets to the sword? Is the Elijah of 1 Kings also the Elijah of the Jewish Grace After Meals? "May God in his mercy send us the prophet Elijah, may his memory be blessed, and may he bring us good tidings, help, and comfort." This same sense of Elijah is present in the many Elijah songs: "The prophet Elijah, the Tishbite from Gilead, may he come to us soon with the son of David, the Messiah."

My Aunt Amy does what many devout members of The Church of Jesus Christ of Latter-day Saints do. She compiles the genealogy of her ancestors. She will send the names of those she links in the family pedigree to the temple, where *the faithful will be baptized for them*. She is anxious to see that her family is sealed together for the eternities. After a difficult search, when her work seemed at a dead end, she finally achieved a breakthrough that pushed her records back another generation. How was she able to discover the missing family link? Her answer is the answer of many devout. "It was the spirit of Elijah."

Joseph Smith, the first prophet of Mormonism, saw Elijah in the Mormon temple in Kirtland, Ohio, in 1836 (*Doctrine and Covenants* 110). The words of Malachi about turning the hearts of fathers to children are also in the *Book of Mormon* (3 Nephi 25:5). What seems mysterious, or even "mythterious," is the transportation through time of the prophet who confronted the prophets of Baal to the spirit who helps the devout do genealogy and will bless the homes of believing Jews at the seder table.

The Elijah whose kiss marks true love seems like a kindly old man, not a prophet of fire and sword. But didn't Elijah also provide for the woman and her son and heal the dead son with a kiss? There may be some mythical connection.

I am not suggesting that Elijah does not help, in a very practical way, those whose hearts turn to their fathers. I am not suggesting that Elijah will not someday occupy his place at the Passover seder and drink from the cup reserved for him. I am suggesting that Elijah does even more. He is the source to whom people look when asked what they believe or why they believe.

To say that literature is in any way myth adds to it the sacred. It becomes more than just literature. To study the Bible as literature would somehow be less than studying it as mythic literature, for in reading mythic literature we are not bound by the conventions of historical method and science in the search for belief and truth. It is as though we look for our belief in scripture rather than believing because of what is written in a holy text.

In that spirit it may be for the writer of stories to explain the travel through time and belief of Elijah. We'll end where we began, with *The Gates of the Forest* by Elie Wiesel. This monologue is set in a cave as two young men hide during the Holocaust:

> "For years," Gabriel went on, "I would cry and pray God to renew joy in the heart of Israel and to rebuild the Temple, His dwelling. I spurred my vision to traveling faster and farther into space, seeking to pierce the veil that conceals the future and to penetrate its most profound secrets. I wanted to discover the sanctuary of the Messiah, to grip him by the shoulders and bring him forcibly to earth. One night I stood before the prophet Elijah and demanded his help. Elijah is the prophet of harshness and wrath. When he was alive no one dared approach him for fear of being scarred. Even kings, especially kings, masters sated with power and glory, trembled before him. When it was time for him to die, the Angel of Death drew back and declared himself unable to take him. That is why he is the only one of the elect that rose, alive, to heaven. God sent His chariot of fire to fetch him, and Elijah has never returned it; he needs it for his wanderings. The prophet of the thundering word has become prophet of consolation. He made an agreement with God on Mount Carmel, saying, 'I shall go against my feelings and be angry with your people, who are even more mine than yours, but on one condition only: You will let me return among your unhappy children in a different role, to warm the dwellings of the poor and to lighten their burdens by foretelling their end.' Needing Elijah's services, God accepted this condition. And because He likes those who stand up to Him, He gave to Elijah an important mission. 'You shall be the only one to know the hour when the Messiah will go down to earth to mend My creation, to make a link between Myself and man, between the voice and its echo, between the voice and its source. You shall be the announcer.' It is for this reason, too—in order to be ready to appear on the horizon—that Elijah has kept the chariot of fire. And this is why it is to him that I presented the urgency of the situation and the dangers threatening our people. Madmen—unconscious and conscious—I told him, are preparing to kill them in cold blood; indeed, they have already begun. If the Messiah doesn't hurry, he may be too late; there will be no one left to save. I spoke to him of Jewish

children, with dreams in their eyes, massacred in front of their speechless parents, who went to join them in the grave. I recalled the phrase from the Talmud: 'Ever since the destruction of the Temple the power of prophecy has been given to children.' 'Soon,' I said, 'there will be none of them left; our only prophets will be dead children.' And I also said to him, 'To you everything is simple because your are an angel. Try being a man among men or a child among men and you will see why to wait any longer would be a crime'"

Myth continues. It grows. Evidence is in the work of Brazilian author Paulo Coelho, whose books are becoming some of the most translated in the world. The note about the author on the Amazon.com website notes that his books have sold more than 21 million copies in 74 countries and have been translated into 34 languages. His book *The Alchemist* leads the way but is closely followed by *The Fifth Mountain*, a modern writer's story of Elijah.

Coelho does what we all do with myth: He fills in the blanks. We all take understated reticent biblical narrative and let our world add and embellish and create an even more imaginative story. I have found that students like *The Fifth Mountain*, especially after *The Alchemist*, a story about following a dream. *The Fifth Mountain* is a demonstration of mythmaking at its best.

Bible as myth is an important subject, yet no matter how careful a teacher is, some students may still equate *myth* with *fiction*. Here are some ideas for the teacher to follow in discussion:

1. Read the Cannanite myth in this chapter to the class.
2. Read the confrontation on Mt. Carmel (1 Kings 18–19)
3. Ask if there is any evidence that the Canaanite myth is in the story of Elijah on Mt Carmel.
4. Are the Canaanite gods symbolically in the wood, stones, dust, and water consumed by the fire from heaven?
5. What Canaanite gods does Jezebel worship?
6. When God tells Elijah that the LORD was not in the earthquake and fire is Elijah being reminded about Canaanite gods?
7. Is Mt. Carmel part of Canaanite mythology?

Chapter 18

THE GOSPEL OF MARK: READING A NEW GENRE

The Gospels of the New Testament are the center of Christian belief. They are also a unique literary genre. Although there is some debate about the newness and uniqueness of the genre because of a literary pattern of Jewish lives of the prophets or pagan biographies, there is no doubt that the Gospels are a unique literature in today's context. They are the founding literature of Christian belief and carry as much, if not more, emotional or religious attachment for a Christian than any part of the Bible that is studied in our modern classroom.

The word *gospel* identifies this new genre and partially explains the strength of belief associated with this text. It is a translation of the Greek *euangelion*, which literally means "good news" or "good announcement." The good news for Christians is the mission of Jesus, which allowed the redemption of the world from sin. A gospel is a proclamation of this good news. It is a testimony or testament of the mission of Jesus. It has as its purpose to convince readers that the good news is for them.

It is easy to see how reading any gospel in a literature class could easily lead to a theological discussion. This is allowed in public schools. What is not allowed is devotional reading, and this is the way the Gospels are usually read by religious people.

On the other hand, much of the reading in the scholarly community is in the context of a search for the historical Jesus. Who was Jesus, really? This is the question that seems to motivate many in the academic community who read the Gospels as a piece of evidence to be evaluated and analyzed in the context of other literary and sometimes physical evidence. This kind of study reaches outside the established canon of four gospels to some twenty-plus texts that can be considered part of the genre we call gospel.[14] The devotional reader requires no external evidence but the text itself. It is a matter of faith.

At the same time, the Gospels include fascinating examples of literary principles. There are parables, perhaps a tragic hero, and, in fact, three of the gospels are stories. Ryken, in *How to Read the Bible as Literature*, identifies at least fourteen different genres *within* the Gospels, any of which could be taught in a literature classroom (136–137). Matthew, Mark, and Luke are called the Synoptic Gospels because they offer a mostly linear synopsis of the life and teachings of Jesus. "Many suggest that Mark has created a new type of literature, a gospel—a narrative acclamation of the "good news" of what God has done and "will do through Jesus of Nazareth" (Rhodes et al. 3):

> Whatever Mark intended, he surely produced a narrative that makes a claim upon readers. This claim is strengthened by the fact that his story concerns real people, is based on actual events, and makes predictions about future events. And Mark has apparently brought all his storytelling capacities to bear on this task.

I choose Mark as a gospel for classroom study because is seems to be the most comprehensive of the Synoptic Gospels. Luke retells or reproduces about 50% of Mark. Matthew reproduces about 90%. In addition, Mark seems to have the least unique material, about 7%. John has the most unique material—it is about 92% exclusive. Since Mark is so close to Matthew and Luke, many scholars believe that both Matthew and Luke used Mark and perhaps another source in writing their Gospels. The fact that Mark is the oldest of the Gospels and a primary source for other Gospel writers is even more reason to use it in the classroom.

There are two excellent teacher resources for teaching Mark. Helpful at any level is Rhodes et al., *Mark as Story: An Introduction to the Narrative of a Gospel*. This book takes the traditional approach and examines narrator, setting, plot, and characters. Another good resource is Anderson and Moore's *Mark & Method: New Approaches in Biblical Studies*. This book is a ways of reading resource with chapters on narrative criticism, reader-response criticism, deconstruction, feminist criticism, and social criticism. This book has been particularly helpful in undergraduate courses.

Both of these resources offer a similar suggestion. Read the Gospel of Mark independently and completely. Most Gospel reading is a flight from one text to another. "Short passages are read aloud in church services and expounded in sermons. They regularly form the basis for Sunday school lessons" (Anderson 1). This kind of reading is appropriate in its place, but if that is the only kind of reading students do, they may not "realize that each of the four evangelists is a fell-fledged author in his own right. Each paints a unique portrait of Jesus" (Anderson 1). And this unique portrait is also for a unique audience, as the four Gospel writers seem to address different audiences with a similar message.

The suggestions in *Mark as Story* are more explicit and helpful:

- Read Mark as story rather than as history.
- Read Mark independently from the other Gospels.
- Avoid reading modern cultural assumptions into Mark's first-century story.
- Avoid reading modern theologies about Jesus back into Mark's story. (Rhodes 5–6)

The Story's Theme

The first part of the story is the development of a very public hero. He attracts people with miracles and new ideas. Students may notice the number of times they encounter the term *multitude* or see crowds gather for one reason or another. The attention he attracts is from different groups. Some are friendly and others are not.

He attracts the attention of Jews looking for a messiah, someone to save them from political oppression. He attracts the attention of the two major Jewish groups at the time, the Sadducees and the Pharisees, as well as the scribes. He seems to be able to do things they can't do, and he says things that offend them. When he confronts them, he debates them and wins.

He attracts the attention of the Romans, who occupy Judea. This land is not governed by the native inhabitants except as they are allowed to govern by Rome. An occupying army would do well to worry about insurrection, and Jesus sounds like a revolutionary and is attracting considerable attention.

Attracting attention can be dangerous. The danger leads to the death of Jesus in the final chapters. All the groups that are attracted to him in some way are involved in the death scenes. Each groups interprets or understands the death in its own way.

In the first few chapters of Mark, the narrator puts forward the major themes of the story. It is around some of the seven themes proposed by Louis in *Literary Interpretations of Biblical Narratives* (296–329) that students can begin to discuss the text. It is a way of making the obvious literary point that most stories have one or more themes. Teachers can use the themes proposed by Louis as discussion questions.

The first theme is the "mystery" of Jesus. What is mysterious to the people Jesus encounters? Is it the new teachings? Is it the idea that many don't know who he is? He talks about a kingdom. Do his listeners understand him, or is this part of the mystery?

Jesus is a healer in the second theme. Louis points out that the healings are initially physical, but as the narrative progresses there is more emphasis on spiritual healing, forgiveness, and cleansing from sin. In the end he is mocked while on the cross for saving others and seemingly being unable to save himself (312). What do the healings have in common? What is the effect of the healings on the different groups of people that he attracted?

The secrecy of Jesus is the third theme. It is apparent more at the beginning of the story than at the end when he arrives in Jerusalem. Louis points out that only once did he ask that a miracle be made public (312). This is when he tells the man from whom he has cast spirits to "Go home to thy friends, and tell them how great things the Lord hath done for thee, and hath had compassion on thee" (Mark 5:19). This is such an interesting exception to the secrecy that it is an important question for students when teaching this particular scene, and it will be seen later. At this point it is interesting to ask students about the secrecy. Why does Jesus ask people to keep a secret that is obviously intended for the entire world?

The fourth theme shows Jesus as a revolutionary (perhaps tragic) hero. He is new and revolutionary in the eyes of all of the audiences he attracts. These revolutionary ideas led to his death. In that case he may be seen as an archetypal tragic hero, something the class can discuss from the materials that follow. In the meantime, the question is obvious. What makes Jesus revolutionary? Why does he seem to break the rules and overturn some traditions (Louis 313)?

The other themes proposed by Louis also have excellent potential for discussion: Jesus as bridegroom, the lack of understanding of those who hear Jesus speak, and the development of the disciples.

Spirits into Swine

All four themes mentioned above in the Gospel of Mark are part of a particularly interesting story that can be approached from many directions. The story in Mark 5:1–20 can be read as a literal story about how Jesus exorcized devils from a man possessed. It can also be read in such a way that the evil spirits or devils are a metaphor for the sins that can entrap the unwary. Those caught by these metaphorical evil spirits can find release in Jesus, the story would seem to be saying. It can also be read as an underlying political commentary on the occupation of the country by the Romans.

¹And they came over unto the other side of the sea, into the country of the Gadarenes. ²And when he was come out of the ship, immediately there met him out of the tombs a man with an unclean spirit, ³Who had *his* dwelling among the tombs; and no man could bind him, no, not with chains: ⁴Because that he had been often bound with fetters and chains, and the chains had been plucked asunder by him, and the fetters broken in pieces: neither could any *man* tame him. ⁵And always, night and day, he was in the mountains, and in the tombs, crying, and cutting himself with stones. ⁶But when he saw Jesus afar off, he ran and worshiped him, ⁷And cried with a loud voice, and said, What have I to do with thee, Jesus, *thou* Son of the most high God? I adjure thee by God, that thou torment me not. ⁸For he said unto him, Come out of the man, *thou* unclean spirit. ⁹And he asked him, What *is* thy name? And he answered, saying, My name *is* Legion: for we are many. ¹⁰And he besought him much that he would not send them away out of the country. ¹¹Now there was there nigh unto the mountains a great herd of swine feeding. ¹²And all the devils besought him, saying, Send us into the swine, that we may enter into them. ¹³And forthwith Jesus gave them leave. And the unclean spirits went out, and entered into the swine: and the herd ran violently down a steep place into the sea, (they were about two thousand;) and were choked in the sea. ¹⁴And they that fed the swine fled, and told *it* in the city, and in the country. And they went out to see what it was that was done. ¹⁵And they come to Jesus, and see him that was possessed with the devil, and had the legion, sitting, and clothed, and in his right mind: and they were afraid. ¹⁶And they that saw *it* told them how it befell to him that was possessed with the devil, and *also* concerning the swine. ¹⁷And they began to pray him to

depart out of their coasts. [18]And when he was come into the ship,
he that had been possessed with the devil prayed him that he might
be with him. [19]Howbeit Jesus suffered him not, but saith unto him,
Go home to thy friends, and tell them how great things the Lord
hath done for thee, and hath had compassion on thee. [20]And he
departed, and began to publish in Decapolis how great things Jesus
had done for him: and all *men* did marvel.

To start with the political reading, there is an obvious question:
Why is there a large (2000) herd of swine in a country where the food
laws prohibit the eating of pork? The swine is clearly an unclean animal, a good place to send unclean spirits, but what are they doing in
the country? One answer may be that they were being raised as food
for the Roman legions that occupied the country. This is a hint. What
other references are there to the occupying Romans in this narrative?
The unclean spirits are called "legion," a major unit in the Roman
army of 4,000 to 6,000 men.

It may be that the unclean spirits are the Roman army of occupation, and this army is fed to the very swine that sustain it; then both the
unclean legion and the unclean animals drown in the sea. The is revolutionary rhetoric. It is a thinly disguised story about how bad Rome
is, and it would attract the attention of the Romans and the Jews. The
irony is that it is the only miracle in Mark that Jesus asks be publicized
in the "Decapolis," or ten cities. This purposefully attracts the attention of the Roman authorities. Why would Jesus want to do this?

To read the story where the unclean spirits are a metaphor for
sinful behavior, teachers may wish to show the ten-minute video translation of the story produced by the American Bible Society, "Out of
the Tombs." The video uses the exact language of the Bible and is
probably best described as an MTV version. The ABS has not been
without criticism for seemingly making evil look good. The criticism
seems to have made the video even more popular.

What makes the video good in a literature class is that it is a literal
translation cast in a modern context that strives for a metaphorical
reading of the unclean spirits, the swine, and the symbolic exorcism.
Over the years it has been a good vehicle for discussion.

Archetype Tragic Hero

One of the compelling questions of Mark is whether or not the
death of Jesus could have been avoided. His miracles, stories, and
preaching seem to provoke the people most dangerous to him. It may

even be that from a literary perspective, our hero has some tragic flaw. This is a difficult concept for a devotional reader, unless he or she is quietly reminded that in Christian theology Jesus had to die to accomplish his purpose.

To get at this question, students should understand "the first great theorist of dramatic art," Aristotle (Perrine 1052):

> A tragedy . . . is the imitation in dramatic form of an action that is serious and complete, with incidents arousing pity and fear wherewith it effects a catharsis of such emotions. The language used is pleasurable. . . . The chief characters are noble personages ('better than ourselves,' says Aristotle), and the actions they perform are noble actions (1052).

Aristotle defines the characteristics of a tragic character. Then students are invited to see if the hero of Mark exemplifies these characteristics of Greek tragedy. The characteristics are summarized here from Perrine (1052–1055):

1. The tragic hero is a man of noble stature.

2. Although the tragic hero is preeminently great, he is not perfect.

This is a difficult one for students. I try to put it this way: Is the character in Mark perfect? This is much different than asking if Jesus is perfect. The idea is that he does do some things in this narrative that invite trouble. He may be perfect, but he is antagonizing some very dangerous people.

3. The hero's downfall, therefore, is partially his own fault, the result of his own free choice, not the result of pure accident or villainy or some overriding malignant fate.

Here again I remind students that Jesus had to die to accomplish his purpose.

4. Nevertheless, the hero's misfortune is not wholly deserved. Many students breath a sigh of relief when this is emphasized.

5. The tragic fall is not pure loss. Alhough it may result in the protagonist's death, it involves some increase in awareness, some gain in self-knowledge.

6. Though it arouses solemn emotions—pity and fear, says Aristotle, but compassion and awe might be better terms— tragedy, when will performed, does not leave its audience in a state of depression.

Whether or not the narrative of Mark is tragedy, the discussion allows students a new look at the Gospel and a vivid look at Aristotle's definition of tragedy. For the first time many students will understand that a tragic ending is not necessarily a sad ending. In fact the catharsis of a tragic ending is usually much more uplifting than comedy.

One of the reasons the end of Mark's Gospel is so interesting is because it is somewhat problematical. In some of the oldest manuscripts, the narrative ends with Mark 16:8. This gives the story a different direction, especially if discussed as a Greek tragedy. This ending would define the narrative as tragedy, for there would be no post-resurrection appearances. *The Interpreter's Dictionary of the Bible*, "Mark, Gospel of" proposes four reasons that the Gospel as written by Mark ends with 16:8 (Cranfield 276). These reasons provide for a good multiple choice class discussion:

1. It was never finished, because Mark was prevented in one way or another from finishing it.

2. The conclusion was lost or destroyed by some mischance.

3. The conclusion was deliberately suppressed.

4. Verse 16:8 was intended to be the end of the gospel.

Although Cranfield may not have *the* answer to his multiple choices, it is interesting for a teacher to have his opinion on this to facilitate class discussion:

> Of these 1 is unlikely: and 2 is not very likely, since it involves assuming both that Mark was unavailable to rewrite the conclusion and also that the gospel had not been in use long enough for someone else to be able to restore the conclusion from memory. Since the fact of resurrection appearances was clearly an element of the primitive preaching (cf. 1Corinthians 15:5-7; and also Acts 1:22; 2:32; 3:15; 10:41; 13:31), 4, though it has received a good deal of support, should surely be rejected. It is extremely improbable that Mark intended to conclude his gospel without recording at least one resurrection appearance. The most probable answer to the question is 1. (276)

Note

14 Teachers interested in gospels outside the Christian canon will enjoy *The Complete Gospels*, edited by Robert J. Miller. This work is mainly by the Fellows of the Jesus Seminar and includes new translations of the Bible's four Gospels plus the Gospels of Thomas and Mary, the Saying Gospel Q, the Secret Gospel of Mark, and twelve other gospels from the first three centuries.

FINDING THE BIBLE IN OUR WORLD:
BORROWINGS FROM BARTLETT AND OTHERS

T his is a place to start for students on a search for the Bible in our world. All citations are from the King James Version.

The Hebrew Bible / Old Testament.

Genesis 2:18	It is not good that the man should be alone.
Genesis 3:19	In the sweat of thy face shalt thou eat bread.
Genesis 3:19	For dust thou art, and unto dust shalt thou return.
Genesis 3:20	The mother of all living.
Genesis 4:9	Am I my brother's keeper?
Genesis 4:13	My punishment is greater than I can bear.
Genesis 7:12	And the rain was upon the earth forty days and forty nights.
Genesis 15:15	In a good old age.
Genesis 16:12	His hand will be against every man, and every man's hand against him.
Genesis 18:11	Old and well stricken in age.
Genesis 37:23	They stript Joseph out of his coat, his coat of many colours.
Genesis 49:4	Unstable as water, thou shalt not excel.
Exodus 2:22	I have been a stranger in a strange land.

Exodus 3:8 and Jeremiah 32:22	A land flowing with milk and honey.
Exodus 10:21	Darkness which may be felt.
Exodus 16:3	When we sat by the fleshpots (of Egypt).
Leviticus 19:18	Love thy neighbour as thyself.
Deuteronomy 8:3	Man doth not live by bread only.
Deuteronomy 19:21	Eye for eye, tooth for tooth, hand for hand, foot for foot.
Deuteronomy 29:28	The secret things belong unto the Lord.
Deuteronomy 32:10	He kept him as the apple of his eye.
Joshua 23:14	I am going the way of all the earth.
Judges 5:7	I arose a mother in Israel.
Judges 15:8	He smote them hip and thigh.
Judges 20:8	The people arose as one man.
Ruth 1:16	Whither thou goest, I will go; and where thou lodgest, I will lodge: thy people shall be my people, and thy God my God.
1 Samuel 4:9	Quit yourselves like men.
1 Samuel 13:14	A man after his own heart.
2 Samuel 1:23	In their death they were not divided.
2 Samuel 1:25	How are the mighty fallen!
2 Samuel 1:26	Thy love to me was wonderful, passing the love of women.
2 Samuel 12:7	Thou art the man.
2 Samuel 14:14	As water spilt on the ground, which cannot be gathered up again.
2 Samuel 23:1	The sweet psalmist of Israel.
1 Kings 18:21	How long halt ye between two opinions?
1 Kings 19:12	A still, small voice.
2 Kings 4:40	Death in the pot.
Job 1:1	One that feared God and eschewed evil.
Job 1:6	Satan came also.
Job 1:21	The Lord gave, and the Lord hath taken away
Job 2:4	All that a man hath will he give for his life.
Job 4:13 & 33:15	Night, when deep sleep falleth on men.
Job 5:7	Man is born unto trouble.
Job 5:13	He taketh the wise in their own craftiness.
Job 6:25	How forcible are right words!

Job 10:21	The land of darkness and the shadow of death.
Job 11:17	Clearer than the noonday.
Job 12:8	Speak to the earth, and it shall teach thee.
Job 16:2	Miserable comforters are ye all.
Job 18:14	The king of terrors.
Job 19:20	I am escaped with the skin of my teeth.
Job 28:13	The land of the living.
Job 29:13	I caused the widow's heart to sing for joy.
Job 29:15	I was eyes to the blind, and feet was I to the lame.
Job 32:9	Great men are not always wise.
Job 35:16	He multiplieth words without knowledge.
Job 37:22	Fair weather cometh out of the north.
Job 38:2	Who is this that darkeneth counsel by words without knowledge?
Job 38:7	The morning stars sang together, and all the sons of God shouted for joy.
Job 39:25	He smelleth the battle afar off.
Job 41:24	His heart is as firm as a stone.
Psalm 8:2	Out of the mouth of babes and sucklings.
Psalm 8:5	Thou hast made him a little lower than the angels.
Psalm 17:8	Keep me as the apple of the eye, hide me under the shadow of thy wings.
Psalm 18:10	10 he did fly upon the wings of the wind.
Psalm 19:1	The heavens declare the glory of God; and the firmament showeth his handiwork.
Psalm 19:10	Sweeter also than honey and the honeycomb.
Psalm 23:2	He maketh me to lie down in green pastures: he leadeth me beside the still waters.
Psalm 23:5	My cup runneth over.
Psalm 33:15	He fashioneth their hearts alike.
Psalm 39:3	My heart was hot within me.
Psalm 39:5	Every man at his best state is altogether vanity.
Psalm 41:1	Blessed is he that considereth the poor.
Psalm 46:1	God is our refuge and strength, a very present help in trouble.
Psalm 55:6	Oh that I had wings like a dove!
Psalm 55:14	We took sweet counsel together.
Psalm 57:7	My heart is fixed.

Psalm 72:9	His enemies shall lick the dust.
Psalm 73:20	As a dream when one awaketh.
Psalm 84:7	They go from strength to strength.
Psalm 90:9	We spend our years as a tale that is told.
Psalm 93:4	The noise of many waters.
Psalm 104:15	Wine that maketh glad the heart of man.
Psalm 107:27	They reel to and fro, and stagger like a drunken man, and are at their wits' end.
Psalm 116:11	All men are liars.
Psalm 119:99	I have more understanding than all my teachers
Psalm 137:2	We hanged our harps upon the willows.
Psalm 137:5	If I forget thee, O Jerusalem, let my right hand forget her cunning.
Psalm 139:14	I am fearfully and wonderfully made.
Proverbs 1:20	Wisdom crieth without; she uttereth her voice in the street.
Proverbs 4:7	With all thy getting get understanding.
Proverbs 6:6	Go to the ant, thou sluggard; consider her ways, and be wise.
Proverbs 7:22	As an ox goeth to the slaughter.
Proverbs 9:17	Stolen waters are sweet, and bread eaten in secret is pleasant.
Proverbs 10:1	A wise son maketh a glad father.
Proverbs 10:15	The destruction of the poor is their poverty.
Proverbs 10:25	The liberal soul shall be made fat.
Proverbs 13:12	Hope deferred maketh the heart sick.
Proverbs 13:24	He that spareth his rod hateth his son.
Proverbs 14:9	Fools make a mock at sin.
Proverbs 14:34	Righteousness exalteth a nation.
Proverbs 15:1	A soft answer turneth away wrath.
Proverbs 15:13	A merry heart maketh a cheerful countenance.
Proverbs 16:18	Pride goeth before destruction, and an haughty spirit before a fall.
Proverbs 17:22	A merry heart doeth good like a medicine.
Proverbs 17:27	He that hath knowledge spareth his words.
Proverbs 17:28	Even a fool, when he holdeth his peace, is counted wise.
Proverbs 18:22	Whoso findeth a wife findeth a good thing.

Proverbs 20:1	Wine is a mocker, strong drink is raging.
Proverbs 20:3	Every fool will be meddling.
Proverbs 20:12	The hearing ear and the seeing eye.
Proverbs 21:9	It is better to dwell in a corner of the housetop than with a brawling woman in a wide house.
Proverbs 22:1	A good name is rather to be chosen than great riches.
Proverbs 22:6	Train up a child in the way he should go; and when he is old he will not depart from it.
Proverbs 22:28 & 23:10	Remove not the ancient landmark.
Proverbs 23:2	Put a knife to thy throat.
Proverbs 23:5	Riches certainly make themselves wings.
Proverbs 23:7	As he thinketh in his heart, so is he.
Proverbs 25:25	As cold waters to a thirsty soul, so is good news from a far country.
Proverbs 26:27	Whoso diggeth a pit shall fall therein.
Proverbs 27:5	Open rebuke is better than secret love.
Proverbs 27:6	Faithful are the wounds of a friend.
Proverbs 29:8	Where there is no vision, the people perish.
Proverbs 30:8	Give me neither poverty nor riches.
Proverbs 31:28	Her children arise up and call her blessed.
Ecclesiastes 1:2 &12:8	Vanity of vanities, . . . all is vanity.
Ecclesiastes 1:4	One generation passeth away, and another generation cometh.
Ecclesiastes 1:8	The eye is not satisfied with seeing.
Ecclesiastes 1:9	There is no new thing under the sun.
Ecclesiastes 1:5	The sun also ariseth.
Ecclesiastes 1:14	All is vanity and vexation of spirit.
Ecclesiastes 1:18	He that increaseth knowledge increaseth sorrow.
Ecclesiastes 3:1	To everything there is a season, and a time to every purpose under the heaven.
Ecclesiastes 4:2	Let thy words be few.
Ecclesiastes 5:12	The sleep of a labouring man is sweet.
Ecclesiastes 7:1	A good name is better than precious ointment.
Ecclesiastes 8:15	Eat, and to drink, and to be merry.
Ecclesiastes 9:10	Whatsoever thy hand findeth to do, do it with thy might.

Ecclesiastes 9:11	The race is not to the swift, nor the battle to the strong.
Ecclesiastes 11:1	Cast thy bread upon the waters; for thou shalt find it after many days.
Ecclesiastes 12:7	Then shall the dust return to the earth as it was; and the spirit shall return unto God who gave it.
Ecclesiastes 12:12	Of making many books there is no end; and much study is a weariness of the flesh.
Ecclesiastes 12:13	Let us hear the conclusion of the whole matter: Fear God, and keep his commandments; for this is the whole duty of man.
Song of Solomon 2:11,12	For, lo! the winter is past, the rain is over and gone; the flowers appear on the earth; the time of the singing of birds is come, and the voice of the turtle is heard in our land.
Song of Solomon 6:4 & 10	Terrible as an army with banners.
Song of Solomon 8:6	Love is strong as death; jealousy is cruel as the grave.
Song of Solomon 8:7	Many waters cannot quench love, neither can the floods drown it.
Isaiah 1:3	The ox knoweth his owner.
Isaiah 1:5	The whole head is sick, and the whole heart faint.
Isaiah 1:18	Come now, and let us reason together.
Isaiah 2:4 and Micah 4:3	They shall beat their swords into ploughshares, and their spears into pruning-hooks; nation shall not lift up sword against nation, neither shall they learn war any more.
Isaiah 3:15	Grind the faces of the poor.
Isaiah 3:16	Walk with stretched-forth necks and wanton eyes, walking and mincing as they go.
Isaiah 4:20	Woe unto them that call evil good, and good evil.
Isaiah 6:5	I am a man of unclean lips.
Isaiah 8:19	Wizards that peep and that mutter.
Isaiah 9:15	The ancient and honorable.
Isaiah 11:6	The wolf also shall dwell with the lamb, and the leopard shall lie down with the kid.
Isaiah 14:12	Son of the morning.
Isaiah 21:9	Babylon is fallen.
Isaiah 21:11	Watchman, what of the night?
Isaiah 22:13	Let us eat and drink; for to-morrow we shall die.

Isaiah 28:10	For precept must be upon precept, precept upon precept; line upon line, line upon line; here a little, and there a little.
Isaiah 30:7	Their strength is to sit still.
Isaiah 35:1	The desert shall rejoice, and blossom as the rose.
Isaiah 38:1	Set thine house in order.
Isaiah 40:6	All flesh is grass.
Isaiah 40:15	A drop of a bucket.
Isaiah 48:22	There is no peace.
Isaiah 53:7	He is brought as a lamb to the slaughter.
Isaiah 63:3	I have trodden the wine-press alone.
Isaiah 64:6	We all do fade as a leaf.
Jeremiah 6:14 & 8:11	Peace, peace; when there is no peace.
Jeremiah 7:3 & 26:13	Amend your ways and your doings.
Jeremiah 8:22	Is there no balm in Gilead? Is there no physician there?
Jeremiah 13:23	Can the Ethiopian change his skin, or the leopard his spots?
Jeremiah 17:1	Written with a pen of iron, and with the point of a diamond.
Ezekiel 18:2 and Jeremiah 31:29	The fathers have eaten sour grapes, and the children's teeth are set on edge.
Ezekiel 21:21	Stood at the parting of the way.
Daniel 5:27	Thou art weighed in the balances, and art found wanting.
Daniel 12:4	Many shall run to and fro, and knowledge shall be increased.
Hosea 8:7	They have sown the wind, and they shall reap the whirlwind.
Joel 2:28	Your old men shall dream dreams, your young men shall see visions.
Joel 3:14	Multitudes in the valley of decision.
Zechariah 9:12	Prisoners of hope.
Zechariah 13:6	I was wounded in the house of my friends.

The Apocrypha

2 Esdras 14:25	I shall light a candle of understanding in thine heart, which shall not be put out.

The New Testament

Matthew 4:4	Man shall not live by bread alone.
Matthew 5:13	The salt of the earth.
Matthew 5:14	Ye are the light of the world. A city that is set on an hill cannot be hid.
Matthew 5:43	Love thy neighbour.
Matthew 6:1	Do not your alms before men, to be seen of them.
Matthew 6:3	Let not thy left hand know what thy right hand doeth.
Matthew 6:20	Lay up for yourselves treasures in heaven.
Matthew 6:21	Where your treasure is, there will your heart be also.
Matthew 6:22	The light of the body is the eye.
Matthew 6:24	No man can serve two masters.
Matthew 6:24	Take no thought for your life, what ye shall eat, or what ye shall drink.
Matthew 6:28	Consider the lilies of the field, how they grow; they toil not, neither do they spin.
Matthew 7:6	Neither cast ye your pearls before swine.
Matthew 7:7	Ask, and it shall be given you; seek, and ye shall find; knock, and it shall be opened unto you.
Matthew 7:9	Or what man is there of you, whom if his son ask bread, will he give him a stone?
Matthew 7:12	Therefore all things whatsoever ye would that men should do to you, do ye even so to them.
Matthew 7:13	Wide is the gate and broad is the way that leadeth to destruction.
Matthew 7:14	Strait is the gate and narrow is the way.
Matthew 7:20	By their fruits ye shall know them.
Matthew 7:25	Founded upon a rock.
Matthew 8:20	The foxes have holes, and the birds of the air have nests.
Matthew 9:37	The harvest truly is plenteous, but the labourers are few.
Matthew 10:16	Be ye therefore wise as serpents, and harmless as doves.
Matthew 10:30	The very hairs of your head are all numbered.
Matthew 12:33	The tree is known by his fruit.
Matthew 13:46	Pearl of great price.
Matthew 13:57	A prophet is not without honour, save in his own country and in his own house.

Matthew 14:27	Be of good cheer: it is I; be not afraid.
Matthew 15:14	If the blind lead the blind, both shall fall into the ditch.
Matthew 15:27	The dogs eat of the crumbs which fall from their masters' table.
Matthew 16:2	When it is evening, ye say it will be fair weather: for the sky is red.
Matthew 16:3	The signs of the times.
Matthew 16:23	Get thee behind me, Satan.
Matthew 16:26	What is a man profited, if he shall gain the whole world, and lose his own soul?
Matthew 17:4	It is good for us to be here.
Matthew 19:6	What therefore God hath joined together, let not man put asunder.
Matthew 19:19	Love thy neighbour as thyself.
Matthew 19:24	It is easier for a camel to go through the eye of a needle, than for a rich man to enter into the kingdom of God.
Matthew 20:12	Borne the burden and heat of the day.
Matthew 22:5	They made light of it.
Matthew 22:14	For many are called, but few are chosen.
Matthew 22:21	Render therefore unto Caesar the things which are Caesar's.
Matthew 23:24	Blind guides, which strain at a gnat, and swallow a camel.
Matthew 23:27	Whited sepulchres, which indeed appear beautiful outward, but are within full of dead men's bones.
Matthew 23:37	As a hen gathereth her chickens under her wings.
Matthew 24:6	Wars and rumours of wars.
Matthew 24:6	The end is not yet.
Matthew 24:15	Abomination of desolation.
Matthew 25:29	Unto every one that hath shall be given, and he shall have abundance; but from him that hath not shall be taken away even that which he hath.
Matthew 26:41	The spirit indeed is willing, but the flesh is weak.
Mark 2:27	The Sabbath was made for man, and not man for the Sabbath.
Mark 3:25	If a house be divided against itself, that house cannot stand.
Mark 4:9	He that hath ears to hear, let him hear.
Luke 2:14	Glory to God in the highest, and on earth peace, good will toward men.

Luke 3:5	Every valley shall be filled, and every mountain and hill shall be brought low; and the crooked shall be made straight, and the rough ways shall be made smooth.
Luke 3:9	The axe is laid unto the root of the trees.
Luke 4:23	Physician, heal thyself.
Luke 6:26	Woe unto you, when all men shall speak well of you!
Luke 8:17	Nothing is secret.
Luke 10:5	Peace be to this house.
Luke 10:7	The labourer is worthy of his hire.
Luke 10:37	Go, and do thou likewise.
Luke 11:23	He that is not with me is against me.
Luke 12:19	Eat, drink, and be merry.
Luke 19:22	Out of thine own mouth will I judge thee.
John 1:46	Can there any good thing come out of Nazareth?
John 3:8	The wind bloweth where it listeth.
John 7:24	Judge not according to the appearance.
John 8:32	The truth shall make you free.
John 8:44	There is no truth in him.
John 9:4	The night cometh when no man can work.
John 12:8	The poor always ye have with you.
John 14:1	Let not your heart be troubled.
John 14:2	In my Father's house are many mansions.
John 15:13	Greater love hath no man than this, that a man lay down his life for his friends.
Acts 8:20	Thy money perish with thee.
Acts 9:5	It is hard for thee to kick against the pricks.
Acts 19:38	The law is open.
Acts 20:35	It is more blessed to give than to receive.
Acts 26:26	For this thing was not done in a corner.
Acts 26:28	Almost thou persuadest me to be a Christian.
Romans 2:11	There is no respect of persons with God.
Romans 3:18	Fear of God before their eyes.
Romans 3:31	God forbid.
Romans 4:18	Who against hope believed in hope.
Romans 6:19	Speak after the manner of men.
Romans 6:23	The wages of sin is death.

Romans 8:28	All things work together for good to them that love God.
Romans 8:31	If God before us, who can be against us?
Romans 10:2	A zeal of God, but not according to knowledge.
Romans 12:13	Given to hospitality.
Romans 12:16	Be not wise in your own conceits.
Romans 12:18	If it be possible, as much as lieth in you, live peaceably with all men.
Romans 12:20	If thine enemy hunger, feed him; if he thirst, give him drink: for in so doing thou shalt heap coals of fire on his head.
Romans 12:21	Overcome evil with good.
1 Corinthians 5:3	Absent in body, but present in spirit.
1 Corinthians 7:31	The fashion of this world passeth away.
1 Corinthians 9:22	All things to all men.
1 Corinthians 13:1-4	Though I speak with the tongues of men and of angels, and have not charity, I am become as sounding brass, or a tinkling cymbal. Though I have all faith, so that I could remove mountains, and have not charity, I am nothing. Charity suffereth long and is kind; charity envieth not; charity vaunteth not itself, is not puffed up.
1 Corinthians 13:11	When I was a child, I spake as a child . . . When I became a man, I put away childish things.
1 Corinthians 13:12	Now we see through a glass, darkly.
1 Corinthians 14:40	Let all things be done decently and in order.
1 Corinthians 15:33	Evil communications corrupt good manners.
1 Corinthians 15:52	In the twinkling of an eye.
2 Corinthians 3:6	Not of the letter, but of the spirit; for the letter killeth, but the spirit givelight.
2 Corinthians 3:12	Plainness of speech.
2 Corinthians 5:7	We walk by faith, not by sight.
2 Corinthians 6:2	Now is the accepted time.
2 Corinthians 12:7	A thorn in the flesh.
Philippians 4:7	The peace of God, which passeth all understanding.
Colossians 2:21	Touch not; taste not; handle not.
1 Thessalonians 1:3	Labour of love.
1 Thessalonians 4:11	Study to be quiet.
1 Thessalonians 5:21	Prove all things; hold fast that which is good.

1 Timothy 1:8	Not greedy of filthy lucre.
1 Timothy 3:13	Busybodies, speaking things which they ought not.
1 Timothy 6:10	The love of money is the root of all evil.
1 Timothy 6:12	Fight the good fight.
1 Timothy 6:29	Science falsely so called.
2 Timothy 2:15	A workman that needeth not to be ashamed.
2 Timothy 4:7	I have fought a good fight, I have finished my course, I have kept the faith.
Hebrews 5:12	Such as have need of milk, and not of strong meat.
Hebrews 11:1	Faith is the substance of things hoped for, the evidence of things not seen.
Hebrews 12:1	A cloud of witnesses.
Hebrews 12:6	Whom the Lord loveth he chasteneth.
Hebrews 13:8	Yesterday, and to-day, and forever.
James 1:19	Be swift to hear, slow to speak, slow to wrath.
James 3:5	How great a matter a little fire kindleth!
James 3:8	The tongue can no man tame; it is an unruly evil.
1 Peter 1:13	Hope to the end.
1 Peter 2:17	Fear God. Honour the king.
1 Peter 3:8	Be ye all of one mind.
1 Peter 4:8	Charity shall cover the multitude of sins.
2 Peter 1:19	And the day star arise in your hearts.
2 Peter 2:22	The dog is turned to his own vomit again.
1 John 3:17	Bowels of compassion.
1 John 4:18	There is no fear in love; but perfect love casteth out fear.
Revelation 2:10	Be thou faithful unto death.
Revelation 2:27	He shall rule them with a rod of iron.
Revelation 7:9	All nations and kindreds and tongues.
Revelation 22:13	I am Alpha and Omega, the beginning and the end, the first and the last.

Bartlett, John. 1901. *Familiar Quotations*.

Appendix B

Gold, Frankincense, and Myrrh: Gifts of Wise Men

This example of symbols is included in the appendix because it is laden with Christian Christmas meaning. In fact, the visit of the wise men is celebrated in many Christian cultures on the twelfth day of Christmas, or Epiphany. The three kings visit children at night, leaving gifts like Santa Claus on Christmas Eve. The celebration of Christmas has become a lightning rod in some schools, so teacher discretion is advised. The best guideline is to note that teaching about religion is legal, but teaching religion is not. The use of this and any other material should have a clear educational purpose, like teaching the literary symbols of a Bible narrative, and not have a devotional purpose. When material has a devotional purpose, the courts have ruled that it primarily advances a religion and is unconstitutional, as establishing a religious practice.

> Star-led, the Magi,
>   Christ their King adoring,
> Gold, myrrh and incense at his feet bestow;
>   We on his birthday
> Bring our hearts' oblation:
>   O come, let us adore him,
>   O come, let us adore him,
>   O come, let us adore him, Christ the Lord.
>   —Verse 4 of *Adeste Fideles*
>   (O Come All Ye Faithful)
>   from *The Westminster Hymnal*, 1839

The Christmas pageants and Christmas carols include the Magi in the Nativity even though they came into the house (Matthew 2:11) and not into the stable or manger as the shepherds did. In the seldom-sung fourth verse of "O Come All Ye Faithful," Christians honor them and their gifts. The record of these Magi, or wise men from the East, is only twelve verses long (Matthew 2:1–12). The Bible doesn't say where they came from or how many of them there were. Their mission was to witness and worship, much like the Christmas eve shepherds.

Many assume that these wise men followed a star. The text isn't clear here. It says they had "seen his star in the east, and are come to worship him" (Matthew 2:2). Most assume from this verse that they followed a star, but a close reader may be left with doubts. The passage says they saw a star, not that they followed it.

Their effect was to begin the tradition of Christmas presents as they presented the first gifts of Christmas while witnessing a gift to the world. These Magi are the literary subjects of legends and operas that build on the scant facts of these twelve verses. Perhaps they were from Arabia or Mesopotamia, but "from the east" is all the text says. Perhaps the clue is in Psalm 72:10–15, which could be saying that the three were from Tarshish, Sheba, and Seba, but this is an allusion away from the text and a meaning added by Christian readers. We guess there were three because of the three gifts they brought the baby, but some commentators suggest on two gifts, golden frankincense (a rare and pure frankincense) and myrrh. Perhaps the real clues to their identity and mission are in their gifts of gold, frankincense, and myrrh. From a literary point of view these gifts are the center of the story and symbols that give these twelve verses context and meaning. They are important for literary Bible readers trying to look beneath the story at symbolic meanings. With all that is not mentioned and left to us to imagine in this reticent literature, the gifts must be important because they *are* mentioned.

Looking specifically at the gifts of the Magi should not detract our attention from the fact that these wise men were very different from the others that came the night of the nativity. Perhaps shepherd and scholar visiting is itself symbolic. The shepherds were the simple local folks, who were given a miraculous revelation as they tended sheep. The wise men were sophisticated foreign scientists of the day who had studied astrology and astronomy. Perhaps the symbolic meaning of the two groups of visitors is that Jesus is appealing to both the simple and the intellectual of the world.

Based on the questions the wise men asked of Herod, "Where is he that is born King of the Jews?" the assumption is that they were not Hebrews, but all that is really known beyond the twelve verses is legend mingled with history. For example, Herodotus, writing about 450 B.C.E, suggests that the Magi were of a priestly caste of the Medes (Persia), which specialized in the interpretation of dreams. It may be that when Herodotus was writing, Magi were Zoroastrian priests.

Other magi in the New Testament and in New Testament times are not treated by the writers with the same favor as those who visited the baby. Simon (Acts 8:9–24), Elymas (Acts 13:6–11), and Atomos in Josephus, *The Antiquities of the Jews* (20.7.2) are sorcerers or magicians. It is their sorcery that seems to distinguish them from the worshiping Magi.

The passage in Matthew indicates that the Magi were scientists who understood the stars to reveal wonders and even God's will. Other passages also make this point. In Genesis 37:9, Joseph dreams of stars that make obeisance to him and riles his brothers by repeating the dream; Joel 2 speaks of wonders in the heavens; the stars of heaven fall in Mark 13:25; there are wonders in heaven in Acts 2:17-21; behind the sixth seal in Revelation 6:13, the stars of heaven fall to earth. It is important to notice that these allusions are outside the wise men text and may or may not hold. It may be that a look at symbolic stars would be interesting to students.

Matthew carefully writes his gospel in terms of the Christian view of the fulfillment of prophecy. As the events of the New Testament are said to fulfill the Old in Matthew, we are reminded in Numbers 24:17 that "There shall come a Star out of Jacob, and a Sceptre shall rise out of Israel." Old Testament prophecy notes that "Nations shall come to thy light, and kings to the brightness of thy rising" (Isaiah 60:3). Even with these few words there are still details "missing" about the visit of these wise men from the East. With all that is "missing," the key must still be in the gifts of gold, frankincense, and myrrh.

Gold has become a synonym for value. *Precious* is probably the best adjective for a metal easily refined that doesn't corrode or tarnish. In the Bible we read of pure gold, fine gold, and choice gold. It comes from Nubia (Sudan) by way of Egypt. Nubia means *gold* in ancient Egyptian. Gold also came from Ophir (1 Kings 9:28, 10:11; Job 22:24) and from Havilah and Parvaim (Genesis 2:11–12; 2 Chronicles 3:6). What is important is not where gold comes from—although it may give a clue as to the home and the possible royal status of the wise men—but what gold means. It is the precious metal of jewelry and a commodity traded on international exchanges where people watch by the hour for fluctuations in price. Gold may be a symbol beyond a pearl of great price.

Myrrh, a fragrant gum from the rockrose, was carried from Gilead to Egypt by the Ishmaelites in Genesis 37:25. It was carried with the balm of Gilead. Myrrh was one of the "choice fruits of the land" that Jacob had his sons carry to Joseph in Egypt (Genesis 43:11). Indications are that in biblical times it was sometimes in solid form and sometime used as an oil. Esther used myrrh in its oil form as a beauty treatment (Esther 2:12). It was also an important ingredient in making anointing oil and was used in the anointing oil as Aaron and his sons were consecrated to the priesthood (Exodus 30:22–30). Perhaps the most important use of myrrh was its apparent function in Egyptian embalming. It was prized as early as 2000 B.C.E. according to ancient Ugaritic records found at Ras Shamra. Herodotus, writing about 450 B.C.E. noted its apparent use in Egyptian embalming. The reason this may be the most important fact to understand about myrrh is because it was not only offered and refused by Jesus as "wine mingled with myrrh" (Mark 15:23) to act as pain relief to the suffering Jesus, but myrrh was brought by Nicodemus for Jesus' burial (John 19:39).

Frankincense is also a gum resin. It is a fragrant resin from trees belonging to the genus Boswellia and has a balsamlike odor when burned. I've never had a problem teaching about the symbols, except for the time that burning frankincense set off the fire alarms in the school! Frankincense was probably used by the Egyptians in the 15th-century B.C.E. It was at this time that Queen Hatshepsut sent an expedition to what is now probably Somalia to get some "perfume of the gods."

The trade in aromatics prompted Herodotus to write, "The whole country is scented with them and exhales an odor marvelously sweet." This was when Athens was at its peak of power in 450 B.C.E. At the time of Jesus, the trade would have been no less. Production could have amounted to 3,000 tons a year. The amount didn't seem to depress the price in the time of Rome, when Nero spent the equivalent of a year's Arabian production on the funeral of Poppaea.

The recipe for the Temple incense, a "perfume which thou shalt make... unto the holy for the Lord," includes frankincense (Exodus 30:34–37). This incense, or frankincense and oil, was added to grain offerings and burned (Leviticus 2:1–2, 2:14–16; 6:14–18). It was not added to a sin offering (Leviticus 5:11) or to a grain offering of jealousy (Numbers 5:15). It should also be noted that frankincense was put on the Showbread in the Temple (Leviticus 24:7) and, because of its use, it was stored in the Temple (1 Chronicles 9:29; Nehemiah 13:5, 9).

Knowing what the gifts of the Magi were helps to establish that they represent ideas, they are symbols. Knowing the symbols, we may ask what the wise men knew that would prompt them to offer such valuable gifts to a young baby. The gifts first of all represent that which is valuable. They are also gifts often associated with death. This makes them unusual gifts for a young child. These symbols of sacrifice, death, authority, burial, and preservation of the body tell us what the wise men may have known. The gifts teach us how to look at symbols and expand our reading.

The Three Kings

Who are these that ride so fast o're the desert's
     sandy road,
That have tracked the Red Sea shore, and have
     swum the torrents broad;
Whose camels' bells are tinkling through the long
     and starry night—
For they ride like men pursued, like the vanquished
     of a fight?
      —from *Hymns*
      edited by Frederick William Faber, 1848

There are some beautiful pictures of frankincense in Abercrombie's *National Geographic* article, "Arabia's Frankincense Trail." Much in this example comes from this article. This is an example of what anyone can do when turned loose with a good Bible dictionary and biblical encyclopedia. The search for the symbolic for students is as easy as looking in reference books and then reading the information into the biblical text. Granted, there are some contextual pitfalls, but the dictionary and encyclopedia are places to start.

Appendix C

Samson as Archetype

Samson's hair is interesting and students will like looking at this symbol, but Samson himself can provide a good example of the archetype character, a prototype or model upon which other literary or historical characters are made and measured. Samson is the typical character who makes the mold for others. He is the bad guy we like. He is like Robin Hood or Jesse James, two outlaws that we celebrate in song, verse, and movie who are really quite foul characters, whose popularity probably persists because of their legendary resistance to established authority.

I usually begin the discussion with two questions:

1. Can you name any modern bad guys that we like? (The list students come up with usually includes some sports, rock music, or movie celebrities. They are usually people who rub against authority.)

2. If you were to bring Samson home for a family dinner, what good things would you tell your family about him so he wouldn't be judged by all the bad things your family has probably heard about him?

After the discussion I point out that we usually tell of the exploits of these folk heros in a way that no one seems to seriously disapprove of some pretty nasty behavior.

In his *Introduction to Biblical Literature*, O. B. Davis includes a list of characteristics of the folklore character bad guys. Samson seems to set the pattern. This list can be used for group work, with each group deciding how Samson matches the description:

1. Most such heroes possess one particular ability in which they far surpass anyone around them.

2. They are frequently "rascals" who entertain us by tricking their enemies—and sometimes their friends.

3. Very often they are also rascals in their disregard of local proprieties, particularly property rights and sexual ethics. Their stories are generally told, however, in such a style that the audience is not invited to disapprove seriously of these shortcomings, if at all.

4. They are self-directed, willful individuals who, for good or ill, make their own decisions and follow them through despite advice or warning. Such decisions are generally impulsive, because these heroes are not given to extended contemplation of consequences.

5. Often the stories about their lineage, birth, or infancy contain strange or marvelous details that may suggest they are destined for the roles they play.

6. In the end, such heroes are betrayed by people they trust.

7. They are primitives: childlike and childish, trusting and untrustworthy, innocent and homicidal, romantic and unrestrained, attractive and dangerous. (141)

Appendix D

Samson as Foil

Students who take the Bible seriously as a religious text have a question after reading Samson. How did he make the cut? They want to know how an antiheroic brawler and womanizer qualifies as a judge in Israel and why his exploits should achieve the status of scripture. Even secular readers wonder about the context of this tale and other grim tales in Judges.

In his excellent teaching resource, *Introduction to Biblical Literature*, O. B. Davis suggests that Samson is a "parody of his great predecessor, Moses" (Davis 141). This suggests that Samson is a foil for Moses. This idea requires some license because a foil should really be within the same narrative, not just the same book or collection of books. This problem aside, the opportunity is there to teach about a foil. It is an easy concept for students to understand and helps them become more imaginative readers.

It helps to look at jewelry in the mall. The stones sparkle in the display case. They even seem to look larger under the advantage of skillfully used lighting. The lights create a foil for the jewels. The lights make the jewels look even better than they are. Take the jewelry out into the honest light of day, and it can look a bit ordinary. It can look a bit small in a big world, whereas it looked big in a small case. In C. Hugh Holman's *A Handbook to Literature*, the definition of *foil* takes the word back to its origins. "A *foil* is literally a sheet of bright metal that is placed under a piece of jewelry to increase its brilliance. In literature, by extension, the term is applied to any person or sometimes a thing that through strong contrast underscores or enhances the distinctive characteristics of another" (187).

It may be that Samson makes the heroic Moses look even better, stronger, more heroic. This is the point that Davis makes in his comparison of Samson and Moses (141–14). It may be overstated a bit, but we'll let Davis speak for himself on this literary point:

A foil is literally a sheet of bright metal placed under a piece of jewelry to increase its brilliance.	A literary foil is a person who through strong contrast underscores or enhances the distinctive characteristics of another.
Moses	Samson
Moses speaks with God face to face.	Samson's only contacts with God are through his mother and father.
Moses obeys the Word against his own fearful inclinations.	Samson never obeys anyone and is apparently incapable of reasonable fear or any inclinations but the most immediate physical ones.
Moses works for the unity of Israel.	As a lusty brawler, Samson, without apparently working at all, contributes to just the opposite.
Moses makes a solemn historical covenant with God in behalf of his people.	Samson asks God for a last surge of strength so that he can be revenged for his lost eyesight.
Moses makes his God the public reference point for all his actions.	Samson gives God credit for none of his exploits.
Moses staunchly counteracts the pressures of emotion or sentiment.	Sexual desire and irritation easily and invariably overcome any principles that Samson may have.
Moses gives and explains the law.	Samson is either unaware of or simply disregards the law.
Moses composes songs in praise of God and His deliverance of Israel.	Samson tosses off riddles and barnyard sayings.
The life of Moses, in spite of certain incongruous episodes, is serious and lofty.	The life of Samson, in spite of its spectacular ending, is really rather funny.
Moses is a might man of God.	Samson is a mighty buffoon.

It is the "certain incongruous episodes" in the life of Moses that are diminished by his foil, if Samson were indeed in the same narrative. As a foil, Samson makes Moses even better, to the point that we easily look past "certain incongruous episodes."

LITERARY HISTORY OF PSALM 23: COMPARATIVE TRANSLATIONS AND METAPHOR

This literary history of the most translated passage in the English Bible was published by Charles C. Butterworth in *Literary Lineage of the King James Bible, 1340-1611*. The translations since the KJV in 1611 were added by this author and are listed as passages, not as interlinear text. Butterworth underlined the lines that found their way to the KJV. His point is that the poetic metaphors stuck and became the "authorized" version. They became *the* translation. I use this to teach metaphor. I also use this when asking if this Psalm has improved since 1611.

Psalm 23 is cited as a "Psalm of Confidence" or a "Psalm of Thanksgiving" in some translations. It may have been a "Psalm of Pilgrimage" to the Temple, according to some commentators. Whatever else it is, it is a psalm of metaphor:

Shepherd:
: The image is of a shepherd who leads the sheep rather than driving them. This is the principle metaphor of the poem.

Green Pastures:
: Our mental image is that green pastures are scarce in the land of this psalm. Scarcity increases value and creates a symbol.

Still Waters:	The still waters are a sharp contrast to the washes and gullies that are mostly dry yet flood with the sudden showers. The washes offer little refreshment and the still waters offer safety and nourishment.
Darkness, or Valley of the Shadow of Death:	There are deep ravines in the land of the psalm that are dangerous to people and sheep.
Staff or rod:	The shepherd has a staff to protect sheep from other animals and a crook for guiding sheep.
Table:	Perhaps since the psalm suggests dwelling in the house of the LORD forever, this is the table where a sacrifice was eaten by the Temple priests.
Enemies:	Even the enemies are symbolic, since the psalm doesn't explain exactly what danger is apparent. It would take some confidence to eat in the presence of an enemy.
Cup Runneth Over:	This metaphor describes abundant blessings and happiness. It is more than the cup can hold.
Anointed with Oil:	The head of an honored guest could be anointed with oil. The symbolism of olive oil is rich in the Bible as kings are anointed in the Hebrew Bible and the rich anointed in the New Testament.
House of the Lord:	The place of sacrifice and worship would offer temporary happiness. The psalmist suggests that life with a shepherd LORD is like living in the Tabernacle forever.

Butterworth provides a literary history of other familiar texts for teachers interested in exploring the history of language. One misconception students often have on this point is that translators were trying to improve earlier versions. It is probably more accurate to assume that each translator sees the text through a template of the times and is trying to help the psalm communicate to contemporary readers.

One reason this example is in the appendix is that for many readers it is laden with sanctity—so much so that academic study is difficult. Some religious traditions use this psalm as a prayer or part of the litergy. For this reason, it is difficult to use in some schools. A liturgical or devotional reading would not comply with current Bible-reading guideline for the schools. A secular reading, teaching language history and metaphor, would meet the guidelines. Even given the cautions, I have found that this is an excellent comparative reading.

Rol	1340	Lord gouerns me	and nathynge sall me want:
Mid	1340	Our Lord gouerneth me,	and nothyng shal defailen to me;
WHf	1382	The Lord gouerneth me,	and no thing to me shal lacke;
WPv	1395	The Lord gouerneth me,	and no thing schal faile to me;
LhP	1410	Oure lord gouerneth me	and nothyng schal lacke me;
P30	1530	The lorde is my pastore & feader:	wherfore I shal not wante.
GJP	1534	The Lorde fedeth me:	wherfore I can want nothinge.
Cov	1535	<u>The Lorde is my shepherde,</u>	I can wante nothinge.
R36	1536	The Lorde ruleth me,	& nothynge shall fayle me
Grt	1539	The Lorde is my shepherde,	therfore can I lack nothing.
PLG	1540	The Lorde gouerneth me,	and I shall lacke nothynge:
Gnv	1560	The Lord *is* my shepherd,	<u>I shall not want.</u>
B68	1568	God is my sheephearde,	therfore I can lacke nothyng:
RhD	1610	Our Lord ruleth me,	and nothing shal be wanting to me:
KJV	1611	The Lord *is* my shepheard,	I shall not want.

Rol	1340	in sted of pasture thare he me sett.
Mid	1340	in the stede of pasture he sett me ther.
WHf	1382	in the place of leswe where he me ful sette.
WPv	1395	in the place of pasture there he hath set me.
LhP	1410	in place of pasture there he hath sett me.
P30	1530	¶He made me to feade in a full plentuous batle grownde:
GJP	1534	¶He settith me in a goodly lusty pasture:
Cov	1535	He fedeth me in a grene pasture,
R36	1536	in a place of pasture there hathe he set me.
Grt	1539	He shall fede me in a grene pasture,
PLG	1540	in a place of pasture euen there hath he set me.
Gnv	1560	He maketh me to rest in grene pasture,
B68	1568	he wyll cause me to repose my selfe in pasture full of grasse,
RhD	1610	in place of pasture there he hath placed me.
KJV	1611	<u>He maketh me to lie downe in greene pastures:</u>

Rol	1340	¶On the watere of rehetynge forth he me broght;
Mid	1340	¶He norissed me vp water of fyllyng;
WHf	1382	Ouer watir of fulfilling he nurshide me;
WPv	1395	He nurschide me on the watir of refreischyng;
LhP	1410	He hath browghte me foorth up on the water of rehetynge;
P30	1530	& dyd dryve and retche me at layser by the swete ryvers.
GJP	1534	and retcheth me forthe vnto swete still runninge waters.
Cov	1535	and ledeth me to a fresh water.
R36	1536	¶He hathe broughte me vpon a fresshe water:
Grt	1539	& leade me forth besyde the waters of comforte.
PLG	1540	¶Vpon ye water of refection hathe he norished me,
Gnv	1560	& leadeth me by the stil waters.
B68	1568	and he wyll leade me vnto calme waters.
RhD	1610	¶Vpon the water of refection he hath brought me vp:
KJV	1611	<u>he leadeth me beside the still waters.</u>

Rol	1340	my saule he turnyd.
Mid	1340	he turned by soule fram the fende.
WHf	1382	my soule he conuertide.
WPv	1395	he conuertide my soule.
LhP	1410	he conueertede my soule.
P30	1530	¶He restored my lyfe
GJP	1534	¶He refressheth my soule/
Cov	1535	He quickeneth my soule,
R36	1536	he conuerteth my soule.
Grt	1539	He shall conuerte my soule,
PLG	1540	my soule hath he conuerted.
Gnv	1560	<u>He restoreth my soule,</u>
B68	1568	He wyll conuert my soule:
RhD	1610	he hath conuerted my soule.
KJV	1611	He restoreth my soule:

Rol	1340	¶He led me on the stretis of rightwisnes: for his name.
Mid	1340	¶He led me vp the bistiyes of rightfulnes for his name.
WHf	1382	He broghte doun be vpon the sties of rightwisnesse: for his name.
WPv	1395	Heledde me forth on the pathis of rightfulnesse: for his name.
LhP	1410	He ladde me upon the pathes of rightwesnesse: for his naame.
P30	1530	and led me by the pathes of rightwisnes: <u>for his names sake.</u>
GJP	1534	and directeth me in the right waye / for his names sake.
Cov	1535	& bringeth me forth in the way of rightuousnes for his names sake.
R36	1536	¶He hathe ledde me vpon the pathes of iustyce for his names sake.
Grt	1539	& brynge me forth in the pathes of ryghteousnes for hys names sake.
PLG	1540	¶He hath led me forth vpon the pathes of ryghteousnes, euen for hys owne name sake.
Gnv	1560	& leadeth me in the paths of righteousnes for his Names sake.
B68	1568	he wyll bring me foorth into the pathes of righteousnesse for his name sake.
RhD	1610	¶He hath conducted me vpon the pathes of iustice, for his name.
KJV	1611	<u>he leadeth me in the pathes of righteousnes,</u> for his names sake.

Rol	1340	¶ffor whi, if i had gane in myddis of the shadow of ded;
Mid	1340	¶For vif that ich haue gon amiddes of the the shadowe of deth;
WHf	1382	For whi and if I shal go in the myddel of the shadewe of deth;
WPv	1395	For whi though Y schal go in the myddis of schadewe of deeth;
LhP	1410	For whi though y go in myddes the schadwe of deeth;
P30	1530	¶Ye if I shulde go thorow the myddes of deth:
GJP	1534	¶For albe it I shulde go vnto the valye of the dedely shadewe/
Cov	1535	Though I shulde walke now in the valley of the shadowe of death,
R36	1536	¶For although I walke in ye myddes of the shadowe of deathe/
Grt	1539	<u>Yee though I walke thorow ye valley of the shadow of death,</u>
PLG	1540	¶For though I walke in ye myddes of the shadowe of death,
Gnv	1560	Yea, thogh I shulde walke through the valley of the shadow of death,
B68	1568	Yea though I walke through the valley of the shadowe of death,
RhD	1610	For, although I shal walke in the middes of the shadow of death,
KJV	1611	Yea though I walke through the valley of the shadowe of death,

Rol	1340	i sall noght dred illes, <u>for thou ert with me.</u>
Mid	1340	y shal nought douten iuels; for thou art wyth me.
WHf	1382	I shal not dreden euelis, for thou art with me.
WPv	1395	Y schal not drede yuels, for thou art with me.
LhP	1410	y schal nought dreede yueles, for thou art with me.
P30	1530	yet wolde I feare non evel: for thou art with me:
GJP	1534	yet fere I none euyll/ for thou art with me:
Cov	1535	yet I feare no euell, for thou art with me:
R36	1536	I shal feare no harme, for thou art with me.
Grt	1539	<u>I will feare no euell</u>, for thou art wt me:
PLG	1540	I wyll feare no euell, for yu art wt me.
Gnv	1560	I wil feare no euil: for thou art with me:
B68	1568	I wyll feare no euyll: for thou art with me,
RhD	1610	I wil not feare euils: because thou art with me.
KJV	1611	I will feare no euill: for thou *art* with me,

Rol	1340	¶Thi wand and thi staf; thai haf confortyd me.
Mid	1340	¶Thy discipline and thyn amendyng conforted me.
WHf	1382	Thi yerde and thy staf; tho han confortid me.
WPv	1395	Thi yerde and thi staf; tho han coumfortid me.
LhP	1410	Thy yerde and thi staf; they han comforted me.
P30	1530	thy staffe and thy shepe hoke counfort me
GJP	1534	ye thy staffe and shepehoke ar my counforte,
Cov	1535	thy staffe & thy shepehoke comforte me.
R36	1536	¶Thy stafe and thy rodde: they comfortyd me.
Grt	1539	<u>thy rodde & thy staffe</u> comforte me.
PLG	1540	¶Thy rodde & thy sraff, those haue comforted me.
Gnv	1560	thy rod and thy staffe, <u>they comfort me.</u>
B68	1568	thy rodde and thy staffe be thynges that do comfort me.
RhD	1610	¶Thy rod and thy staffe: they haue comforted, me.
KJV	1611	thy rod and thy staffe, they comfort me.

Rol	1340	¶Thou has grayid in my syght the bord; agayns thaim that angirs me.
Mid	1340	¶Thou madest radi grace in my sight ogayns hem that trublen me.
WHf	1382	Thou hast maad redi in thi sighte a bord; agen hem that trublyn me.
WPv	1395	Thou hast maad redi a boord in my sight; agens hem that troblen me.
LhP	1410	Thou hast greythed a table in my syght; agen hem that trowbleth me.
P30	1530	¶Thou shalt sprede and garneshe me a table/ ye and that in the syght of myn enymes:
GJP	1534	¶Thou spredest me a table in the presence of my aduersaryes/
Cov	1535	<u>Thou preparest a table before me</u> agaynst mine enemies:
R36	1536	¶Thou haste preparyd a table in my syght agaynst them that trouble me.
Grt	1539	Thou shalt prepare a table before me agaynst them yt trouble me:
PLG	1540	¶Thou hast prepared a table before me, agaynst them that trouble me.
Gnv	1560	Thou doest prepare a table before me in the sight of mine aduersaries:
B68	1568	Thou wylt prepare a table before me in the presence of myne aduersaries:
RhD	1610	¶Thou hast prepared in my sight a table, against them; that truble me.
KJV	1611	Thou preparest a table before me, <u>in the presence of mine enemies</u>:

Rol	1340	¶Thou fattid my heued in oyle;
Mid	1340	¶Thou makest fatt myn heued wyth mercy;
WHf	1382	Thou hast myche fatted in oile myn hed;
WPv	1395	Thou hast made fat myn heed with oyle;
LhP	1410	Thou madest fatt myn heued in oyle;
P30	1530	thou shalt souple my hed with oyntment/
GJP	1534	thou sowplest my head with oyntment
Cov	1535	<u>thou anoyntest my heade with oyle,</u>
R36	1536	¶Thou hast soupled myne hede in oyle
Grt	1539	yu hast anoynted my head with oyle,
PLG	1540	¶Thou hast soupled my headin oyle:
Gnv	1560	thou doest anoint mine head with oyle
B68	1568	thou hast annoynted my head with oyle,
RhD	1610	¶Thou hast fatted my headwith oyle:
KJV	1611	thou anointest my head with oyle,

Rol	1340	and my chalice drunkynand what it is bright.
Mid	1340	and my drynk makand drunken ys ful clere.
WHf	1382	and my chalis makende ful drunden, hou right cler it is.
WPv	1395	and my cuppe, fillinge greetli, is ful cleer.
LhP	1410	and my dronkelew coppe is right cleer.
P30	1530	& my full cuppe shall laughe vpon me.
GJP	1534	and fillest my cuppe.
Cov	1535	& fyllest my cuppe full.
R36	1536	and my cuppe beynge full, is ryght goodly.
Grt	1539	& my cuppe shalbe full.
PLG	1540	my cuppe also is full & exceadynge fayre.
Gnv	1560	*and* my cup runneth ouer.
B68	1568	and my cup shalbe brymme full.
RhD	1610	and my chalice inebriating how goodlie is it!
KJV	1611	<u>My cuppe runneth ouer.</u>

Rol	1340	¶And thi mercy sall folow me; <u>all the dayes of my lif</u>.
Mid	1340	¶And thy merci shal folwen me alle daies of mi lif;
WHf	1382	And thi mercy shal vnderfolewe me; alle the dayis of my lif.
WPv	1395	And thi merci schal sue me; in alle the daies of my lijf.
LhP	1410	And thy mercy schal folwe me; alle the dayes of my lyf.
P30	1530	¶Ye/ and thy mercy & ientlenes shall folowe me all my lyfe:
GJP	1534	¶Thy goodnes therfore & thy benigne mercye are with me through all my lyfe
Cov	1535	Oh let thy louynge kyndnes & mercy folowe me all the dayes off my life,
R36	1536	¶And thy mercye shall folowe me all the dayes of my lyfe.
Grt	1539	But (*thy*) louynge kyndnes and mercy shall folowe me all the dayes of my lyfe:
PLG	1540	¶And thy mercy shall go wyth me all the dayes of my lyfe.
Gnv	1560	Douteles kindenes, & mercie shal follow me all the dayes of my life,
B68	1568	Truely felicitie and mercie shal folowe me all the dayes of my lyfe:
RhD	1610	¶And thy mercie shal folow me al the dayes of my life:
KJV	1611	<u>Surely goodness and mercie shall followe me</u> all the dayes of my life:

Rol	1340	¶And that i won in the hows of lord; in length of dayes.
Mid	1340	¶And that ich wonne in the hous of our Lord in lengthe of daies.
WHf	1382	And that I dwelle in the hous of the Lord; in to the lengthe of dayis.
WPv	1395	And that Y dwelle in the hows of the Lord; in to the lengthe of daies.
LhP	1410	And that y wonye in the hous of oure lord; in to the lengthe of dayes.
P30	1530	I shall sitte in the house of the lorde a longe tyme.
GJP	1534	that I myght dwell in thy house for euer.
Cov	1535	that I maye dwell in the house of the Lorde for euer.
R36	1536	¶And yt I may inhabyte in ye house of ye lorde for ye length of my dayes.
Grt	1539	<u>& I will dwell in the house of the Lord for euer.</u>
PLG	1540	¶That I also maye dwell in the house of the Lorde longe and many dayes.
Gnv	1560	and I shal remaine a long season in the house of the Lord.
B68	1568	and I wyll dwell in the house of God for a long tyme.
RhD	1610	¶And that I may dwel in the house of our Lord, in longitude of dayes.
KJV	1611	and I will dwell in the house of the Lord for euer.

KJV   1611 {A Psalm of David.} ¹The LORD *is* my shepherd; I shall
           not want. ²He maketh me to lie down in green pastures:
           he leadeth me beside the still waters. ³He restoreth my
           soul: he leadeth me in the paths of righteousness for his
           name's sake. ⁴ Yea, though I walk through the valley of
           the shadow of death, I will fear no evil: for thou *art* with
           me; thy rod and thy staff they comfort me. ⁵Thou preparest
           a table before me in the presence of mine enemies: thou
           anointest my head with oil; my cup runneth over. ⁶Surely
           goodness and mercy shall follow me all the days of my
           life: and I will dwell in the house of the LORD for ever.

WEB   1833 (The English Noah Webster Bible) ¹A Psalm of David.
           The LORD [is] my shepherd; I shall not want. ²He maketh
           me to lie down in green pastures: he leadeth me beside
           the still waters. ³He restoreth my soul: he leadeth me in
           the paths of righteousness for his name's sake. ⁴Yes,
           though I walk through the valley of the shades of death,
           I will fear no evil: for thou [art] with me; thy rod and thy
           staff they comfort me. ⁵Thou preparest a table before me
           in the presence of my enemies: thou anointest my head
           with oil; my cup runneth over. ⁶Surely goodness and
           mercy shall follow me all the days of my life: and I will
           dwell in the house of the LORD for ever.

YLT   1862 (Young's Literal Translation) ¹A Psalm of David. Je-
           hovah [is] my shepherd, I do not lack, ²In pastures of ten-
           der grass He causeth me to lie down, By quiet waters He
           doth lead me. ³My soul He refresheth, He leadeth me in
           paths of righteousness, For His name's sake, ⁴Also—when
           I walk in a valley of death-shade, I fear no evil, for Thou
           [art] with me, Thy rod and Thy staff—they comfort me.
           ⁵Thou arrangest before me a table, Over-against my ad-
           versaries, Thou hast anointed with oil my head, My cup
           is full! ⁶Only—goodness and kindness pursue me, All the
           days of my life, And my dwelling [is] in the house of Je-
           hovah, For a length of days!

DBY   1884 (The English Darby Bible) ¹Jehovah is my shepherd;
           I shall not want. ²He maketh me to lie down in green pas-
           tures; he leadeth me beside still waters. ³He restoreth my

soul; he leadeth me in paths of righteousness for his name's sake. [4]Yea, though I walk through the valley of the shadow of death, I will fear no evil: for thou art with me; thy rod and thy staff, they comfort me. [5]Thou preparest a table before me in the presence of mine enemies; thou hast anointed my head with oil; my cup runneth over. [6]Surely, goodness and loving-kindness shall follow me all the days of my life; and I will dwell in the house of Jehovah for the length of the days.

DRA   1899 (Douay-Rheims American Version) [1]A psalm for David. The Lord ruleth me: and I shall want nothing. [2]He hath set me in a place of pasture. He hath brought me up, on the water of refreshment: [3]He hath converted my soul. He hath led me on the paths of justice, for his own name's sake. [4]For though I should walk in the midst of the shadow of death, I will fear no evils, for thou art with me. Thy rod and thy staff, they have comforted me. [5]Thou hast prepared a table before me against them that afflict me. Thou hast anointed my head with oil; and my chalice which inebreateth me, how goodly is it! [6]And thy mercy will follow me all the days of my life. And that I may dwell in the house of the Lord unto length of days.

ASV   1901 (American Standard Version) [1]Jehovah is my shepherd; I shall not want. [2]He maketh me to lie down in green pastures; He leadeth me beside still waters. [3]He restoreth my soul: He guideth me in the paths of righteousness for his name's sake. [4]Yea, thou I walk through the valley of the shadow of death, I will fear no evil; for thou art with me; Thy rod and thy staff, they comfort me. [5]Thou preparest a table before me in the presence of mine enemies: Thou hast anointed my head with oil; My cup runneth over. [6]Surely goodness and lovingkindness shall follow me all the days of my life; And I shall dwell in the house of Jehovah for ever.

BBE   1949/64 (The English Bible in Basic English) [1]The Lord takes care of me as his sheep; I will not be without any good thing. [2]He makes a resting-place for me in the green fields: he is my guide by the quiet waters. [3]He gives new life to my soul: he is my guide in the ways of righteousness because of his name. ⁴Yes, though I go through the valley of deep shade, I will have no fear of evil; for you are with me, your rod and your support are my comfort. ⁵You make ready a table for me in front of my haters: you put oil on my head; my cup is overflowing. ⁶Truly, blessing and mercy will be with me all the days of my life; and I will have a place in the house of the Lord all my days.

RSV   1952 (Revised Standard Version) ¹The LORD is my shepherd, I shall not want; ²he makes me lie down in green pastures. He leads me beside still waters; ³he restores my soul. He leads me in paths of righteousness for his name's sake. ⁴Even though I walk through the valley of the shadow of death, I fear no evil; for thou art with me; thy rod and thy staff, they comfort me. ⁵Thou preparest a table before me in the presence of my enemies; thou anointest my head with oil, my cup overflows. ⁶Surely goodness and mercy shall follow me all the days of my life; and I shall dwell in the house of the LORD for ever.

NAS   1977 (New American Standard Bible) ¹The LORD is my shepherd, I shall not want. ²He makes me lie down in green pastures; He leads me beside quiet waters. ³He restores my soul; He guides me in the paths of righteousness For His name's sake. ⁴Even though I walk through the valley of the shadow of death, I fear no evil; for Thou art with me; Thy rod and Thy staff, they comfort me. ⁵Thou dost prepare a table before me in the presence of my enemies; Thou hast anointed my head with oil; My cup overflows. ⁶Surely goodness and lovingkindness will follow me all the days of my life, And I will dwell in the house of the LORD forever.

NKJ   1982 (New King James Version) ¹The LORD *is* my shepherd; I shall not want. ²He makes me to lie down in green pastures; He leads me beside the still waters. ³He restores my soul; He leads me in the paths of righteousness For His name's sake. ⁴Yea, though I walk through the valley of the shadow of death, I will fear no evil; For You *are* with me; Your rod and Your staff, they comfort me. ⁵You prepare a table before me in the presence of my enemies; You anoint my head with oil; My cup runs over. ⁶Surely goodness and mercy shall follow me All the days of my life; And I will dwell in the house of the LORD Forever.

NIV   1984 (New International Version) ¹The LORD is my shepherd, I shall not be in want. ²He makes me lie down in green pastures, he leads me beside quiet waters, ³he restores my soul. He guides me in paths of righteousness for his name's sake. ⁴Even though I walk through the valley of the shadow of death, I will fear no evil, for you are with me; your rod and your staff, they comfort me. ⁵You prepare a table before me in the presence of my enemies. You anoint my head with oil; my cup overflows. ⁶Surely goodness and love will follow me all the days of my life, and I will dwell in the house of the LORD forever.

NJB   1985 (New Jerusalem Bible) ¹Yahweh is my shepherd, I lack nothing. ²In grassy meadows he lets me lie. By tranquil streams he leads me ³to restore my spirit. He guides me in paths of saving justice as befits his name. ⁴Even were I to walk in a ravine as dark as death I should fear no danger, for you are at my side. Your staff and your crook are there to soothe me. ⁵You prepare a table for me under the eyes of my enemies; you anoint my head with oil; my cup brims over. ⁶Kindness and faithful love pursue me every day of my life. I make my home in the house of Yahweh for all time to come.

NAB   1986 (New American Bible) ¹The LORD is my shepherd; there is nothing I lack. ²In green pastures you let me graze; to safe waters you lead me; ³you restore my strength. You guide me along the right path for the sake of your name. ⁴Even when I walk through a dark valley, I fear no harm for you are at my side; your rod and staff give me courage. ⁵You set a table before me as my enemies watch; You anoint my head with oil; my cup overflows. ⁶Only goodness and love will pursue me all the days of my life; I will dwell in the house of the LORD for years to come.

NRS   1989 (New Revised Standard Version) ¹The LORD is my
         shepherd, I shall not want. ²He makes me lie down in
         green pastures; he leads me beside still waters; ³he re-
         stores my soul. He leads me in right paths for his name's
         sake. ⁴Even though I walk through the darkest valley, I
         fear no evil; for you are with me; your rod and your staff—
         they comfort me. ⁵You prepare a table before me in the
         presence of my enemies; you anoint my head with oil;
         my cup overflows. ⁶Surely goodness and mercy shall fol-
         low me all the days of my life, and I shall dwell in the
         house of the LORD my whole life long.

RWB   1995 (English Revised 1833 Webster Bible) ¹The LORD *is*
         my shepherd; I shall not want. ²He maketh me to lie down
         in green pastures: he leadeth me beside the still waters.
         ³He restoreth my soul: he leadeth me in the paths of righ-
         teousness for his name's sake. ⁴Yea, though I walk through
         the valley of the shadow of death, I will fear no evil: for
         thou *art* with me; thy rod and thy staff they comfort me.
         ⁵Thou preparest a table before me in the presence of my
         enemies: thou anointest my head with oil; my cup runneth
         over. ⁶Surely goodness and mercy shall follow me all the
         days of my life: and I will dwell in the house of the LORD
         for ever.

NAU   1995 (New American Standard Bible) ¹The LORD is my
         shepherd, I shall not want. ²He makes me lie down in
         green pastures; He leads me beside quiet waters. ³He re-
         stores my soul; He guides me in the paths of righteous-
         ness For His name's sake. ⁴Even though I walk through
         the valley of the shadow of death, I fear no evil, for You
         are with me; Your rod and Your staff, they comfort me.
         ⁵You prepare a table before me in the presence of my en-
         emies; You have anointed my head with oil; My cup over-
         flows. ⁶Surely goodness and lovingkindness will follow
         me all the days of my life, And I will dwell in the house
         of the LORD forever.

NLT   1996 (New Living Translation) ¹The LORD is my shepherd;
         I have everything I need. ²He lets me rest in green mead-
         ows; he leads me beside peaceful streams. ³He renews

my strength. He guides me along right paths, bringing honor to his name. [4]Even when I walk through the dark valley of death, I will not be afraid, for you are close beside me. Your rod and your staff protect and comfort me. [5]You prepare a feast for me in the presence of my enemies. You welcome me as a guest, anointing my head with oil. My cup overflows with blessings. [6]Surely your goodness and unfailing love will pursue me all the days of my life, and I will live in the house of the LORD forever.

TEHILIM (Book of Psalms) Chapter 23 [1]A Psalm of David. HaShem is my shepherd: I shall not want. [2]He maketh me to lie down in green pastures; He leadeth me beside the still waters. [3]He resoreth my soul; He guideth me in straight paths for his name's sake. [4]Yea, though I walk through the valley of the shadow of death, I will fear no evil, for Thou art with me; Thy rod and Thy staff, they comfort me. [5] hou preparest a table before me in the presence of mine enemies; Thou hast anointed my head with oil; my cup runneth over. [6]Surely goodness and mercy shall follow me all the days of my life; and I shall dwell in the house of HaShem for ever.

WORKS CITED

Abercrombie, Thomas J. "Arabia's Frankincense Trail." *National Geographic* Oct. 1985: 474–513.

Ackerman, James S., and Thayer S. Warshaw. *The Bible as/in Literature*. Glenview: ScottForesman, 1995.

Adams, Dickinson W., ed. *Jefferson's Extracts from the Gospels: "The Philosophy of Jesus" and "The Life and Morals of Jesus."* The Papers of Thomas Jefferson, Second Series. Princeton: Princeton UP, 1983.

Ajami, Mansour. *The Alchemy of Glory: The Dialectic of Truthfulness and Untruthfulness in Medieval Arabic Literary Criticism*. Washington, DC: Three Continents, 1988.

"Altared States." *Xena: Warrior Princess*. Videocassette. Universal Television Enterprises, Santa Monica. 22 Apr. 1996.

Alter, Robert. *The Art of Biblical Narrative*. New York: Basic, 1981.

———. *The Art of Biblical Poetry*. New York: Basic, 1985.

———. *The World of Biblical Literature*. New York: Basic, 1992.

Alter, Robert, and Frank Kermode. *The Literary Guide to the Bible*. Cambridge: Belknap, 1987.

Anderson, Janice Capel, and Stephen D. Moore. *Mark & Method: New Approaches in Biblical Studies*. Minneapolis: Fortress, 1992.

Ap-Thomas, D. R. ""Elijah on Mount Carmel." *Palestine Exploration Quarterly* 92 (1960): 146–55.

Aristotle. *The Rhetoric of Aristotle:Translated, with an Analysis and Critical Notes*. Trans. J.E.C. Welldon. New York: Macmillan, 1886.

As It Was in the Beginning. John Romer. Testament: The Bible and History. Videocassette. Films for the Humanities, Princeton, 1988.

Baldwin, Charles Sears. *How to Write: A Handbook Based on the English Bible*. London: Macmillan, 1906.

Barna Research Group. "The Faith Practice of America." 8 March 1999. <http://www.barna.org>.

Barna Research Group. "Barna Research On Line." (7/8/2000). http://www.barna.org.

Basho and Moritake. "Two Japanese Haiku." *Literature: Structure, Sound, and Sense*. Ed. Laurence Perrine. New York: Harcourt, 1983. 727.

Beem, Beverly. "The Wisdom of Achsah: A Reading of Judges 1:11–15." Unpublished essay, 2000.

Berra, Yogi. *The Yogi Book: I Really Didn't Say Everything I Said*. New York: Workman, Publishing, 1999.

"Bible Questions." *The Best of Art Linkletter's Kids Say the Darndest Things*. Videocassette. CBS/Darndest Partnership/Big Sky Productions, Los Angeles, 1994.

"Bible Questions." *Tonight Show with Jay Leno*. NBC. Los Angeles. 6 November, 1997.

Bible Works for Windows. 4.0. Big Fork, MT: Hermeneutika Bible Research Software, 1999.

Bleefeld, Bradley R., and Robert L. Shook. *Saving the World Entire and 100 Other Beloved Parables from the Talmud*. New York: Plume, 1998.

Blomberg, Craig L. *Interpreting the Parables*. Downers Grove: InterVarsity Press, 1990.

Bloom, Harold and David Rosenberg. *The Book of J*. New York: Grove, 1990.

Bodoff, Lippman. "God Tests Abraham, Abraham Tests God." *Bible Review* Oct. 1993: 53–56+.

The Book of Job. Trans. Stephen Mitchell. San Francisco: North Point, 1987.

The Book of Job. Trans. Raymond P. Scheindlin. New York: Norton, 1998.

Browning, W.R.F. *A Dictionary of the Bible*. New York: Oxford UP, 1997.

Bullinger, E. W. *Figures of Speech Used in the Bible: Explained and Illustrated*. Grand Rapids: Baker, 1968.

Butterworth, Charles C. *Literary Lineage of the King James Bible, 1340–1611*. Philadelphia: U of Pennsylvania, 1941.

Buttrick, George Arthur, ed. *The Interpreter's Dictionary of the Bible: An Illustrated Encyclopedia*. 4 vol. New York: Abingdon, 1962.

Campbell, Antony F., and Mark A. O'Brien. *Sources of the Pentateuch: Texts, Introductions, Annotations*. Minneapolis: Fortress, 1993.

Carter, Stephen L. *The Culture of Disbelief: How American Law and Politics Trivialize Religious Devotion*. New York: Basic, 1993.

Clines, David. "Deconstructing the Book of Job." *The Bible as Rhetoric*. Ed. Martin Warner. New York: Routledge, 1990. 65–80.

The Complete Parallel Bible with the Apocryphal/Deuterocanonical Books: New Revised Standard Version—Revised English Bible—New American Bible—New Jerusalem Bible. New York: Oxford UP, 1993.

Coogan, Michael David, ed. *The Oxford History of the Biblical World*. New York: Oxford UP, 1998.

Cranfield, C.E.B. "Mark, Gospel of." *The Interpreter's Dictionary of the Bible*. Ed. George Arthus Buttrick. Vol. 3. Nashville: Abingdon, 1962. 267–77.

Cremin, Lawrence. *American Education: The National Experience, 1783–1876*. New York: Harper, 1970.

Cross, Frank Moore. *Canaanite Myth and Hebrew Epic: Essays in the History of the Religion of Israel*. Cambridge: Harvard UP, 1973.

Daniell, David. *William Tyndale: A Biography*. New Haven: Yale UP, 1994.

Davis, O. B. *Introduction to Biblical Literature*. Portsmouth: Boynton, 1988.

Dershowitz, Alan M. *The Genesis of Justice : Ten Stories of Biblical Injustice That Led to the Ten Commandments and Modern Law*. New York: Warner, 2000.

Despland, Michel. *Kant on History and Religion with a Translation of Kant's 'On the Failure of All Attempted Philosophical Theodicies.'* Montreal: McGill-Queen's UP, 1973.

DeVoto, Bernard, ed. *Mark Twain: Letters from The Earth*. Greenwich: Crest, 1964.

Driver, G. R. *Canaanite Myths and Legends*. Edinburgh: Clark, 1956.

Dundes, Alan. *Sacred Narrative: Readings in the Theory of Myth*. Berkeley: U of California P, 1984.

A Father and Two Sons. Videocassette. American Bible Society, New York, 1994.

Ferguson, George. *Signs & Symbols in Christian Art*. New York: Oxford UP, 1961.

Ford, Massyngberde. *Revelation: Introduction, Translation, and Commentary*. Anchor Bible. Garden City, NY: Doubleday, 1975.

Freedman, David Noel, ed. *The Anchor Bible Dictionary*. 6 vols. New York: Doubleday, 1992.

Friedman, Richard Elliott. *Who Wrote the Bible?* New York: Harper, 1987.

Frye, Northrop. *The Great Code: The Bible and Literature*. New York: Karvest, 1982.

Gabel, John B., and Charles B. Wheeler. *The Bible as Literature: An Introduction*. New York: Oxford, 1996.

Gallup, Alec, and Wendy W. Simmons. "Six in Ten Americans Read the Bible at Least Occasionally." The Gallup Organization, 20 Oct. 2000. 6 April 2001. http://www.gallup.com/poll/releases/pr001020.asp.

Gallup, George, and Frank Newport. "The Bible Is Still Widely Read and Studied. 1990 Telephone Survey GO 922021." 1–4 Nov. 1990 (8 Jul. 1994).

The Gallup Organization. "Religion." 2001. 6 Apr. 2001 http://www.gallup.com/poll/Indicators/indreligion3.asp

Graves, Robert, and Raphael Patai. *Hebrew Myths: The Book of Genesis*. New York: Greenwich, 1983.

The Great Books Reading & Discussion Program: Reader Aid (First Series). Chicago: Great Books, 1985.

Greenspoon, Leonard J. "The New Testament in the Comics." *Bible Review* 9.6 (Oct. 1991): 40.

Grossman, Cathy Lynn. "The Bible Business: More People Curling Up with the Good Book." *USA Today* 27 May 1998: D1.

Gutjahr, Paul C. *An American Bible: A History of the Good Book in the United States, 1777–1880*. Stanford: Stanford UP, 1999.

Hammond, Gerald. "English Translations of the Bible." *The Literary Guide to the Bible*. Ed. Robert Alter and Frank Kermode. Cambridge: Harvard UP, 1987.

Harris, Stephen L. *Understanding the Bible*. 4th ed. Mountain View, CA: Mayfield, 1997.

Hayes, John H., and Carl R. Holladay. *Biblical Exegesis: A Beginner's Handbook*. Atlanta: Knox, 1987.

Haynes, Charles C., and Oliver S. Thomas and John B. Leach and Alyssa Kendall. *Finding Common Ground : A First Amendment Guide to Religion*. Ed. Charles C. Haynes. Nashville: Freedom Forum First Amendment Center, 1996.

Hirsch, E. D. Jr., and Joseph F. Kett, eds. *The Dictionary of Cultural Literacy*. Boston: Houghton, 1991.

History of the English Language. The English Programme. Knowing about Language. Videocassette. Films for the Humanities, Princeton, 1991.

Holman, C. Hugh. *A Handbook to Literature*. 4th ed. Indianapolis: Bobbs-Merrill, 1980.

Iwasaki, Scott. "I'm No Rock Star, but I've Got the Hair." *Deseret News* [Salt Lake City] 18 May 2001: W7, 10.

Jasper, David, and Stephen Prickett, eds. *The Bible and Literature: A Reader*. Malden, : Blackwell, 1999.

Jeffrey, David Lyle, ed. *A Dictionary of Biblical Tradition in English Literature*. Grand Rapids: Eerdmans, 1992.

Jensen, Robin M. "How Jews and Christians See Differently." *Bible Review* Oct. 1993.

"Jonah, Book of." *Dictionary of Biblical Imagery*. Ed. Leland Ryken et al. Downers Grove, : InterVarsity Press, 1998. 458–59.

Joseph. Dir. Roger Young. Perf. Ben Kingsley, Paul Mercurio, Martin Landau, Lesley Ann Warren. Videocassette. Turner, 1995.

Joseph and His Brethren. Dir. Irving Rapper. Perf. Geoffrey Horen, Robert Morley, and Belinda Lee. 1962. Videocassette. Vanguard, 1989.

Joseph and His Brothers. New Media Bible. The Genesis Project. Videocassette. Corporation of the President of the Church of Jesus Christ of Latter-Day Saints, 1996.

Joseph Mega-Remix. The Premiere Collection Encore. Andrew Lloyd Webber. Videocassette. PolyGram, New York, 1992.

Kirsch, E. D., and Joseph F. Kett, eds. *The Dictionary of Cultural Literacy*. Boston: Houghton, 1991.

Klein, William W., Craig L. Blomberg, and Robert L. Hubbard. *Introduction to Biblical Interpretation*. Dallas: Word, 1993.

Kohlenberger III, John R., ed. *The NIV Interlinear Hebrew-English Old Testament*. Grand Rapids: Zondervan, 1987.

Kugel, James L. *The Great Poems of the Bible*. New York: The Free Press Division of Simon & Schuster, 1999.

Kushner, Harold S. *When Bad Things Happen to Good People*. New York: Avon, 1981.

"Lewd, Indecent? Atheist Fights to Remove Bible From Schools." *The Salt Lake Tribune* 24 Sep. 1992: A4.

Lewis, C. S. *The Literary Impact of the Authorized Version*. Philadelphia: Fortress, 1963.

Logos Bible Software 2.0e, The Logos Library System. Oak Harbor, WA: Logos Research Systems, 1996.

Long, John R. "Aesop's Fables Online Collection." 1999. 28 Jan. 2000. http://www.pacificnet.net/~johnr/aesop/

Long, V. Philips. *The Art of Biblical History*. Foundations of Contemporary Interpretation 5. Grand Rapids: Zondervan, 1994.

Longman, Tremper III. *Literary Approaches to Biblical Interpretation*. Foundations of Contemporary Interpretation 3. Grand Rapids: Academe, 1987.

Louis, Kenneth R. R., Gros, ed. *Literary Interpretations of Biblical Narratives: The Bible in Literature Courses*. Nashville: Abingdon, 1974.

Mack, Burton L. *Who Wrote the New Testament? The Making of the Christian Myth*. San Francisco: HarperCollins, 1989.

Matthews, Victor H. *Manners and Customs in the Bible*. Peabody: Hendrickson, 1991.

McCary, P. K., interp. *Black Bible Chronicles: From Genesis to the Promised Land*. New York: African American Family, 1993.

McCullough, W. S. "Serpent." *The Interpreter's Dictionary of the Bible*. Ed. George Arthur Buttrick. Vol. 4. Nashville: Abingdon, 1962. 289–90.

McDowell, Josh. *Historical Evidences for the Christian Faith*. San Bernardino: Here's Life, 1972.

McGuffey's Eclectic Readers: Primer through the Sixth Revised Editions. New York: Wiley, 1909.

Milgrom, Jacob. "Nazirite." *Encyclopaedia Judaica*. CD-ROM. 1997.

Miller, Robert J., ed. *The Complete Gospels*. San Francisco: Polebridge, 1994.

Murphy, Cullen. "Women and the Bible." *The Atlantic Monthly* Aug. 1993.

Nash, Robert J. *Faith, Hype, and Clarity: Teaching about Religion in American Schools and Colleges*. New York: Teachers College, 1999.

National Council of Teachers of English and International Reading Association. *Standards for the English Language Arts*. Urbana: NCTE, 1996.

"Noah's Flood (The Chester Play)." *The Norton Anthology of English Literature*. Ed. M. H. Abrams. 7th ed. Vol. 1. New York: Norton, 2000. 381–91.

Nord, Warren A., and Charles C. Haynes. *Taking Religion Seriously across the Curriculum.* Alexanderia, VA: Association for Supervision & Curriculm Development, 1998.

Nord, Warren A. and Charles C. Haynes. *Taking Religion Seriously Across the Curriculum.* Nashville: Association for Supervision and Curriculum Development and First Amendment Center, 1998.

Oscarson, Glen E. "The Foils of Joseph." Student Paper at Brigham Young University. English, Provo, UT, 2000.

Out of the Tombs. Videocassette. American Bible Society. New York, 1991.

Padgett, Ron, ed. "Allegory." *The Teachers' & Writers' Handbook of Poetic Forms.* 1987. 7.

Perrine, Laurence. *Literature: Structure, Sound, and Sense.* New York: Harcourt, 1983.

Potok, Chaim. *Davita's Harp.* New York: Knopf, 1985.

———. *Wanderings: Chaim Potok's History of the Jews.* New York: Fawcett Crest, 1978.

Rhodes, David, Joanna Dewey, and Donald Michie. *Mark as Story: An Introduction to the Narrative of a Gospel.* 2nd ed. Minneapolis: Fortress, 1999.

Riemer, Jack. "The Binding of Isaac: Rembrandt's Contrasting Portraits." *Bible Review* 6 (Dec. 1989): 26.

Robertson, Shanda. "The Law: Case History of Teaching Bible in the Public Schools." Report prepared for author, 2000.

Rollins, Richard M. *The Long Journey of Noah Webster.* Philadelphia: U of Pennsylvania, 1980.

Romer, John. *Testament: The Bible and History.* New York: Holt, 1988.

Rosenbaum, Stanley N. "It Gains a Lot in Translation." *Approaches to Teaching the Hebrew Bible as Literature in Translation.* Ed. Barry N. Olshen and Yael S. Feldman. New York: MLA, 1989. 40–44.

Ryken, Leland. *How to Read the Bible as Literature.* Grand Rapids: Academe, 1984.

———. *Words of Delight.* Grand Rapids: Baker, 1987.

Ryken, Leland et al., eds. *Dictionary of Biblical Imagery.* Downers Grove: InterVarsity, 1998.

Ryken, Leland, and Tremper Longmann III. *A Complete Literary Guide to the Bible.* Grand Rapids: Zondervan, 1993.

Samson and Delilah. Dir. Nicolas Roeg. Perf. Dennis Hopper, Eric Thal, and Elizabeth Hurley. Videocassette. Turner, 1996.

Sanders, James A. "Understanding the Development of the Biblical Text." *The Dead Sea Scrolls after Forty Years*. Ed. Hershel Shanks. Washington: Biblical Archaeology Society, 1990. 56–73.

"Satire." *Dictionary of Biblical Imagery*. Ed. Leland Ryken et al. Downers Grove: InterVarsity Press, 1998. 762.

Schwartz, Regina M. "Teaching a Sacred Text as Literature, Teaching Literature as a Sacred Text." *Profession* (1998).

Seaberry, Manica, and David E. Anderson. "Biblical Literalists." *Salt Lake Tribune* Dec. 1998: B2.

Smith, William Robertson. *Kinship and Marriage in Early Arabia*. Boston: Beacon, 1966.

Stein, Robert H. *Difficult Sayings in the Gospels: Jesus' Use of Overstatement and Hyperbole*. Grand Rapids: Baker, 1985.

Sternberg, Meir. *The Poetics of Biblical Narrative*. Bloomington: Indiana UP, 1985.

Strong, James. *The New Strong's Exhaustive Concordance of the Bible*. Nashville: Nelson, 1990.

Tate, Randolph W. *Biblical Interpretation: An Integrated Approach*. Peabody: Hendrickson, 1991.

Trible, Phyllis. *Texts of Terror: Literary-Feminist Readings of Biblical Narratives*. Philadelphia: Fortress, 1984.

Vaughan, Curtis, editor. *The Word: The Bible From 26 Translations*. Gulfport, MS: Mathis, 1993.

Vickers, Brian. "The Songs and Sonnets and the Rhetoric of Hyperbole." *John Donne, Essays in Celebration*. Ed. A. J. Smith. London: Harper, 1972.

The Visit. Videocassette. American Bible Society. New York, 1994.

Wachlin, Marie Goughnour. "The Bible: Why We Need to Teach It; How Some Do." *English Journal* 87.3 (March 1998).

Wadsworth, Michael, ed. *Ways of Reading the Bible*. New Jersey: Barnes & Noble, 1981.

Walker, Steven C. *Seven Ways of Looking at Susanna*. Values in Literature Monograph 1. Provo: Brigham Young University, 1984.

Warshaw, Thayer S. *Handbook for Teaching the Bible in Literature Classes*. Nashville: Abingdon, 1978.

Welch, John W. *Chiasmus in Antiquity*. Provo: Brigham Young University, 1999.

"Which—and Whose—Ten Commandments?" *Deseret News* [Salt Lake City] 28 June 1999: A2.

Whiston, William, and Paul L. Maier. *The New Complete Works of Josephus*. Grand Rapids: Kregel, 1999.

Wiesel, Elie. *The Gates of the Forest*. New York: Frenaye, 1966.

"Women, Blacks, Teens Can Find Bibles Edited for Them." *Deseret News* [Salt Lake City] 26 September 1998.

Wordsworth, William. "My Heart Leaps Up." *Favorite Poems: William Wordsworth*. New York: Dover, 1992. 34.

INDEX OF BIBLICAL CITATIONS

Genesis
Genesis 1:1, *60*
Genesis 1:1-2:3, *70-72*
Genesis 1-3, *75*
Genesis 1:3, *11*
Genesis 1:4, *60, 140-141*
Genesis 2:4-25, *70, 72-73*
Genesis 2:11-12, *279*
Genesis 2:16-17, *75*
Genesis 2: 19-20, *12*
Genesis 3:14, *98*
Genesis 3:22, *97*
Genesis 6:4, *106*
Genesis 7:2-3, *156*
Genesis 8:8-12, *212*
Genesis 9, *106*
Genesis 9:13, *107*
Genesis 10, *46*
Genesis 11:4, *60*
Genesis 12:6, *155*
Genesis 12-24, *87*
Genesis 14:18, *236*
Genesis 18:23-33, *89*
Genesis 22, *83*
Genesis 22:1-19, *79*
Genesis 31:32, *239*
Genesis 37:9, *279*
Genesis 37:25, *280*
Genesis 37-45, *222*
Genesis 38, *221, 222*
Genesis 43:11, *280*
Genesis 45:1-15, *222*
Genesis 49:17, *101*

Exodus
Exodus 3:2, *242*
Exodus 4:3, *100*
Exodus 4:10, *217*
Exodus 7:9-10, *100*
Exodus 7:12, *100*
Exodus 7:15, *100*

Exodus 12:12, *237*
Exodus 13:21, *242*
Exodus 14:2, *237*
Exodus 14:22, *60*
Exodus 18:10-11, *237*
Exodus 20, *46*
Exodus 20:1-17, *36*
Exodus 20:3, *237*
Exodus 20:4, *59*
Exodus 24:4, *242*
Exodus 30:22-30, *280*
Exodus 30:34-37, *280*
Exodus 32:4, *237*
Exodus 32:6, *237*
Exodus 33:12-23, *243*
Exodus 33:17-23, *243*
Exodus 34:6-8, *243*
Exodus 33:22, *242*
Exodus 34:22-26, *238*
Exodus 34:10, *98*

Leviticus
Leviticus 2:1-2, *280*
Leviticus 2:14-16, *280*
Leviticus 6:14-18, *280*
Leviticus 5:11, *280*
Leviticus 7:15, *134*
Leviticus 9:24, *242*
Leviticus 11-15,
Leviticus 19:14, *59*
Leviticus 24:7, *281*

Numbers
Numbers 5:15, *280*
Numbers 5:22, *60*
Numbers 6, *109, 111*
Numbers 6:24-26, *40*
Numbers 21:9, *98, 99*
Numbers 24:17, *279*
Numbers 25:1-5, *238*

Deuteronomy
    Deuteronomy 8:3, *12, 60*
    Deuteronomy 11:16-17, *241*
    Deuteronomy 32:33, *100*

Joshua
    Joshua 4:3, 102
    Joshua 4:3, 242
    Joshua 22:17-19, *238*
    Joshua 24:2, *239*
    Joshua 24:14,15, *239*

Judges
    Judges 1:11-15, *137-140*
    Judges 3:12-30, *47-48*
    Judges 3:24, *136*
    Judges 4, *180, 181-182*
    Judges 4:8, *179*
    Judges 4:9, *179*
    Judges 5, *181, 182-185*
    Judges 5:7, *179, 187*
    Judges 5:12, *187*
    Judges 5:24, *187*
    Judges 5:25, *116*
    Judges 5:27, *187*
    Judges 5:30, *187*
    Judges 13-16, *109*
    Judges 13:5, *109*
    Judges 13:5, *111*
    Judges 13:7, *111*
    Judges 14, *12-17*
    Judges 16:17, *111*

1 Samuel
    1 Samuel 1, *142*
    1 Samuel 8:7, *60*
    1 Samuel 9:2, *215*
    1 Samuel 16:7, *215*
    1 Samuel 16-17, *191-196*
    1 Samuel 16-30, *199*
    1 Samuel 17, *58*
    1 Samuel 18, 19, 20, 23, *199*
    1 Samuel 24, 26, *199*

2 Samuel
    2 Samuel 1-6, *199*
    2 Samuel 11-18, *199*
    2 Samuel 19:1-8, *199*
    2 Samuel 23:1-5, *199*

2 Samuel 3:26-30, *205*
2 Samuel 6: 12-23, *200*
2 Samuel 11-12, *200-203*
2 Samuel 13:1–20, *199*
2 Samuel 14:25, *199*
2 Samuel 5:2–6, *199*
2 Samuel 18:9, *199*
2 Samuel 16:5-13, *205*
2 Samuel 18:1-15, *205*
2 Samuel 21:19, *135*
2 Samuel 19:16-23, *205*
2 Samuel 20:4-13, *205*
2 Samuel 23: 1-5, *204*

1 Kings
    1 Kings 1-2, *198*
    1 Kings 2, *199*
    1 Kings 2: 1-10, *204-205*
    1 Kings 3:16-28, *134*
    1 Kings 9:28, *279*
    1 Kings 10:11, *279*
    1 Kings 10:1, *137*
    1 Kings 16:33, *236*
    1 Kings 17-19, *233*
    1 Kings 17:31, *242*
    1 Kings 18:13, *240*
    1 Kings 18-19, *xi, 253*
    1 Kings 18:21, *244*
    1 Kings 18:22, *240*
    1 Kings 18:25, *246*
    1 Kings 18:30, *239*
    1 Kings 19:9-14, *243*
    1 Kings 19:10, *240*
    1 Kings 22:6, *240*
    1 Kings 34, *245*

2 Kings
    2 Kings 1:8, *249*
    2 Kings 2:11, *247*
    2 Kings 10:18-28, *241-242*
    2 Kings 14:25, *213*
    2 Kings 15 and 16, *47*
    2 Kings 18:4, *99, 101*
    2 Kings 22:2, *39*

1 Chronicles
    1 Chronicles 9:29, *281*
    1 Chronicles 11-29, *199*

1 Chronicles 20:5, *135*
1 Chronicles 21:26, *242*

2 Chronicles
2 Chronicles 3:6, *279*
2 Chronicles 7:1, *242*

Nehemiah
Nehemiah 13:5,9, *281*

Esther
Esther 2:12, *280*
Esther 4:3, *59*

Job
Job 2:3, *175, 177*
Job 3:25, *175*
Job 19:25-27, *147, 174*
Job 19:28, *60*
Job 22:24, *279*
Job 27:1-6, *176*
Job 28:20-26, *117*
Job 31:5-7, *176*
Job 38:1-42, *172*
Job 41:31, *115*
Job 42:7, *176*
Job 42:7-17, *172*
Job 42:10, *177*

Psalms
Psalm 1:6, *116*
Psalm 2:4, *115*
Psalm 7:17, *107*
Psalm 8, *147*
Psalm 8:3-8, *117*
Psalm 19:1, *115*
Psalm 20:7, *116*
Psalm 23, *47, 124-126, 136, 147-148,*
    289, 301
Psalm 23:3, *117*
Psalm 33:6, *12*
Psalm 37, *10*
Psalm 46:3, *60*
Psalm 49:5, *137*
Psalm 51:2, *115*
Psalm 55: 6-8, *212*
Psalm 58:4, *100*
Psalm 72:10-15, *278*
Psalm 76, *120*

Psalm 78:2, *137*
Psalm 90:9, *59*
Psalm 97:1, *116*
Psalm 102:1-11, *117-118*
Psalm 107:27, *59*
Psalm 127:1, *60*
Psalm 147:3, *60*
Psalm 148:5, *12*

Proverbs
Proverbs 1:6, *137*
Proverbs 3:3, *39*
Proverbs 3:13-18, *96*
Proverbs 6:20, *116*
Proverbs 12:4, *116*
Proverbs 18:19, *146*
Proverbs 23:32, *100*
Proverbs 31:10-31, *129-130*

Ecclesiastes
Ecclesiastes 1:18, *131*
Ecclesiastes 12:9-10, *12*
Ecclesiastes 10:1, *59*

Song of Solomon
Song of Solomon 2:1, *95*

Isaiah
Isaiah 1:18, *59*
Isaiah 6:5, *217*
Isaiah 14:29, *100*
Isaiah 38:1, *59*
Isaiah 38:14, *212*
Isaiah 40:15, *60*
Isaiah 52:8, *60*
Isaiah 54:13, *149*
Isaiah 59:11, *212*
Isaiah 60:3, *279*

Jeremiah
Jeremiah 1:6, *217*
Jeremiah 2:5-9, *120*
Jeremiah 2:27, *120*
Jeremiah 8:17, *100*
Jeremiah 10:3-4, *134*
Jeremiah 51:34, *214*

Ezekiel
Ezekiel 1, *107*

Ezekiel 1:28, *107*
Ezekiel 7:16, *212*

Daniel
Daniel 5:5, *59*
Daniel 8:23, *137*

Joel
Joel 2, *279*

Jonah, *207-211*

Habakkuk
Habakkuk 2:6, *137*
Habakkuk 3:11, *107*

Nahum 2:7, *212*

Malachi
Malachi 3:11, *235*
Malachi 4:5, *247*
Malachi 4:6, *106*

Ecclesiasticus
Ecclesiasticus 43:11-12, *108*

Susanna, *49-55*

Sirach 43:11, *108*
Sirach 50:7, *108*

1 Maccabees
1 Maccabees 2:58, *248*

Matthew
Matthew 2:1-12, *278*
Matthew 2:2, *278*
Matthew 3:12, *60*
Matthew 3:15, *212*
Matthew 4:4, *60*
Matthew 5:13, *59*
Matthew 5:9, *60*
Matthew 6:24, *59*
Matthew 7:6, *59*
Matthew 7:14, *59*
Matthew 10:16, *99, 101*
Matthew 10:27, *59*
Matthew 10:29, *218*

Matthew 12:39-41, *213*
Matthew 12:43-45, *230*
Matthew 13:46, *59*
Matthew 17:12-13, *249*
Matthew 17:16, *249*
Matthew 19:30, *219*
Matthew 23:23, *60*
Matthew 25:14-30, *162*

Mark
Mark 5:1-20, *259*
Mark 5: 19, *258*
Mark 6:14-15, *249*
Mark 9:2-8, *249*
Mark 13:25, *279*
Mark 16:8, *262*
Mark 15:23, *280*

Luke
Luke 1:17, *248*
Luke 2:14, *60, 143*
Luke 15:29, *60*
Luke 8:10-13, *162-163*
Luke 9:28-36, *249*
Luke 10:29-37, *164-165*
Luke 11:24-26, *230*
Luke 23:46, *191*

John
John 1:1, *11, 60*
John 1:19-23, *249*
John 3:14, *100*
John 10:10, *219*
John 19:39, *280*

Acts
Acts 1:22, *262*
Acts 2:32, *262*
Acts 3:15, *262*
Acts 10:41, *262*
Acts 13:31, *262*
Acts 2:17-21, *279*
Acts 8:9-24, *279*
Acts 9:3, *60*
Acts 10:34, *59*
Acts 13:6-11, *279*
Acts 17:6, *60*
Acts 17:22-34, *10*

Romans
    Romans 2:29, *59*
    Romans 11:4, *240*
    Romans 13:1, *60*

1 Corinthians
    1 Corinthians 9:22,
    1 Corinthians 13, *46, 126-128, 147*
    1 Corinthians 15:5-7, *262*

2 Corinthians
    2 Corinthians 3:6, *60*

Ephesians
    Ephesians 2:1-10, *46*

Hebrews
    Hebrews 11, *46*

James
    James 5:11, *170*

1 Peter
    1 Peter 3:8, *60*

Revelation
    Revelation 3:5, *60*
    Revelation 6:13, *279*
    Revelation 11:3, *250*
    Revelation 12:10, *60*
    Revelation 12:9-15, *101*
    Revelation 20:2, *101*
    Revelation 20:10, *101*
    Revelation 22:1, *60*

General Index

Aaron, 100
Abraham, 77–94
ACLU, 24–25
Adam, 73, 75
Akedah, 77–94
Allegory, 207, 214
Ark, 106, 155–156
Author, 38–40, 155–158

Baal, 233–238; *see also* Elijah
Barak, 179–187
Bathsheba, 200–203

Canaanite gods, 234–238
Case law, 13–20
Chiasmus, 119–122
Christ, *see* Jesus
Christians, 34, 36, 37, 88
Creation, 69–76
Cultural DNA, xi, 12

David, 189–206
Dead Sea Scrolls, 39–40, 142, 150
Deborah, 179–187
Delilah, 109–112
Dove, 212

Eden, 72
El, 233–238
Elijah, ix–x, 233–238, 240–253
Elisha, 213
Eve, 75

Fire, x, 242
First Amendment, 13–32
Fish, 102–104
Foil, 226–227, 285–287
Frankincense, 277–281
Freedom Forum First Amendment
     Center, 22–24

Goliath, 193–196, 198, 199
Gospel of Mark, 255–263

Hair, 109–112
Hebrew Bible, 35–38

Isaac, 77–94
Ishmael, 82–83
Islam. *See* Moslems

Jacob, 101, 225
Jael, 179–187
Jesus, 102–103, 162, 213, 255–263
Jews, 35, 36, 37, 56, 87–88, 130
Joab, 201, 205
Job, 167, 187
Joint Statement of Current Law, 24–28
Jonah, 207–220
Joseph, 221–227

Law, *See* Caselow

McGuffey's Eclectic Primer, 9–10
Midrash, 161, 245
Moses, 285–287
Moslems, 81, 88

National Council of Teachers of
     English, 21
Nazirite, 109–112
Noah, 106, 108

Parable, 159–166
Parallelism, 114–118
Poetry, 113–131
     psalm, 124–126
     lament, 122–124
     chiasm, *See* Chiasmus

Qur'an, 81, 83, 118, 223

Rainbow, 104–109

Samson, 109–112
Satire, 207, 214–220
Saul, 192–197
Serpent, 98–101
Sisera, 179–187
Surveys
    Barna, 2–4
    Gallup, 1–2
    Wachlin, 5
Susanna, 49–56
Symbols, 95–112

Ten Commandments, 7–8, 35–36
Testament, 35
Translation, 42–43, 133–148
Tree of life, 96–97
Tree of knowledge, 97

U.S. Department of Education, 28–30

About the Author

Roger Baker is currently an Associate Professor of English at Brigham Young University. He has presented on the topics of teaching Bible narratives in public schools at national conferences such as CCCC and NCTE, as well as at the Utah Council of Teachers of English. Currently, Roger is researching death wishes in the Bible. This research coincides with the research he is doing on the Bible concordance of Alexander Cruden, which is the longest published index ever and has influenced how the Bible is read.